The Transformation of the Classical Heritage
Peter Brown, General Editor

ASCETICISM AND SOCIETY
IN CRISIS

SUSAN ASHBROOK HARVEY

ASCETICISM AND
SOCIETY IN CRISIS

John of Ephesus
and the
Lives of the Eastern Saints

UNIVERSITY OF CALIFORNIA PRESS
Berkeley • Los Angeles • London

University of California Press
Berkeley and Los Angeles, California
University of California Press, Ltd.
London, England
© 1990 by
The Regents of the University of California

Library of Congress Cataloging-in-Publication Data

Harvey, Susan Ashbrook.
    Asceticism and society in crisis : John of Ephesus and the Lives
of the Eastern Saints / Susan Ashbrook Harvey.
        p. cm.—(The Transformation of the classical heritage ; 17)
    Based on the author's thesis.
    Includes index.
    Bibliography: p.
    ISBN 0-520-06523-9 (alk. paper)
    1. John, Bishop of Ephesus, ca. 507–589. Lives of the Eastern
saints.   2. Christian saints—Middle East—Biography.   3. Jacobites
(Syrian Christians)—Biography.   4. Asceticism—History—Early
church, ca. 30–600.   5. Monophysites—Middle East—History.
I. Title.   II. Series.
BR65.J7653L5834   1990
275.6'02'0922—dc20
[B]   89-4822
                                                                       CIP

Part of chapter 3 appeared as "Asceticism in Adversity: An Early Byzantine Experience,"
    Byzantine and Modern Greek Studies 6 (1980) 1–11.

Part of chapter 7 appeared as "The Politicisation of the Byzantine Saint," *The Byzantine
    Saint*, ed. S. Hackel, Studies Supplementary to Sobornost 5 (1981), pp. 37–43.

Part of chapter 6 appeared as "Women in Early Syriac Christianity," *Images of Women in
    Antiquity*, ed. A. Cameron and A. Kuhrt (London 1983), pp. 288–98.

To my parents
"Did not our hearts burn within us on the road . . . ?"
Luke 24:32

CONTENTS

ACKNOWLEDGMENTS

This study has been completed with the help of many people, and I am grateful to all concerned. Some contributions must, however, be noted. The thesis phase of this book was kindly supported at different times by the Marshall Aid Commemoration Commission and the American Association of University Women. The final production has been undertaken with the gracious assistance of the American Council of Learned Societies, the University of Rochester, and Brown University.

I began my work with John of Ephesus for a doctoral thesis, and I remain deeply indebted to my supervisors, Sebastian P. Brock and Frances M. Young. They have taught, exhorted, encouraged, and inspired me to an extent I can hardly measure; and they continue to do so, with deep generosity. Were my debt to them less, I would feel less keenly the inadequacies of this study. Peter Brown, Martin Goodman, Robin Anne Darling Young, Marjorie Curry Woods, Ella Schwartz, Sidney Griffith, and John V. A. Fine, Jr. have all given freely of their knowledge, skills, and time, while also providing nourishment for the spirit and great gifts to the heart. I thank all of them; needless to say, shortcomings remain my own. In addition, I am grateful to Doris Kretschmer, Mary Lamprech, and Franci Duitch of the University of California Press for their patient and good-natured guidance in the production of this book; to Timothy Seid of Brown University for his kind technical assistance; and to Susan Lundgren for her thoughtful skill in preparing the index. Finally, my husband Jim has been unfailingly supportive; his sustaining presence accounts for more than I can say.

PREFACE

The Mediterranean world of late antiquity has in recent years gained popularity with scholars and the lay public both. A lacuna has been present in our studies thus far, however, in the case of a major and compelling writer from this era, John of Ephesus. Living in the sixth century, John led a varied career as a Monophysite monk, missionary, writer, and church leader. Two significant works by John remain extant: his *Ecclesiastical History* and his *Lives of the Eastern Saints*. John wrote in Syriac and his focus is often the eastern Byzantine provinces, especially his homeland Mesopotamia. But John's career took him throughout the empire of his day, and he knew the imperial court of Constantinople as intimately as he knew the villages of Amida's regions. John's writings are important in part because they concern a personal encounter with the full Byzantine world of his time, and in part because few writers from late antiquity have opened that world so vividly as he.

John lived through the period spanning the Monophysite movement's greatest successes and defeats. In his youth the Monophysites represented a formidable source of energy and creativity in the Byzantine realm; in his old age, John saw them not simply defeated but stalemated: discredited by the Chalcedonians on the Byzantine throne and incapacitated by their own internal bickerings. Within and beyond this frame of activity were the people of John's world. For John's home, the eastern provinces of Byzantium, the sixth century was above all a time of suffering. Their lands provided the battleground for war between Byzantium and Persia. Their monasteries and church communities, Monophysite in faith, endured persecutions by the Chalcedonian government. Famine and plague were chronically ubiquitous. It was a century when tragedy both accountable and capricious was the fabric of daily life.

John has received uneven treatment by modern scholars. Appreciation for his significance was first shown in the pamphlet by J. P. N. Land, *Joannes Bischof von Ephesos der erste syrische Kirchenhistoriker* (Leiden, 1856). Subsequent studies culminated in the monumental work of A. Djakonov, *Ioann Efesskiy* (Petrograd, 1908)—still the only monograph devoted to John. Further efforts followed, primarily textual, and critical editions of John's writings were published in the 1920s and 1930s, accompanied by translations into English for the *Lives of the Eastern Saints* and into Latin for the *Ecclesiastical History*. Nonetheless, John's works continued to be utilized mainly by Syriac scholars, while historians of the late Roman and early Byzantine periods persisted in sidestepping his contribution.

In recent decades, however, scholars of late antiquity have turned to a more comprehensive treatment of the materials available to us, and a greater appreciation for Syriac sources has been apparent. An upsurge in the interest shown for John of Ephesus' *Ecclesiastical History* has accompanied this wider view, and not least because John's records contrast with the contemporary accounts of the Greek literati.

For the most part, John's *Lives of the Eastern Saints* have not shared the limelight. The *Lives* have been used primarily for the information they contain about certain key figures and events in the ecclesiastical crises of the sixth century. Such selective treatment bypasses both what John's *Lives* are about and what they have to offer—as may be seen in two notable exceptions to this situation, Peter Brown's "Eastern and Western Christendom in Late Antiquity: A Parting of the Ways" and Evelyne Patlagean's *Pauvreté économique et pauvreté sociale à Byzance 4e–7e siècle*.

This study is an attempt to bring John's *Lives of the Eastern Saints* into view. They provide a different perspective from that of his *History*. Rather than a chronological record of important events, one finds here what is often lacking in such records: the daily world of ordinary people, and how they coped with war, plague, famine, and persecution. Here one sees, above all, Syrian asceticism fully developed. Its practitioners are at home in the small world of the villager, and sometimes, too, in the larger one of the imperial court. But the Syrian ascetics also reflected their times. By the end of the sixth century, even the vitality of this movement had been worn down.

John of Ephesus and his *Lives of the Eastern Saints* provide an opportunity to learn about life in a time and place of drastic events. Here we can see the ways in which those who have chosen extreme lives are forced by external circumstances into extremities even more severe. In writing the stories of holy men and women whom he had known, John shows us the confrontation between extreme experience and the human necessity of shaping that experience through narrative.

The hesitation that scholars have shown in the instance of John's *Lives* in fact stems largely from its literary form. For despite John's personal acquaintance with his subjects, and despite his professed intention to record in the *Lives* only what he himself has seen or can verify, hagiography alters both an author's material and its presentation. The nature of hagiography does not invalidate the historicity of John's *Lives*, but it does require that we read the text with a particular understanding.

Hagiography is a literary genre in which form is as important as content in understanding the text. Its task is to render the world of human experience comprehensible. It does this in two ways: first, by celebrating the saint (whether real or legendary) as one through whom God acted in the realm of human life; and second, by using a standardized language of literary *topoi* that identified the saint as saint and interpreted the saint's work as that of divine agency. Recognizing the formulaic, non-historical language of hagiography opens the route for treating the standardization itself as historical material. These texts offer us historical information, even in the most stringent sense, only if we can ask the appropriate questions. Standardization in hagiographical language is not a static matter. Favorite themes change; and the criteria of sanctity itself change in accordance with fluctuations in the values of society. Standard hagiographical themes, their periods of fashion and forms of expression, reveal the subconscious concerns of their societies and serve to establish a larger sense of order for those whom they are written to guide.

How, then, can we approach hagiography so as to evaluate the interaction of formulaic and historical material? The text must be heard on its own terms as well as in its hagiographical context; one must separate the standardized material from the author's perspective and establish how and why the author is using the hagiographic medium. There are clues internal to the text: the author's style, emphases, choices and viewpoints, and the author's position as distinct from the subject's. There are also external clues by which to measure the internal evidence: other sources—hagiographical, archaeological, archival, historiographical—and other information can be brought to bear upon the text. The consistency and coherence of a text, the interplay between an author's intent and content, analyses of comparative and contrasting material—all of these matters are tools by which we can listen more carefully to a text. In the listening, we can discern what the text is saying, and what we can learn from it.

John of Ephesus' *Lives of the Eastern Saints* is a work of hagiography in the historical rather than the legendary tradition of saints' lives. Unlike many works of this kind, John's collection is not primarily stereotyped or didactic. It is a work incorporating a strikingly personal element, as John not only participated in much of what he sets down but also is actively present in his role as author. In the present study, John himself stands at the center. As will be seen, his individualistic manner is constantly apparent; more than a matter of style, John produces a form of hagiography peculiarly his own. His circumstances do much to encourage his individuality.

The purpose of the present study is to explore the relationship and interaction between asceticism and society in the sixth-century Byzantine East. In particular, we are concerned with how this relationship works for the Monophysite ascetics, what factors influenced it, and what the consequences and implications may have been.

How do we see the particular historical circumstances reflected in the ascetic experience John describes hagiographically? As John tells us, it was a time when stylites descended from their pillars to enter the arena of religious controversy; anchorites returned to towns and cities to care for the laity in the absence of exiled church leaders; exile became a part of monastic practice; the needs of the laity overrode the sentiments of bishops in the formation of a separate church hierarchy; and women took leadership roles they would otherwise have shunned. The situation of religious controversy was compounded by war with Persians, invasions by Huns, extended famine, bubonic plague, and collective hysteria. We can see the contrast of Mesopotamia in its calamity with the expansion and prosperity experienced elsewhere in the Byzantine Empire during the first half of the sixth century; we can see also the contrast of provincial life to that of the cosmopolitan centers, whether Antioch, Jerusalem, or Constantinople. Our goal here is to break the religious experience down into its component parts, in search of the meaning ascribed to the larger event.

Establishing the historicity of John's text is thus neither the methodology nor the point of this study, nor does it attempt to prove a thesis. Rather, it seeks to see a situation: What is the story John tells? How are we to understand it? This is not a book about John of Ephesus as a historian. I chose to write about his *Lives* because they are not the history of his time but rather the story of the people who live in his world. I will utilize his *Ecclesiastical History* only as a complementary supplement to the *Lives*. My purpose is to understand what Syriac spirituality meant to these people, both those who practiced an ascetic career and those who did not.

Consequently, this is also not a book about the Monophysite movement, nor is its originating point of reference the Council of Chalcedon in 451. Rather, the point of origin is Syrian asceticism, its roots and development. In this particular instance, the ascetics are also Monophysites. While the church crisis colored their situation, as the book emphasizes, they are not themselves the entire Monophysite body (far from it), nor are they the reason for the separation of the churches. Their spirituality, their asceticism, and their responses to the crises of their times do not depend on their Monophysitism but rather on their Syriac heritage. The continuity of that heritage is ultimately more important than the change brought by persecution.

Because the material is generally unfamiliar to scholars and students of late antiquity, this study starts with an introduction to the Syrian Orient of the sixth century. I do this by focusing on particular texts that illustrate the themes important for John of Ephesus; there is a context in which the ascetic practice John records makes sense in practical as well as symbolical terms. Syrian asceticism did not develop through a sequence of events. It developed in a collective experience, in which individuals and communities pursued a variety of goals for various reasons. The people rather than the events were the determining factors, and they overlapped, clashed, and harmonized in patterns rather than in a clear progression. The same is true of the spirituality studied in this book. Events affected it and forced people to make certain decisions or changes; those circumstances are central to this study insofar as they reveal the people and their spirituality more clearly.

The first chapter then introduces John himself, his writings, and the literary issues of the *Lives*. The following chapters focus on those events that shaped John's collection: the development of asceticism in a time of crisis (chapter 2); the plague of madness in the city of Amida, as a collective societal response to the years of calamity (chapter 3); the impact of exile on monastic practice, and the functioning of monastic communities as refugee camps (chapter 4); mission, the breakdown of Byzantine imperial ideology in the East, and the formation of separate churches (chapter 5); the fluctuating position of women (chapter 6); and, finally, an assessment of John's hagiographical purpose (chapter 7).

In using John's *Lives* to the end, we will work with the awareness that John is writing hagiography for a specific reason and with a specific intent. In order to see what John is doing and how and why he does it, the *Lives* will be treated throughout this study together with contrasting and complementary writings of late antiquity, both Greek and Syriac. We will seek to clarify the singular experience contained in the work. These are particular people in a particular world. To see them on their own terms and to hear their story as truly theirs is to touch history as a living thing.

Hagiography is about a theology of activity. The careers of the saints are one expression of this theology. The writing of hagiography is another.

Since no one can speak for John of Ephesus better than he himself, I have illustrated this study with his own words as much as possible. For the most part I quote from the translation of E. W. Brooks, though occasionally I have altered the text or, where noted, substituted my own.

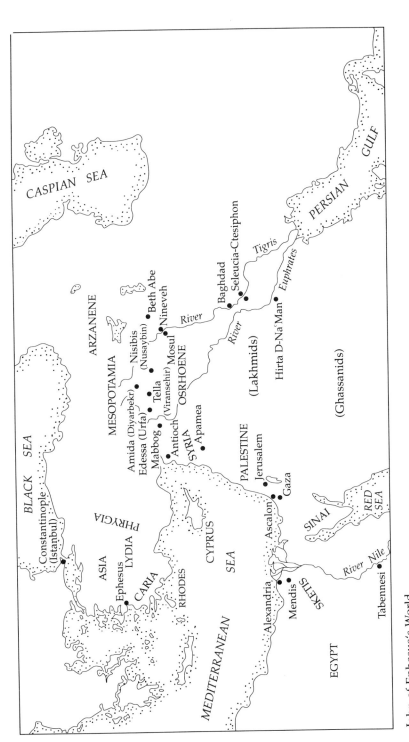

John of Ephesus's World

INTRODUCTION: JOHN'S WORLD

LANGUAGE AND CULTURE

Syriac began as a dialect of Aramaic, spoken in the region of Edessa early in the first century of the Christian Era.[1] It grew quickly as both the primary vernacular and literary language of the Syrian Orient: the Roman provinces of Mesopotamia, Syria, Osrhoene, and their neighboring Persian provinces. But it became, too, the lingua franca over a much wider area of the eastern Roman frontier. It was used by traders throughout the East, in Persia and into India, and as far into the Latin West as Gaul.[2] Over time, Syriac built an impressive cultural and literary strength in its own right.[3] Its survival to this day in southeastern Turkey, Iran, Iraq, Syria, Lebanon, and parts of India has been largely due to its hold as a religious force in the liturgies of the Syriac-speaking churches. Although the Middle Ages under Islamic domination brought a serious decline in Syriac literature, apart from that for liturgical or ecclesiastical use, recent generations have brought a renewal of it once again.[4]

Throughout its existence, Syriac has been a language in tension with other, more influential languages. Perhaps more than any other factor, this has shaped its history. It may have been spurred to full development as a reaction against its religious setting in the first century: the Jewish and pagan connotations of Aramaic and Greek facilitated Syriac's adoption as a cultural vehicle for Christianity, particularly in a geographical area where the population prided itself on the primacy of an early affirmation of the Christian faith, in contrast (or so Edessans claimed) to the

Greco-Latin realm.[5] Indeed, Syriac has remained for the most part a Christian language, producing a primarily religious literature. Furthermore, unlike Greek, which struggled in late antiquity to reconcile Hellenic tradition and Christian context in its literary forms, Syriac developed as a Christian medium; relatively young as a literary language, it was free of the archaizing pressure exerted on Hellenic literature. Once begun, its development came quickly.[6]

The Syrian Orient was less submissive to the ascendency of Hellenic aesthetics than the provinces of Asia Minor, in part because after the Roman conquests this area had maintained a degree of political autonomy longer than had the western provinces. Its culture represented the inheritance of the ancient Near East—Babylon, Assyria, Palestine, and influence from the Arab peninsula.[7] During the early Christian period, Hellenism was present as a strand within this sophisticated matrix, and our earliest Christian texts from this region circulated in both Greek and Syriac versions.[8] Hellenic philosophy appears in the theological speculations of Bardaisan of Edessa (d. 222) and in some of the heretical movements, especially Marcionism and, later, Arianism (causing Ephrem Syrus to rail against the "poison . . . of the Greeks").[9] But it does not emerge as a dominant force until the fifth and sixth centuries. The Syrian Orient was Christianized mainly through semitic Judaism rather than pagan religion or philosophy; its religious culture continued to reflect that heritage and differed from those of the Greco-Latin churches accordingly.[10] There was, too, a further cultural factor involved: the Syrian Orient was the trading crossroad that brought East and West together. The wealth of artistic and religious influences that mingled in this area generated a literary fertility evident in the Greek as well as in the Syriac writing produced in the eastern Roman provinces.[11]

Thus in the syncretism of the late antique Greco-Roman world, Syriac language and culture were in a position to give as well as to take— unlike, for example, their Coptic counterparts in Egypt or the Armenians to the north.[12] The position of Syriac was strengthened further by the growth of its own academies during the second half of the fourth century. Edessa was the first city of the Syrian Orient to gain recognition as a center of scholarship, though the school in Edessa had been transferred from its original location at Nisibis. In the fifth century, religious persecutions against the Nestorians led to the spread of Syriac schools into Persia, where they flourished perhaps most illustriously again at Nisibis.[13] The existence of the Syriac academies was to some degree responsible for the way in which Hellenism infiltrated Syriac culture. The use of Syriac as the teaching language and the consequent task of trans-

lating Greek literature, particularly under pressure for theological dialogue, caused a gradual impact, one in which Greek gained the greater
privilege in the eyes of the Syriac literati during the fifth and sixth
centuries.[14]

Despite the antipathy of Greek culture to outside ("barbarian") influences, Syriac succeeded in creating a two-way interaction. Although
translations of Syriac texts into Greek are minimal compared with those
in reverse, what was chosen to be translated from Syriac is important.[15]
Syriac hymnography made an early and lasting impression on Greek
literature. The fourth-century hymns of Ephrem Syrus were translated
into Greek during the poet's own lifetime; the form and imagery he developed probably provided the inspiration for the later Greek *kontakion*,
especially as crafted by Romanos Melodos.[16] Not unrelated, perhaps,
was the attraction felt toward certain Syriac mystical writings, a tradition culminating with Isaac of Nineveh in the seventh century and John
the Solitary in the eighth. These were translated and used in Byzantine
monasteries, deeply affecting Byzantine spirituality.[17]

But hagiography was undoubtedly the sphere in which Syriac made
its greatest contribution because its legends and themes were more important than its literary forms. Influence could be exerted not through
translations or aesthetic issues—both areas in which Greek was grudgingly receptive—but through the stories themselves. The legends of Euphemia and the Goth, Alexius the Man of God, Sergius and Bacchus,
Cosmas and Damian, Pelagia the Penitent, to name but the obvious ones,
are all examples of stories originating in the Syrian Orient (Cosmas and
Damian may in fact have been Arabs),[18] which were told and retold in a
variety of versions, in numerous languages, and which sparked related
motifs that flourished too.[19]

During the fifth century, the influence of Hellenism increased in Syriac culture, language, and literature, fueled above all by the Christological disputes that broke out over the course of that century.[20] The ensuing
pressure for dialogue with the Greek theologians and with the imperial
government at Constantinople led to a change in translation techniques
that mirrored a larger cultural shift: the translation of Greek into Syriac
became increasingly precise, with the emphasis (and thus the prestige)
placed on faithfulness to the Greek text, whatever the result in Syriac.
The need to interact effectively with Greek leaders and theologians created a need for Greek-educated Syrian scholars; indeed, the majority of
Syriac writers and translators between the fifth and seventh centuries
acquired their academic training in Greek-speaking centers.[21]

However, the theological controversies led to more than linguistic change. In the effort to make dialogue more effective, Syrian theologians had to gain skills in Greek intellectual disciplines. By the sixth century, many Syrians reveal marked Hellenic influence on their thought and theological dialectic; significantly, despite the continuing development of Syriac thought,[22] the learned Greek theologian Severus of Antioch provided the "Monophysite" system on which Syrian Orthodoxy has rested ever since.[23]

The full impact of Hellenism on the Syrian Orient can be seen during the sixth century, but the shift was not in itself destructive. The decline of Syriac language and literature came later, under Arab rule, when the linguistic similarity of the two languages surely aided the rapid adoption of the rulers' tongue.[24] The sixth century, instead, witnessed a creative integration of Hellenic and Semitic thought: a situation that briefly shone with promise. This was the cultural juncture at which John of Ephesus wrote his *Lives of the Eastern Saints,* and in which his stories are set.

CULTURE AND RELIGION: EARLY GROUPS AND FEATURES

The most striking feature of early Syrian Christianity, and the most difficult to assess, is its inherent asceticism. For the early church of the Syrian Orient, asceticism was not a marginal phenomenon, an activity of extremists hovering at the fringes of the mainstream Christian church; nor was it an external element, arriving from the "exotic" religions of the East and assimilated into the budding Christian ethos. Extremists there were, and external influences there were. But for the early Christian communities of the Syrian Orient, asceticism was at the heart of Christian understanding and Christian life.[25]

During the fourth century, a common movement prevailed throughout the Christian communities of the Roman Empire: to bring the various forms of Christianity as a whole into conformity, in essence following the characteristics of the "mainstream" Greco-Latin churches. This movement brought a number of changes to the texture of Syriac spirituality. One such change was the idea that asceticism could be a separate vocation within Christianity, distinct from the practices of the laity and from the requirements of the ecclesiastical hierarchy.[26] But in earliest Syrian Christianity, asceticism held a fundamental place. It was basic to the Syrian understanding of the Bible, both in model and in precept; it was essential sacramentally; and it was devotional, practiced to various

degrees by the laity as well as by the consecrated. Moreover this ascetically toned spirituality is found in almost all forms of early Christianity in the Syrian Orient, whatever the particular perspective—"orthodox," Gnostic, Marcionite, or Manichean.[27]

Syrian Christianity inherited from Judaism[28] a religious tradition
that stressed the importance of behavior. Both the Old and the New Tes-
taments gave ample witness that devotion to God meant pursuing God's
purpose with body as well as with soul, starting with the abandonment
of society's comforts—family, home, and community. Moses, Elijah,
Elisha, John the Baptist, and Paul, as well as Christ, were favorite models for the Syrians. Here as elsewhere, the Syrian Orient displayed the
tendency to literalize symbols; that is, the literal and figurative aspects of
interpretation were seen to be the same, and so too were one's actions
and their symbolic meanings.[29] Asceticism as symbolic behavior provided the believer the means for enacting biblical images of salvation.
The significance of asceticism was enhanced by the particular Bible in
use: Tatian's *Diatessaron* was until the fifth century the most popular version of the Gospels in the Syrian Orient, and often the only one. Tatian
not only edited the Gospels into a harmony but further made clear by his
editing and manner of translation (sometimes close to paraphrase) that
renunciation was the model presented in the Gospels and was indeed
demanded of the Christian believer in all circumstances.[30]

The influence of the *Diatessaron* encouraged those who saw the
Christian ideal of renunciation in terms of a dualist understanding: the
material world and the physical body were inferior to those of the spiritual realm, if not outright channels for evil. There were, however, further Biblical models developed in early Christian writings that were not
grounded in a dualist perspective but led nonetheless to an ascetic basis
for Christian life; and these, in the ethos of Syrian spirituality, were seen
to present models for literal, physical translation into the life of the
believer.

In the earliest Christian sources from the Syrian Orient (as elsewhere in the Christian realm), a favorite epithet for Christ was the Heavenly Bridegroom.[31] The marriage feast parables in the Gospels produced
an imagery through which Christian believers understood themselves as
betrothed to Christ, an image developed early on in Syrian baptismal
tradition.[32] By this image, the believer was declared wholly given to
God, body and soul. Celibacy was an ubiquitous value in early Syrian
Christianity. But celibacy was not necessarily a matter of refusing to participate in the imperfection of the physical world. It was a matter of being utterly devoted to God. Body and soul were in this view inseparable.

Thus into the third century, and perhaps longer, celibacy was often a vow taken at baptism, or later after having one or two children.[33] Two categories of celibacy were recognized: the *bthūle,* "virgins," and the *qaddīshe,* "holy ones," the married who practiced continence. Spiritual marriage, the way of the *qaddīshe,* was commonly followed as a means of combining the social functions of marriage with the life of faith.[34] Indeed, when the mainstream church attempted to curtail the practice of spiritual marriage in Christian communities during the late third century and thereafter, the Syrian Orient proved the most difficult to change in this respect. The idea of celibacy was, for Syrian spirituality, more than an ideal; it was fundamental. Hence, in earliest Syrian Christianity, the word *bthūlā,* "virgin," could also mean "Christian," whether male or female, lay or religious.[35]

The growth of the *bnay* and *bnath qyāmā,* consecrated lay offices for both men and women, was also important. Well-established as a part of Syriac Christianity by the third century, these "Covenanters," or "Sons and Daughters of the Covenant," lived a celibate and regulated life—by the fifth century, canonically ruled—and served the Church while living in the Christian community. They functioned together with the normative ecclesiastical structure and were a feature of the Syriac churches that survived into the Islamic period. The Sons and Daughters of the Covenant were organized as a kind of elite congregation within the church, offering a vocational form of Christian life available to the laity.[36] Emphasis on celibacy and service to the church, then, were widely found in Syriac Christianity before the growth of a separate ascetic movement.

The eschatological settings of the marriage feast parables in the New Testament also encouraged the ascetic nature of Syriac Christianity.[37] To engage in activities that furthered the existence of this earthly life only delayed the inevitable—and desired—arrival of the eschaton.[38] Christ as Second Adam had opened the gates of Paradise anew for those who were saved and promised their return to that state of grace lived by the First Adam and Eve before the Fall.[39] To hasten the fulfillment of this event, the believer lived in its expectation and sought in every way possible not to contribute to the continuing existence of this earthly realm, for example, by the procreation of children.

But even further, the Syrian understanding brought a literal living out of life in the eschatological Paradise, as prefigured by Adam and Eve. More than a matter of celibacy, this understanding sometimes led the believer to adopt a life of stark symbolism: living naked in the wilderness exposed to the elements, eating only raw fruit and herbs, dwelling among the wild beasts, and leading an unbroken life of prayer. These precursors of the monastic movement understood the Christian life in its absolute sense; the believer was saved and so no longer part of the fallen world.[40] The believer lived what the true eschatological reality promised. To live as if it had already come was to hasten its actual coming; but there was, too, a palpable sense that to live as if it had already come was to accomplish its actuality.

Early Syrian Christianity evoked extreme action through a spirituality that called for lived symbols. Such action pointed to one more characteristic intensifying the sense that Christianity without asceticism was incomplete (perhaps even unthinkable):[41] that is, the idea of "singleness."[42] A notion rooted in Judeo-Christianity's emphasis on single-minded devotion to God, "singleness" gave particular meaning to the ideal of celibacy. The believer was to be single-mindedly focused on the divine; the believer lived a single, unmarried life to enable that focus. Christ himself had lived such a "single" life of devotion to God's purpose. In Syriac, the word meaning "single one," *ihidāyā*, was also used to connote Christ as the "only begotten" ("single") one of God; it became a word commonly used for and interchangable with other technical terms for the ascetic or the monk. Just as in earliest Syrian Christian terminology the word meaning "virgin," *bthūlā*, could also mean "Christian," so too the word for "single one" (and indeed, for "only begotten") could also mean an ascetic and later a monk.

Thus from various sources Syriac spirituality nourished the conviction that to be a Christian was to be single-minded, and to be celibate, and to live a life of renunciation. The roots of Syrian asceticism, then, surpassed those of dualism. Traditionally, scholars have sought to understand the phenomenon of early Syrian asceticism in terms of a dualistic ethos, which was in fact distinctly bred into the popular religious culture of late antiquity, particularly in the Christian East.[43] The major heretical groups present in the Syrian Orient shared an understanding that separated the spiritual and physical realms and from various angles glorified celibacy. The Marcionites sought to fulfill literally the apostolic injunction that in Christ there is neither male nor female; the Manicheans and some Gnostics understood matter to be evil and so encouraged dissociation from it; baptism was interpreted in some groups as betrothal to Christ, the Heavenly Bridegroom, and thus reduced earthly marriage to adultery.[44]

The presence of such a strongly dualistic mind-set could not but affect the wider popular attitudes of the Syrian Orient during the early Christian centuries. The ideas discussed earlier here—renunciation, celibacy, Paradise fulfilled, and singleness—all lend themselves easily to dualistic developments. Certainly, such developments did take place and are to some extent responsible for the direction that Syrian asceticism took when it emerged during the course of the fourth century as an autonomous and defined movement within the orthodox Christian culture.[45] But it would be misleading to regard heterodox dualism as the only source of Syrian asceticism. On the contrary, the most influential and enduring aspect of early Syrian Christianity was the concept of the essential "oneness" of the believer's self, a "oneness" of body and soul. The importance of religious behavior is here placed in context: what one does with one's body is indistinguishable from what one believes.

CULTURE AND RELIGION: EARLY ASCETIC FORMS

The clearest early expression of this oneness in relation to the divine is seen in the *Odes of Solomon,* perhaps our oldest nonbiblical Syriac text.[46] Scholars have reached no consensus on the original language of these hymns—Greek or Syriac—or on their date: theories range from the late first to the third century, with the late second century being the most likely.[47] But there is no doubt that they are Syrian in provenance, and they illustrate this aspect of Syrian spirituality particularly well. The *Odes* reflect an all-consuming love of God, with the imagery of betrothal as much a bodily experience as a spiritual understanding.[48] There is a sensuousness, an intense physicality to the expression of worship in these hymns, devoid of sexuality despite the bridal imagery that underlies it.[49] So, for example, Ode 40:

2. As a fountain bursts forth its water,
   so my heart bursts forth the praise of the Lord,
   and my lips bring forth praises to Him.

3. And my tongue becomes sweet by His anthems,
   and my limbs are anointed by His odes.

4. My face rejoices in His exultation,
   and my spirit exults in His love,
   and my soul shines in Him.[50]

The act of self-giving is such that the believer is borne into the presence, and even into the very being of God;[51] one of the greatest difficulties a scholar has with these *Odes* is to separate (in some of them) the voice of Christ from that of the believer—to such a degree is the act of union absolute. This union is played out in another image, both physical and spiritual: the believer prays in the form (position) of a cross and in that stance is mystically lifted into the presence of God as was Christ himself.[52] But the image is qualified: it is the cross that leads to resurrection, to the throne of glory, rather than the crucifixion that the believer symbolically becomes in the act of prayer. The distinction is crucial. Nowhere in the *Odes* do we hear of the suffering of Christ, an omission that contributed to the questionable orthodoxy of these hymns. Here the cross holds the symbol of Christ's exaltation, and of supplication; no more, but also no less.[53]

In the fourth century, the imagery of betrothal remained primary. At the same time, the fourth century brought the first real encounter with persecution and martyrdom that the Syrian Orient had known. For the Greco-Latin churches, persecution was a recurrent if sporadic event from Christianity's beginnings. But to the east of Antioch, matters transpired differently. Apart from a brief but contained outbreak in Persia in the 270s,[54] the earliest Syriac Christian martyrdoms occurred between 306 and 310, in the instance of the Edessan martyrs Shmona, Guria, and Habib.[55] Legend later added the prestige of earlier occurrences: during the fifth century, the literary cycle of the Edessan martyrs was expanded to include the *Doctrina Addai*, recounting the martyrdom of Aggai late in the first century;[56] and the *Acts of Sharbil, Babai, and Barsamya*, whose deaths were set in Edessa in 105 (though the events described would better place them in the persecutions of Decius).[57] But we have no evidence that these earlier martyrdoms took place, and the accounts as we have them are clearly part of the literary flowering that fifth-century Edessa engendered.

Thus the Syrian Orient was able to develop its Christianity largely without the threat of martyrdom and its particular framing of devotion to God.[58] Moreover, persecution was less severe when it did come. The final persecution campaigns at the turn of the fourth century witnessed the martyrdom of several Christians in Edessa and other major cities.[59] In the 340s, the Christian communities of Persia suffered more, in widespread campaigns conducted under Shapur II and coinciding with the Roman Empire's change to a favorable policy for Christianity.[60] A result of this chronology is that Syriac martyr passions draw on the ascetic imagery of Syriac spirituality rather than the reverse—as, for example, in the *Life of Antony of Egypt*, where asceticism is named living martyrdom.[61]

Shmona and Guria were two Christian laymen put to death in Edessa around the year 306. An account of their martyrdoms was written soon after.[62] In it, the two men speak without artifice: as Christians, they belong to God. Shmona says, "Our belief is our life in Christ."[63] Such conviction effectively transmutes the meaning of life and death. With words heard in other Christian martyrdoms, Shmona says, "We are not dying . . . but living according to what we believe."[64] What is death is life; to live would mean to be dead. Indeed, Guria recalls the scripture, "He who loses his life for my sake shall find it."[65] They draw comfort from the stories they have heard of martyrs in other times and other places.[66] In sharp contrast to the contemporary accounts of martyrs by Eusebius of Caesarea, they are in no way "prepared" or "trained" to meet this event, as Eusebius' philosopher martyrs had been.[67] Equally striking is the absence of Satan's presence in these stories and in those of the other Edessan martyrs. The officials involved are portrayed as horrid enough but are never identified with the Adversary, as so often happens in Greek and Latin martyrs' passions.[68]

Shortly after these two deaths, the deacon Habib met a similar fate in Edessa. His story, by the same author, is even more emphatic.[69] When Habib refuses to make sacrifice even after severe torture, the governor exclaims in exasperation, "Does your doctrine teach you to hate your bodies?"[70] The governor implies either that Habib can utterly disregard his body or that he delights in the demise of his physical existence to the greater glory of his spiritual one—both ideas dear to Eusebius, as others.[71] But Habib responds with the simplicity of his Syrian predecessors: "We do not hate our bodies. We are taught that he who loses his life shall find it."[72] Rather than distinguishing between his body and his soul, Habib questions what true life and true death are, the question raised by the action of Christ in the resurrection.[73] Both the governor's question and Habib's response were repeated in the later account of the martyrdom of Sharbil, written contemporaneously with Simeon the Stylite's ascent on his pillar and the outcry of similar protest that his action provoked.[74]

Together these texts make no body/soul distinction but rather speak of life and death as matters for which the physical and spiritual meanings are inseparable. And in that statement we have a reasonable summary of what asceticism means, a meaning held equally by both Western and Eastern Christians: to be dead to the world as it is and alive to existence in the kingdom of God, an existence actualized by the ascetic's practice. Here we see life and death each understood as a state of existence in its own right, and each continuous both here and in the hereafter. They are mutually exclusive of one another, both in this world and the next.

In addition to martyrdom, the fourth century brought a shift in the Syrian Orient from Christianity as an ascetic religion to Christianity as a religion with asceticism as a possible vocation. The shift is marked in the writings of Aphrahat the Persian (fl. 336–345) and Ephrem Syrus (d. 373), both "proto-monks" in the movement towards monastic communities.

Aphrahat is primarily concerned with celibacy as the starting point of Christian vocation.[75] It is the mark not only of betrothal to Christ, a joyful gift freely given and freely received,[76] but also of the call to participate in the holy cosmic war against the Adversary.[77] In his *Demonstration* 6, "On the Bnay Qyāmā," Aphrahat interweaves the concepts of betrothal to Christ, renunciation, service, holy war, and eschatology in a rich tapestry of biblical imagery and models representing a tradition he has inherited, the roots of which may well stem from Qumran and early sectarian Judaism.[78] He does not speak of the body as something to be subjugated to the soul—language pervading the roughly contemporary *Life of Antony.* Rather, body and soul are God's, as one; both are for His use and His work.

It is Ephrem who extols the exquisite beauty of betrothal as an image, addressing Christ the Heavenly Bridegroom, "The soul is your bride / the body your bridal chamber."[79] Or again, "O Lord, may the body be a temple for its builder / may the soul be a palace of praise for its architect."[80] For Ephrem, alienation of body and soul is the result of the Fall. In his *Hymns on Nisibis* 69, he writes:

3. . . . for you had joined them together in love, but they had parted and separated in pain.

4. The body was fashioned in wisdom, the soul was breathed in through grace,
love was infused in perfection—but the serpent separated it in wickedness.

5. Body and soul go to court to see which caused the other to sin;
but the wrong belongs to both, for free will belongs to both.

Now, however, the work of the incarnation has reconciled them once again:

14. Make glad the body with the soul; return the soul to the body;
Let them have joy at each other, for they were separated but are returned and joined once more.[81]

Thus Ephrem can rejoice, "We love our bodies, which are akin to us, of the same origin."[82] And he can write this way at the same time that others are describing the startling Syrian ascetics living naked in the wilderness, their hair like eagles' feathers, physically enacting the image of life before the Fall, the true life of the saved believer.[83] It was Ephrem, too, who could exhort that virginity alone without acts of service was an insufficient offering to God, and that chaste marriage combined with

good works could be a better way: "their conduct having filled the place
of virginity. For . . . their spirit was bound in the love of their Lord . . .
with the desire for Him permeating all their limbs."[84]

The common thread that ties the early varieties of Syrian Christianity to an orthodox tradition is the understanding that body and soul
must be united in the act of devotion. What changes over time are the
context and circumstances in which the thread is found. In Syriac martyr
passions, one finds a commentary on the meaning of asceticism: suffering, or hatred of the body, is neither the goal nor the purpose, but devotion of the whole self is. Aphrahat and Ephrem write about the meaning
of devotion to God at a time when Syrian asceticism is shifting toward a
defined movement. The extremity that came to characterize Syrian asceticism during the fifth and sixth centuries is well known. It may be that
its harshness reflects the impact of the earlier dualistic ethos, or indeed
the incorporation of the martyr experience into a spirituality that had
come to bloom without that threat. Yet Aphrahat and Ephrem offer witness that the increasing extremity was not born only out of influence
from a dualistic ethos but also could come from the search to live out,
with one's whole self, betrothal (self-giving) to God.[85]

The two figureheads for Syrian ascetic tradition, praised in the
hymns of their own day as well as in later legend, were Jacob of Nisibis
(d. 338) in Persia and Julian Saba (d. 366/367) in Mesopotamia.[86] Each
took to the wilderness to focus solely on the divine.

Jacob was a solitary in the mountains outside Nisibis.[87] During the
spring, summer, and autumn seasons he lived exposed in the brush with
the sky for his roof. In winter, he stayed in a cave. He ate only wild plants
and denied himself the comfort of fire (for warmth or for cooking) and of
clothing, having only his hair for a tunic. His spiritual excellence brought
rewards: whatever he asked, God granted, blessing him further with the
gift of prophecy. Not surprisingly, Jacob's virtue was discovered by others, and he was ordained bishop of Nisibis. He left his mountains but
did not change his way of life. As bishop, he pursued a career of public
good works and private asceticism. During the Arian crisis, Jacob traveled to the Council of Nicea to battle for orthodoxy. During the Persian
siege of Nisibis he worked among the populace, strengthening their defense and sabotaging the efforts of the Persian soldiers. In the eyes of his
public, his effective leadership was the result of his effective asceticism.

Julian Saba's life followed a parallel but contrasting course.[88] Julian,
too, was an anchorite. He lived in a cave in the desert of Osrhoene and
ate once a week, restricting his diet to meager quantities of barley bread,
salt, and spring water. Prayer and psalmody were his primary activities.
Julian's way of life brought him growing fame and soon a growing band

of disciples. They settled in nearby caves, ate as he did, and under his leadership practiced an asceticism of prayer, psalmody, and labor. Over time Julian's renown spread, and so too did testimonies to the deeds wrought by his prayers. Like Jacob, Julian returned for a time to society to work in opposition to the Arian challenge. Once he was taken seriously ill but worked his own cure by prayer as he had done for many others. Theodoret of Cyrrhus wrote that the illness was a reminder of Julian's humanity.[89] Appropriately, Julian died in the quiet of his desert home.

Both Jacob and Julian found that the course of their ascetic withdrawal led them back to human society: for Jacob, by ordination to the see of Nisibis, and for Julian, by the growth around him of an ascetic community. Both worked to express divine purpose through action. Both saw fit to reenter worldly affairs by intervening in the crises of war and religious controversy. Neither claimed that his holy resolution absolved him of such commitments. Above all, neither softened his private way of life. The example they set terrified their enemies. It was said that armies were turned and dragons slain by their act of prayer.[90]

Jacob and Julian represent the archetypal Syrian saint, and their stories can be seen as blueprints for the hagiographies to follow. Within their mold, the Syrian Orient developed its ascetic tradition, centering on the individual whose life of devotion gained authority in both the divine and human realms. Yet the earlier features of Syriac Christianity were not supplanted. A separate ascetic institution began to arise during the fourth century, but its demarcation was not always clear. The tradition of the lay ascetic remained, the individual who lived a regulated life of chastity and prayer within society and who served the needs of the local congregation. Ephrem Syrus was himself one such individual, working tirelessly for the bishops of Nisibis and Edessa and known for his exceptional efforts on behalf of the needy when Edessa suffered a famine.[91] There continued in Syrian Christianity the understanding that faith required vocational activity and commitment from its adherents. At the same time, the growth of asceticism as an institution raised other issues for the Syrian Christian community.

ASCETICISM AND SOCIETY

During the fourth century monasticism flowered across the Christian realm, and with it a critical role for the ascetic—the holy man or woman—to play in society. By their discipline and their conscious imitation of biblical models, especially from the Gospels, the ascetics enacted the image of Christ. To the public this was more than imitation: in the image of Christ, the holy one could do what Christ had done. The ascetics could intercede for divine mercy, and they could be instruments of divine grace in this world; they were a channel between humanity and God that worked in both directions. The ascetic was the point at which the human and the holy met.[92]

Moreover, the ascetics blurred the lines separating the temporal and spiritual realms. Just as they could intercede effectively with the divine, so too could they intercede with the worldly powers below. It did not take long for the Christian community, great and small, to turn to the holy men or women for cures, exorcisms, advice, justice, and judgments in affairs private and public, personal and civil. Often seen as an attempt to leave the worldly for the spiritual, asceticism in fact carried heavy responsibilities in relation to the larger Christian society.[93]

The wider empire showed developments that paralleled the basic models of Syrian asceticism.[94] In the late third and early fourth centuries Antony had paved the route out to the Egyptian desert as anchorite, and back into the temporal world when he reentered Alexandria on behalf of the Bishop Athanasius.[95] In so doing, he sharpened the task of the ascetic vocation. There had been others before him of devotional practice, recluses who lived the life of prayer. In the desert Antony redefined the ascetic as one who fought the Adversary face-to-face, in the desolate and un-Christianized wilderness. Antony made "the desert a city," sanctifying a place where God had not been present. And he did more: he brought that strength back into Christian society. Indeed, as the prophets of old—Moses, Elijah, John the Baptist—and as Christ himself, Antony faced the wilderness as prelude to a career that involved much public ministry.[96] Soon after, in Cappadocia, Basil of Caesarea both established a form of devotional community dependent on corporate discipline—his monastery / hospice / hospital complex—and caused his friend Gregory of Nazianzus to leave his retreat and enter the church's battlegrounds.[97] It was not a far step from either position to that of the monastic forces utilized by Cyril of Alexandria early in the fifth century.[98]

The Syrian terrain and its vulnerable position as border country between the Roman and Persian Empires made it necessary for the early Syrian anchorites either to remain near to fortified towns or villages, as Jacob of Nisibis had done, or to bond together as a community, however loosely, as in the case of Julian Saba.[99] These factors marked Syrian asceticism with its own distinctive style. In Egypt, clear distance from the outside world was the desert's claim. Although sources indicate continual contact between the ascetics and society, both sides upheld the ideal of that distance as a crucial element for the ascetic's vocation. In the Syrian Orient, proximity to the temporal society was a given. Even in texts describing anchorites, the dramatic isolation eulogized in Egyptian (as well as Palestinian) hagiography is rarely to be found. Furthermore, unlike Cappadocia, the structural patterns of different communities were rarely coordinated and their arrangements with the ecclesiastical organization were less elaborate.

The fifth century brought the full articulation of Syrian asceticism and established its place in relation to Christian society. Again, two figures mark the key developments: Simeon the Stylite (c. 386–459) outside Antioch, and the legendary Man of God in Edessa at about the same time. These two represent the poles of traditional asceticism, the wilderness and the city; and they represent the range of relationships possible for asceticism and society, in the huge cult following of Simeon and its antithesis in the anonymity of the Man of God.

Simeon was the unparalleled star of Syrian asceticism, known in his own day (and perhaps ever after) as the great wonder of the inhabited world.[100] Born in Syria of Christian parents and baptized as a child, Simeon grew up tending his father's flocks. A chance encounter led to his conversion to the ascetic life, and he left his home at once. Simeon passed through two monasteries in Syria, at Tel'ada and Telneshe, in his search for his true vocation, but his propensity for severe and eccentric practice led him into conflict with the developing Syrian monastic structure. Eventually he went his own way, first as a recluse and then, around 412, as stylite, mounting the first of three pillars, each higher than the one before. On the pillar he took up his *stasis*, his stance of continual prayer. The final pillar, on which he spent roughly the last forty years of his life, was about forty cubits high (sixty feet?). It had a platform on top about six-feet square, with a railing to keep him from falling off. Exposed on the mountain with no shelter of any kind, Simeon stood on his pillar midway between heaven and earth until his death at the age of more than seventy years. His career as holy man was spectacular. During his life, his fame had spread from Britain to Persia; the pilgrims who flocked to see him crossed the spectrum of late antique society from peasant to emperor, bringing him problems as mundane as cucumber crops and as complex as foreign policy.

On top of his pillar, Simeon lived exposed to heat, sun, ice, rain, and snow. Once he nearly died from a gangrenous ulcer on his foot. He followed a rigid schedule of stationary prayer, genuflexion, and attention to the pilgrims below. He was tended by disciples who climbed the pillar by ladder to bring him the sparse food he ate once each week when he was not fasting. A monastic community grew up around the pillar base, which served not only the stylite but also the pilgrims who came. Twice a day Simeon would interrupt his prayer routine to hear problems and address exhortations to the crowds below. He judged disputes, addressed the affairs of the Church, proclaimed against heresy, and sent advice to the emperor, foreign kings, and other high officials; he preached, healed, exorcised, prophesied, and blessed the endless crowds.[101]

We possess three contemporary vitae for Simeon. Although we have nothing from his own words that explains why he climbed the pillar, these three sources offer different perspectives on what he was doing and why. Their differences are instructive. Theodoret of Cyrrhus wrote about Simeon in his *Historia religiosa* while the saint was still alive (c. 444), when he had been on the pillar twenty-eight years and his cult was in full glory.[102] Theodoret uses the frame of Hellenic tradition to present Simeon as one for whom body and soul are mutually antagonistic in a battle of wills that forms the central focus for Simeon's career. To seek the resolution of the conflict, Simeon adopted a life of discipline and virtue in order to subjugate his body to his will. He represents the true philosopher, one who seeks the life of virtue by turning his mind wholly to the spiritual world above. In subduing his body to his soul, Simeon achieves an inward harmony through which he can turn the whole of his heart to God. Theodoret calls this the "angelic life"; for him, Simeon's ascent on the pillar represented his search for escape from the physical world. It was the "fatigue," the "unbearable toil"[103] from the weight of the world that drove him to be apart up on his pillar: he sought to "fly heavenward."[104]

Theodoret also takes the time to draw from an apologia apparently prepared by Simeon's monastic community and utilized also by the writers of Simeon's Syriac vita.[105] From this he defends Simeon's career as one that follows the Old Testament prophets: in seeking to reveal the will of God, the prophets often resorted to shocking behavior, which was as essential for their work as the message they spoke. But this is not where Theodoret finds the real key to Simeon's vocation; he focuses instead on the achieved discipline of the virtuous life.

In another vein altogether is the Syriac vita composed by the saint's disciples soon after his death.[106] It represents the saint's official story, the "authorized" version put out either by the community that continued to tend his shrine in its context as a major pilgrimage site or by those close to this community. Here there is no division of body and soul. Here, Simeon's conversion to the religious life is an act of love, the giving of himself into the very hands of God. "[He] cared for nothing except how he might please his Lord. . . . [And] he loved his Lord with all his heart."[107] In Theodoret's story, the capacity to work miracles was something that Simeon gained over time; it accrued to him gradually, as he attained an ever purer discipline. By contrast, in the Syriac vita Simeon was capable of miracles from the moment he gave himself over to God. This was not a grace symbolically earned or achieved; it was the mark of his unity with God.

In the Syriac text, much more space is given to the apologia for Simeon's vocation on the pillar. Major prophets whose actions had shocked their communities—Isaiah walking naked, Hosea marrying the harlot, Jeremiah wearing yoke and thongs—are cited as so many precursors to Simeon's action, and his work is presented specifically as prophetic behavior.[108] Moses and Elijah figure most prominently in this presentation, both as models and as spiritual guides for the stylite.[109] The pillar is climbed because this is what God calls him to do.[110] Here Simeon becomes a stylite not in penitence, not to deny his body nor to discipline it, but because God requires it to fulfill his purpose.

The Syriac text places much emphasis on Simeon's cruciform prayer. But as earlier in the *Odes of Solomon*, this image is not likened to Christ's suffering on the cross. It is used to connote Christ's victorious stance in his triumph over Satan, a victory displayed again through the activity of Simeon on the pillar. The pillar itself is likened to a number of images. It is the high place from which the prophet speaks the word of God; it is the new Mount Sinai from which the new Law is dispensed; it is the crucible that purifies Simeon as gold through fire; it is the altar upon which Simeon is the incense rising heavenward as prayer; it is the mountain on which Simeon is transfigured as Christ himself was once transfigured; but Calvary it is not.[111]

It is only in our third text, the Greek vita written by Antony, an alleged disciple of Simeon, that we hear of Simeon's vocation as one of penance.[112] For Antony, the extremity of Simeon's practice represents his response to his sinful nature as fallen man, and it is sin that holds the focus of this text. Here even the saint's capacity to work miracles does not indicate his victory over sin; it is rather a grace despite Simeon's humanity. In this text Simeon's actions are only the search to achieve adequate repentance through ceaseless abasement and punishment. Unlike the other two sources, this one presents the ugliness of the saint's vocation as exactly that, with no attempt to mitigate its brutality.

The variations in these texts reveal that even the most extreme ascesis did not represent a clear religious stance; the notion of a dualism fundamental to Christian culture can neither account for Simeon's voca-

tion nor convey its meaning.[113] Rather, we are presented with a kaleido-
scope of imagery, one that carries echoes from the entire spectrum of
early Syrian Christianity, heterodox or orthodox.

Simeon's story illustrates another feature of the cult of saints. When
he died, his body was moved to Antioch in an extraordinary procession.
Seven bishops, the military governor of Syria, and an escort of six hundred soldiers accompanied the body to its resting place in the cathedral.
The crowds en route were enormous. The procession took five days to
reach Antioch, a distance of roughly forty miles. After his death, his cult
continued to grow, with particular glory accruing to his shrine at Qal'at
Sim'an housing the relic of his pillar, but figuring also at religious sites
across Christendom, as far away as Gaul.[114] There came, too, the glory of
those who followed Simeon's model: stylites became an important feature of Byzantine spirituality; imitators can be found as late as the mid-
nineteenth century.[115]

Contemporaneously with Simeon's life and cult, the story of the
Man of God appeared in Edessa.[116] The story itself is set in the years
when Rabbula was Edessa's bishop (411–435) and was written perhaps
between 470 and 475, the dates for the composition of the Syriac *Life of
Simeon*. The two stories appear antithetical.

The story of the Man of God is a simple one. We do not know his
name, nor the names of his parents, a noble Roman family. Born to a
childless couple after many years, this son was from the beginning "an
instrument chosen by God." His humility, even as a youth, was unset-
tling; in an effort to help him conform to the ways of the world, his parents finally arranged a marriage for him. But the Man of God fled, and
making his way to Syria, he settled in Edessa as a beggar. The way of life
he took on as his vocation was as simple as it was severe. He lived
among the poor in the vicinity of the church, fasting and praying. He
would accept a little money from the almsgivers, from which he pur-
chased a very little food and gave the rest to others in need. At night he
stayed among the poor, standing in cruciform prayer all night while they
slept.

Eventually the caretaker (*paramonarius*) of the church discovered his
practice, and one night begged, "Who are you and what is your work?"
The saint gestured to the poor who lay sleeping around them, "Ask
those in front of you, and from them you will learn who I am and whence I
am, for I am one of them."[117] It was only with the greatest difficulty that
the caretaker learned the saint's story, and only after the holy man had
bound him to secrecy and refused when the caretaker asked to become
his disciple. But the caretaker began to imitate the Man of God, secretly

following an austere prayer practice of his own and watching over the holy man. One day while the caretaker was away, the saint died; anonymous in death as in life, he was buried in the cemetery of the poor. In great distress, the caretaker poured out the story to Bishop Rabbula, begging that the body be taken back from the graveyard and with proper burial laid "in a known place," [118] to be granted due veneration. But the saint's body could not be found, only the rags in which he had lain.

We have no way of knowing whether or not there is a historical basis to this story. It may have been inspired by such an ascetic, or it may have been a simple didactic tale; either way, the message remains the same. In the story we are shown two responses to the life of this saint. First, the Bishop Rabbula is spurred by the meaning of the saint's presence in the city to undertake service to the poor and destitute, in honor of the saint's identity with them (and indeed, Rabbula was famed for his work with the needy).[119] As for the *paramonarius*, he undertook the continuation of the saint's prayer practice and the telling of the saint's story. But so well did he understand it that he preserved the humility of his master even then. Himself anonymous, he wrote a story that gives us a saint with no teachings, no miracles, no body, no tomb, and no name.[120]

A greater contrast to Simeon would be hard to imagine. On his pillar, Simeon was both in the world and above it. Further, he lived in a space well separated from the urban world; up in the mountains, the world came out to Simeon to seek his aid. As his cult grew, the enclosure built around him and his attendant monastic community created a buffer between the saint and his suppliants that was far more efficient than the height of his pillar. Simeon's practice made him visible to all and thus gave the sense that he was accessible to all.[121] But despite the generosity of his works, Simeon could be reached only by his chosen few. One obtained intercession from Simeon through the intercession of his disciples. The separation was sharp enough to confuse his pilgrims as to whether he was human.[122]

A clear-cut relationship between ascetics and society in the Syrian Orient was emerging, along with a fusion of the eremitic and cenobitic vocations, as the individual virtuosi found their practices increasingly conducted within monastic communities. Rabbula himself published canonical literature for monks and for the Sons and Daughters of the Covenant, dealing with situations both inside the religious community and out in the public sphere.[123] For both groups, in both spheres, he demanded a life of strict separation. There was to be little if any contact with the laity, and no contact between sexes; monastic garments and chaperones helped to demarcate the boundaries of religious life in an urban context. In the monasteries themselves, structures became clear. Both seclusion as a hermit and the use of chains or other "spiritual aids" were restricted to the most worthy in a monastery. Rabbula's legislation was strengthened by civil laws such as those exempting stylites from court appearances, which served to reinforce the practical order of religious and societal interaction.[124]

The Man of God's life would seem to undermine this entire picture. He does not withdraw from the world: he goes to it. He enters the harsh reality of the destitute in a major urban center, "For I am one of them." He lives among men and women, unmarked by clothing, company, or conduct. Without even a name, he has no identity as a holy man. Where the physical separation of the holy was an essential ingredient in the work that Simeon and others like him performed for society, and where the cult of such a saint flourished both during life and after death, the Man of God was invisible in life and death, indistinguishable from the poor in the streets or in the cemetery. Alive he was no one in particular; he could have been anyone, and thus he became everyone. When his body disappeared in death, he was nowhere; he could have been anywhere, and so he was everywhere. The Man of God had just this task as his work: to reveal the presence of the holy in the midst of human life. This he did by the power of his presence alone, sanctifying the world itself and causing good works to be done by those around him—not miracles, but actions of concrete import in human society and possible for any person to perform.

In this text, too, the image of cruciform prayer is crucial. Here again, our saint is given no images of trial, testing, or punishment.[125] Rather, we are once more presented with images of transformation: from the greatness of his noble birth, to the humbleness of the poor, to the holiness of the empty tomb. The holy was where the Man of God was—in the world.

Thus at a time when popular spirituality evoked fervent followings for holy men and women and accorded their monasteries great power and influence, the Man of God provided a balancing voice. Where could the life of true devotion be lived? Where could the holy be found? And who was truly free from the cares of the world? In his story, the Man of God showed no disrespect for either city or monastery. For him, they were one and the same; life itself was vocational. This is in fact the consequence of the story. Simeon presented the holy one as sharply marked out from the general Christian community, by space, behavior, food, and intercessory activity. The Man of God took this division and forged an integration between society and the holy, for the holy could operate anywhere.

The career of Simeon and the story of the Man of God articulate the paradigm of Syrian asceticism as both an external expression and an internal reality. They reflect the variety of earlier ascetic activity in the Syrian Orient, presenting different aspects of its behavior and offering its meaning anew. Directly in their wake came John of Ephesus and the ascetics he celebrates in his *Lives of the Eastern Saints*.

RELIGION AND HISTORY

The Syrian Orient, like the larger Christian world, never contained one overarching "church" identity. During the fourth century the Council of Nicea (325) had helped to spur the general ecclesiastical movement towards conformity, though the Christian realm remained diverse as a body. By the sixth century, Christendom faced the issue of conformity with renewed intensity, and the Syrian Orient was itself a major battlefield for the conflict at hand. When John of Ephesus was born at the turn of the sixth century, the dispute over the Council of Chalcedon (451) continued heatedly, and the anti-Chalcedonian movement was reaching its peak. By the time of John's death in 589, all this had changed. Formally divided into separate church bodies, the Chalcedonian church of the Byzantine Empire and the non-Chalcedonian "Monophysite" church of the Christian Orient now stood autonomously.[126]

The key issue behind the Council of Chalcedon was that of Christological definition: what exactly was the relationship between Christ's divine and human natures?[127] The Monophysites followed Cyril of Alexandria's track in asserting the continuity of the divine subject—in Jesus Christ, the divine Logos really was present in the flesh, in the world. Through the tradition of Alexandrian thought, Cyril posited what were in effect two states for the Logos, the preexistent Logos and the Logos enfleshed. His concentration on the fact that it was the Logos incarnate who suffered left him with the paradox of how Christ could "suffer without suffering." The difficulty in Cyril's way of uniting the human and the divine in Christ lay in how to maintain the full humanity of Christ without being forced to the heterodox position that the Godhead could suffer human weakness and pain.

The Chalcedonians ironically followed the route Nestorius had paved through the tradition of Antiochene thought: protection of the full divinity of the Logos by asserting the full integrity of Christ's humanity. Christ's suffering was here experienced by the man Jesus, fully human in body and soul, devised as the "temple" that the Logos had fashioned for Himself and in which He dwelt. But here the Logos was held intact at the risk of dividing Christ into two separate beings, two natures complete and whole, one divine and one human.

The Council was also concerned with maintaining the theological alliance between East and West, and to some extent it was the concessions to Western thought that created the furor following the Council.[128] The greatest stumbling block to the resolution of theological differences seemed to be the Latin *Tome of Pope Leo*, the papal contribution to the Chalcedonian definition of faith. In order to accommodate the *Tome*, the Council had compromised its theological language, making it more specific. Thus the Chalcedonian definition affirms Christ "in two natures" rather than "out of two natures." Advocates of the Conciliar decision saw the compromise as a matter of sharpening the Creed laid down at Nicea; dissenters saw it as sanctioning innovation by straying from holy tradition into heresy.

The Monophysites accused the Chalcedonians of having divided Christ in two, the error of "Nestorianism" proper, in order to affirm more precisely his humanity; and thus of worshipping a quaternity (as John of Ephesus' subjects refer to it) of Father, Spirit, Christ, and Jesus. In turn, those supporting the Council accused their antagonists of Eutychianism, uniting the two natures into one nature divine, a heresy the Monophysites themselves denounced. The Chalcedonians were concerned to protect the Logos from the blasphemy of asserting that the divine could suffer pain and the weakness of human fallibility. The differences lay in language rather than in concept.[129]

The fact that both sides in the dispute shared the same claims scripturally, patristically, and traditionally—and, above all, that both rightly claimed the authority of Cyril of Alexandria—is critical. In fact, both sides believed the same faith, that declared at the Council of Nicea.[130] But certain key terms shared by the Alexandrian and Antiochene schools of thought did have different connotations for their respective systems,[131] and the deep-seated fear that faith must be absolutely correct, or "orthodox," in order to save, led to a rigid conservatism on both sides. Furthermore, the political interests involved bred a simplistic reductionism from the content of the language to its literal meaning. The arguments became so hardened that the essential points of agreement were obscured.[132]

In the course of the dispute following Chalcedon, considerable movement was made theologically by both sides toward a solution incorporating both the Alexandrian and the Antiochene schools of thought. The efforts of the neo-Chalcedonian theologians, under the sponsorship of Justinian in particular, show how far the work of fusion could progress between the two traditions.[133]

Ironically, Justinian was the emperor who sought a genuine theological resolution to the conflict, rather than a compromise. He saw the problem as one of reconciling the language of the Council with that of Cyril of Alexandria, that is, keeping Chalcedon's authority intact while resolving the knots of the theological discourse. The Council of Constantinople in 553 represented the fruits of his labors. Yet it was also Justinian who forced the political situation to polarize irrevocably and thus to render his theological work ineffectual for the Christian Orient.[134]

The dispute peaked during the sixth century, both theologically and politically. But it is the daily reality of the presence of this dispute that we will find in John of Ephesus' writing. The circumstances in which the battle was fought mediated its meaning for Christian society. Matters did not stand in isolation.

The relative political stability of Anastasius' reign (491–518) seems to have been deceptive. Troubles that had seemed controllable—for example, the flare-up of the Persian campaigns between 502 and 505—began to show themselves as too deeply seated for straightforward solutions. Further complications came from a series of natural disasters occurring throughout the empire at that time: earthquakes, famine, and plague. These put strains on the empire's finances and morale, preventing an amenable context for Anastasius' policies.

The pro- and anti-Chalcedonian factions were not yet completely polarized, but relations worsened as Anastasius proved unable to achieve an equilibrium during his reign; his sympathies for the Monophysite cause forced him gradually into a stronger stance of support than he himself judged wise.[135] The measures he took showed how explosive the situation could be. The Monophysite leader Severus attained the patriarchal seat at Antioch in 512; but in Constantinople, at the same time, riots against the anti-Chalcedonians forced the emperor, without his diadem, to beg for peace in the Hippodrome and to offer abdication. Anastasius' pitiful appearance dampened the violence. But the point had been made: a hapless Syrian monk, taken to be Severus himself, had been beheaded by the rioting mob.[136]

The continuation of these varied problems made a smooth route for Justin's changes in imperial policies, but they also added a sinister tone where it might not otherwise have been felt.[137] Perhaps most decisively in the course of his reign, Justin worked closely with his enigmatic nephew Justinian, who was to succeed him in 527. For some ancient historians (and for some modern ones), these two men comprised one reign.[138]

During Justin's term of office, imperial interests shifted irreparably away from the eastern provinces, for years a stable source of goods, trade, and labor, and focused on the West, a policy that culminated in Justinian's effort to reconquer Italy and North Africa. The policy was initiated on a diplomatic level. Justin and Justinian began to woo the Pope and the Roman people by taking up the Chalcedonian cause. The extent of their commitment was shown in the persecutions against the Monophysites that began in 519 soon after Justin attained office.

The commencement of the persecutions provoked instant reaction on both sides of the theological divide over Chalcedon. Severus' patriarchal reign from 512 to 518 had seen the Monophysite movement at its height, but even to contemporaries the fragility of its hold was clear.[139] Yet Justin's change in religious policy could not have appeared as decisive as it would later prove. First, the Monophysites themselves knew their ascendency had been tenuous, and they expected further battles. And second, the persecutions were conducted against church officials and monastic communities only, leaving the body of the faithful untouched.

By imperial design, the persecutions struck hardest in the Syrian Orient, and particularly in John of Ephesus' home province of Mesopotamia. However, the new measures favoring Chalcedon by force did allow a significant loophole for the dissenters. Egypt was exempted from the persecutions, enabling Monophysites to seek refuge there. Perhaps this exemption was undertaken on economic grounds, since Egypt was Constantinople's bread basket.[140] But Egypt was also the territory of Cyril of Alexandria. Cyril and his successor Dioscurus had drawn profoundly on the authority of their monastic comrades; the Egyptian monks had responded to the Christological crisis with a passionate involvement. Indeed, since the days of Athanasius and Antony, the Alexandrian patriarchate had fostered a heritage of close interaction with the desert ascetics. The people of Alexandria, furthermore, were famed for their volatile religious sentiments; it was a place where controversy thrived.[141]

The Alexandrian heritage suited well the conditions of persecution. The refugee patriarchs, bishops, priests, and ascetics that came together in Egypt's sanctuary of asylum found themselves in a situation that encouraged the spiritual momentum of their cause, combining fears of oppression with the recognition of Egypt's authoritative position among Christians.[142] Thus the persecuted not only fled to Egypt for safety but looked to it to maintain their legitimacy. Egypt, as elsewhere in the East, had not represented a unanimous anti-Chalcedonian faith and had not long before provoked disciplinary measures from Severus;[143] but these differences were now put aside. Egypt, as befitted Cyril's homeland, became the hallmark of orthodox communion for those professing Cyril's "Monophysite" faith.[144]

To a large degree, practical reasons caused the division to harden along geographical and cultural lines. It was essential to the imperial ideology of Byzantium, as developed by Justinian, that the alliance with Rome be upheld and thus that the Latin elements of Chalcedonian theology be supported. It was also of import to the throne, again for ideological reasons, that the patriarchate rankings sanctioned at Chalcedon (Canon 28), giving Constantinople primacy over the eastern sees, be maintained. These two factors were crucial to the emperor's claim to be God's representative, the image of Christ on earth, and also to his claim that the empire was the Christian Empire, the image of the heavenly kingdom. The imperial policies that Justinian brought to the dispute demanded that Chalcedon be affirmed on a par with the three great councils before it, at Nicea, Constantinople, and Ephesus. Chalcedon gave divine sanction to the kind of authority Justinian was claiming and bequeathing to the Byzantine Empire.

On the other hand, the Roman West was of little interest or concern to the eastern provinces. It was remote geographically and culturally, and imperial investment in the West meant economic drain on the East, which had to finance the cost. Moreover, the eastern provinces were far enough away from Constantinople to escape the full brunt of its policies; furthermore, their languages and cultures were sufficiently autonomous to allow a separate activity. They were physically apart and possessed the cultural tools needed for remaining religiously distinct. Finally, their own suffering of calamities during the sixth century of necessity turned their interests inward to their own local situations. These factors made dissent easier, more deep seated, and more self-righteous.

For unforeseeable calamity interfered with Justinian's plans for a revitalized and Chalcedonian empire. A sequence of earthquakes, floods, and famine had nagged the empire from the turn of the sixth century, hitting the eastern provinces particularly hard. The situation came to a head in 542 when the Great Bubonic Plague broke out, bringing an incomprehensible level of disaster. Wherever it struck, production and business halted altogether for the duration of its presence. The survivors were left to restore "normality," while imperial demands continued unabated. But the plague recurred, in Justinian's reign four more times, and it deepened its toll on each occasion. When Evagrius Scholasticus wrote an account of this blight in his *Ecclesiastical History*, he stated with resignation that he wrote in the fifty-second year of the plague. The cumulative effect on population, morale, and economy was as insidious as it was disastrous.[145]

Even so, Justinian's military conquests over the course of his reign might have seemed impressive. But at his death in 565, little concrete gain for his efforts remained, apart from a crippled state. His failures were huge. The wars with Persia had continued, occurring intermittently for the duration of the reign, and their cost was threefold: campaigns had continually to be financed, and fortifications built and strengthened; efforts to end the animosities by diplomatic means involved huge tributary payments; and the opulence of the eastern cities was freely ransacked by the Persians. Moreover, in the West not one of the military victories was to be decisive for any length of time, and the gains proved more costly to hold than they had been to acquire; financially debilitating excursions were launched and relaunched for years. Finally, of least concern to Justinian but of considerable consequence to the empire, his various neighbors to the north required large tributary payments to stay indecisively under control.

Matters disintegrated rapidly on all fronts in the years following Justinian's death. The empire's resources had been drained; his tax collectors had been notoriously efficient. The eastern provinces, for example, already locked in their own plight, were crippled still more by the constant needs of the imperial treasury.[146] To be fair, the economic problems of the empire were already great when Justinian came to power; but he showed no acknowledgment of the delicate situation in his own policies, then or later.[147]

Despite Justinian's lasting accomplishments, notably in art and in law, the glimpse of an empire regained did not conceal its own demise. So violent were the fluctuations between brilliance and obstinacy during Justinian's reign that they evoked an otherwise puzzling incongruity in the writings of his commentators. The apparently unaccountable, even self-defeating, opposite viewpoints in the writings of Procopius, or the complexities in the relationship between Justinian and John of Ephesus, make sense only insofar as they bear witness to the actual contemporary impact of Justinian's reign. Matters were not simply black or white; they were both at once, with no tinge of gray.[148]

With this larger context as their backdrop, the accounts of Amida and its ascetics in John of Ephesus' *Lives of the Eastern Saints* provide considerable supplement to the chronicles of the sixth century. Lists of facts, events, and odd occurrences are translated by John's stories into cohesive parts of real and ongoing life in the eastern empire. Similarly, the people he follows through the wider empire establish for us a sensitivity to the time and space of Justinian's era. Here matters were not just affected by imperial policies but actually take on the imprint of the imperial personalities themselves—not the remote king and queen perceived from Amida's territory, but Justinian and Theodora at work. Thus John opens for us the world in which he lived; it is to that opening we now turn.

· I ·

"THESE HOLY IMAGES":
JOHN OF EPHESUS
AND THE *Lives of the Eastern Saints*

JOHN HIMSELF

John of Ephesus, sometimes known as John of Asia, was born in the early sixth century around the year 507. He was from the territory of Ingilene in north Mesopotamia, which fell under the jurisdiction of the metropolitan city of Amida. The local population was a mixture of Syrians and Armenians. What we know of John's life is drawn from scattered references he makes in his writings; the time and place of major events, at least, can be arranged with fair certainty.[1]

John's many-sided career had a propitious start. Ingila's local stylite had been for some years a monk called Abraham, at the monastery of Ar'a Rabtha. When Abraham died, his brother Maro ascended the vacant pillar. The first miracle of Maro's new career was the saving of John's life.

John's parents had lost all their sons before the age of two, apparently because of a congenital problem. When John succumbed as well, they brought the dying child to Maro. Maro was new to the practice of holy medicine, and the ensuing interchange between stylite, attendants, and parents involved much confusion. The child appeared dead, and Maro's prescription of lentils inspired no confidence in his audience. But when finally the monks were persuaded to place the food in John's mouth, he suddenly revived. The stylite then commanded that the boy be fed as many lentils as he could eat and be brought back to him in two years' time as his own son.[2] Thus by the age of four, John found himself received into the monastic vocation, under the tutelage of a great spiritual father.

Maro died when John was about fifteen years old. The young monk soon left Arʿa Rabtha "because of the proximity of family" and joined Amida's ascetic community, becoming a member of the monastery of Mar John Urtaya in the early 520s.[3] By this time, persecutions against the Monophysites had begun, and the Amidan ascetics were in fact living as a combined group in exile. John's move to their community marked the beginning of his many years of travel and activity as a Monophysite. This was not a matter of conversion to a cause; reflecting the hardened religious positions of his times, John seems never to have considered any other confession. Until the early 540s, John journeyed with his fellow Amidans, much of the time fleeing persecutors and living in makeshift conditions, but also, during periods of relative peace, visiting other monasteries and noted hermits. His travels took him throughout the East, down into Egypt, and across to Constantinople. It was during this period, in the year 529, that John was ordained deacon by John of Tella, himself in exile at the time, as part of an underground program of ordinations meant to replenish the depleted Monophysite clergy.[4]

John of Ephesus first came to Constantinople around the year 540. A large number of Monophysite refugees had settled in the imperial city under the protection of the religiously sympathetic empress Theodora. Upon his arrival, John seems soon to have become known at the court as well as among the Monophysite communities in and around the capital. In 542 the emperor Justinian, champion of Chalcedonian orthodoxy, enigmatically chose John to undertake a campaign of conversion among the pagans and heretics still flourishing in Asia Minor.[5] John's zeal for the task can hardly have served the Chalcedonian interests of the government, for it was while occupied in this way that he was consecrated titular bishop of Ephesus by Jacob Burdʿaya, possibly in 558.[6] Still, his efforts on Justinian's behalf earned him the title Converter of Pagans. On missions through Asia, Lydia, Caria, and Phrygia, John claimed to have converted eighty thousand pagans and schismatics (notably Montanists) and received government aid to found ninety-eight churches and twelve monasteries.[7]

We have no evidence that John ever resided in Ephesus; instead, his base of operation remained at Constantinople. In the 540s he was given a villa by the chamberlain Callinicus just outside the capital, at Sycae, and there he founded a monastery with himself as archimandrite.[8] It served as his home base until its confiscation by the Chalcedonians in 578. By 566, at the death of the Alexandrian patriarch Theodosius, John had become the official leader of the Constantinopolitan Monophysites. But the Monophysites themselves were now beset by internal quarrels, and John was caught in the effort to mediate between factions so opposed that their overriding cause was hopelessly weakened.

The accession of Justin II in 565 brought renewed vigor to imperial Chalcedonian commitment. In 571 the patriarch of Constantinople, John Scholasticus, initiated a new persecution, in which John of Ephesus was an obvious target.[9] From this time until he died, the Monophysite leader suffered imprisonment and exile. Age as well as despair over the state of the church—both within Monophysite ranks and in the wider theological negotiations—left John's health and spirit broken. Nonetheless, he worked on his *Ecclesiastical History,* smuggling the chapters out of prison,[10] until his death, probably in 589.[11]

JOHN'S WRITINGS

Amidst his many activities, John was also an important writer. Most of his two major works, the *Ecclesiastical History* and the *Lives of the Eastern Saints,* remain extant, but large parts of the *Ecclesiastical History,* as well as other pieces, have been lost.

John's earliest work appears to have been a description of the first Monophysite persecutions, perhaps in particular those conducted in the 530s by the patriarch Ephrem of Antioch and Abraham bar Kaili, bishop of Amida.[12] He may also have written a few years later an account of the Great Bubonic Plague that struck the empire in 542, but whether he left this as an independent work is unclear. A further work that has not survived seems to have dealt with theological negotiations in the early 570s, focusing on the general formula of unity discussed by Chalcedonian and Monophysite authorities in 571.[13]

Scholars have long held John's *Ecclesiastical History* as a work of major import for the sixth century. It consists of three parts, the first covering the period from Julius Caesar until the death of Theodosius II, the second spans the period to 571, and the third to 588–589.[14] A few citations from part 1 are incorporated by Michael the Syrian in his *Chronicle;* considerably more of part 2 is quoted in large sections by pseudo-Dionysius of Tell-Mahre in his *Chronicle,* as well as by Michael, and these segments have been supplemented by further scattered references.[15] Part 3 has survived intact.[16]

John's early writings on the persecutions and Great Plague doubtless provided much of the material about those events in part 2 of his *Ecclesiastical History*. For these matters, his accounts of natural disasters, his intimate knowledge of the imperial court under both Justinian and Justin II, his provincial ties, and his detailed rendering of the internal Monophysite disputes, we are most indebted to his *History*.

A careless writer at the best of times, John's enthusiasm outweighed his patience. In the parts of his *History* composed while he was in prison or in exile, this tendency was aggravated by the circumstances. But John shows little regard for the discipline evidenced by fellow Syriac historians of the same time. Both the meticulous concern for detail (of prices and dates in particular) shown by "Joshua the Stylite" in his *Chronicle* and the careful preservation of documents found in pseudo-Zachariah Rhetor's *Ecclesiastical History* are missing in John's *History*.[17]

Yet by virtue of their fervor, John's writings provide an honest record that counterbalances the official (and Chalcedonian) histories, whether "secular" or "ecclesiastical," left by his Greek contemporaries.[18] Perhaps best exemplified by those of Procopius, Agathias, and Evagrius Scholasticus, these formal histories by Greeks constitute works in which literary protocol was at times more important than what was being reported.[19] Despite its many inaccuracies, John's *History* proves true to the nature and experience of his times in a way not possible for those writers more officially or literarily minded.[20]

In the late 560s John wrote and then expanded the *Lives of the Eastern Saints*, a collection of fifty-eight stories of Mesopotamian and Syrian ascetics whom he himself had known or met during his life, and whose religious careers were particularly inspiring.[21] The stories are told as vignettes interspersed with hearsay; their presentation resembles those of the *Historia Lausiaca* by Palladius, the *Historia religiosa* of Theodoret of Cyrrhus, and the later *Pratum spirituale* of John Moschus. E. W. Brooks has called the *Lives* John's "most characteristic" work;[22] it is certainly a personal one.

The major focus of the collection falls between the 520s and 560s. John anchors the chapters primarily by references to each subject's life before and after the commencement of the Monophysite persecutions, his pivotal landmark.[23] The order of the chapters follows the chronology of John's own life, and the shape of the whole reflects the influences at work on John in the development of his career. John's stories, then, are in part his own story.

The fifty-eight chapters of the *Lives* can be divided into two basic clusters: the first revolves around John's experiences as a youth in the

monastic communities of Amida's regions (chaps. 1–23), and the second
concerns his experiences after leaving Mesopotamia, primarily in Egypt
and Constantinople (chaps. 24–57). The final chapter (58) is devoted to
the history of the Amidan monastery of Mar John Urtaya, to which he
felt his greatest bond throughout his career. Odd chapters are out of sequence with this arrangement but probably indicate John's own lack of
organization rather than mishandling in transmission.[24]

The first twenty-three chapters are set mainly in Mesopotamia. They
are, by and large, longer, more detailed, and more personal than the
subsequent chapters. These accounts describe the monastic setting in
which John grew up, the kind of ascetic practices that provided his
models, and the individuals who particularly influenced his vocation.
This portion of the *Lives* includes the following:

Habib (chap. 1), an efficacious monk whose career fits well the pattern
that characterized the holy man of late antiquity;

Z'ura (chap. 2), Habib's disciple who became a stylite but went on, because of the persecutions, to provide an influential presence in
Constantinople;

Abraham and Maro (chap. 4), two brothers whose careers as stylites dom-
inated the religious life of northern Mesopotamia for many years;

John the Nazirite (chap. 3), Paul the Anchorite (chap. 6), Harfat (chap.
11), and Simeon the Solitary (chap. 23), whose anchoretic careers for-
cibly came to accommodate the altered context of persecutions;

Abraham the Recluse (chap. 7) and Mare of Beth Urtaye (chap. 9), who
came to the ascetic vocation late in life;

Simeon the Hermit and Sergius (chap. 5), a solitary and his disciple who
served as vigilanti of Mesopotamia's villages;

Some who undertook the solitary life only to find it leading to involvement in the affairs of the outside world—Addai the Chorepiscopus,
who instituted a profitable wine industry (chap. 8); two monks who
could not avoid their callings as exorcists (chap. 15); Simeon the
Mountaineer, who inadvertently became a missionary (chap. 16);
Thomas the Armenian (chap. 21) and Abraham and Addai (chap. 22),
who discovered their true vocation in founding monasteries;

Virtuosi of private labors in the tradition of Syrian asceticism, who visited Amida's monastic communities to pay them homage (the traveling monks in chaps. 14, 17, 18, 19, and 20);

Mary and Euphemia (chap. 12) and Thomas and Stephen (chap. 13), accounts of paired careers that integrate the life of contemplation and
the life of service; and

Simeon the Persian Debater (chap. 10), notorious bishop of Beth Arsham in Persia.

In the second cluster John expands his setting. Like himself, most of these subjects have their roots in Mesopotamia and were forced out into the larger Roman Empire because of persecution. This section includes a number of Monophysite leaders; in the first section, only Zᶜura and Simeon of Beth Arsham fit this mold. Yet John does not allot these two the same detail that he gives to his "local" celebrities, such as Maro, Euphemia, or Simeon the Mountaineer. This second section is approximately the same length as the first, but where the first section dealt with twenty-nine holy men and women, the second treats more than fifty. These chapters reflect too John's own altered position. He writes with more assertiveness, appropriate to his increasing authority in Monophysite circles during the years covered by these chapters.

This second section comprises the following:

Eminent Monophysite bishops—John of Tella (chap. 24), John of Hephaestopolis (chap. 25), Thomas of Damascus (chap. 26), the Five Patriarchs (chap. 48), Jacob Burdᶜaya (chap. 49), who is again treated with his comissionary Theodore (chap. 50), and Kashish (chap. 51);

Accounts of the ascetic community in Egypt, and particularly of the Monophysite refugees who fled there—the spiritual leader Susan (chap. 27), Mary the Anchorite (chap. 28), a hapless monk who stole and was rehabilitated by John of Ephesus (chap. 32), the wealthy patrician Caesaria (chap. 54) and the members of her household who followed her model John and Sosiana (chap. 55), and Peter and Photius (chap. 56);

Laymen who practiced asceticism in their "worldly" careers—Elijah of Dara (chap. 30), a second Elijah and Theodore (chap. 31), Tribunus (chap. 44), and Theodore the *Castrensis* (chap. 57);

Monophysite refugees who came to Constantinople and performed the ministry of service among its needy populace—Hala (chap. 33), Simeon the Scribe (chap. 34), Mare the Solitary (chap. 36), Aaron (chap. 38), Leontius (chap. 39), Abraham the Presbyter (chap. 40), Bassian and Romanus (chap. 41), Mari, Sergius, and Daniel (chap. 42), four deacons (chap. 43), and Isaac (chap. 45); some of these individuals assisted John on his missions to Asia Minor;

Accounts of what happened to the Amidan monasteries during their exile in the eastern provinces (chaps. 29 and 35), and to those monks who fled to the Monophysite monastic communities in Constantinople (chap. 47);

Paul of Antioch (chap. 46), who established a sizeable network of social
    services in a number of Byzantine cities; and
Two accounts, one set in Amida and one in Constantinople, of holy fools
    (chaps. 52 and 53).

John did not intend to use his *Lives,* as he did his *History,* to record
the Monophysite story, but there is necessarily much overlap between
the two works. Both for him and for his subjects, the persecution of the
Monophysites marked an irrevocable turn in their lives. Further, the
persecution was fundamental to the vision of asceticism John propagated, for his purpose was to show how this drastic change had impact
on the ascetic vocation as he knew it.

In his collection John writes of holy men and women whose ascetic
activities give evidence of power in the temporal as well as spiritual
realms. Often, their capacity for power has been gained in the testing of
abstinence and withdrawal. But it is brought to fullness, as John presents it, only in the context of others: in the congregation of the ascetic
community and, above all, in the needs of the lay society. What we find
in John's *Lives* is a situation that belies an other-worldly focus for asceticism, and indeed the fundamentally timeless, ahistorical concerns of
the hagiographer. Thus the *Lives* must be seen in their context, both literary and historical. John of Ephesus as author offers important clues.

GENRE: CHARACTERISTICS AND CHOICES

Syriac hagiography was a well-developed genre long before John of
Ephesus wrote. The passion narratives of the Edessan martyrs Shmona,
Guria, and Habib; the *Life of Simeon the Stylite;* the *Life of the Man of God;*
the *Acts of Sharbil;* and the *Life of John of Tella* by the monk Elias are examples, exemplary for both content and style. Moreover, the increasing
Hellenization of the fifth and sixth centuries did not diminish the standard. Elias' *Life of John of Tella,* written barely twenty years before John of
Ephesus wrote his *Lives,* is a masterpiece of Syriac literature, with a
prose of elegant simplicity. But Elias' account was above all a product of
the cultural fusion that marked the early sixth century in the Syrian Orient. Excellent Syriac translations of Greek hagiography were also easily
at hand.

John of Ephesus chose for his subjects a free-ranging style of cameo
portraits, the most informal of hagiographical genres and best represented by the earlier *Historia Lausiaca* of Palladius and the *Historia religiosa*

of Theodoret of Cyrrhus. This genre took the form of collections of stories,[25] which might or might not be concerned with a biographical approach; a single incident would often suffice for the author's purpose. The style of these collections tends to be more informal than that of full-length vitae, but sometimes only by way of content; Theodoret's Greek surpasses what we find in many Greek *Lives* as far as language and style are concerned. The collections are notable for their roots in specific monastic communities; what they record are the traditions (often oral) of that community and the author's experiences within it.

John of Ephesus' *Lives of the Eastern Saints* share the main features of this collection genre, although his work is noticeably less serene than the collections of Palladius, of Theodoret, the *Pratum spirituale* of John Moschus, or the *Historia monastica* of the ninth-century Syriac writer Thomas of Marga. Religious controversy of one kind or another was present as a backdrop for each of these authors, but John alone integrates the religious and political upheavals of his time into the foreground of his collection. Nonetheless, John's *Lives* remain a monastic work, like the others of this kind.[26]

Thus John includes discourses on the ascetic life by solitaries and preachings on the temptations a monk or nun must expect to face.[27] He provides an exposition on "the basis of sound training," in which he describes the lengthy process through which a novice must pass before receiving the full habit in an Amidan monastery.[28] And, the final chapter of the *Lives* narrates the history of his own monastery of Mar John Urtaya, from its fourth-century foundation to his present time.[29] Again, his own experiences as a monk in quest of spiritual edification provide the loose (and familiar, in this genre) framework around which the *Lives* are set.

John's literary predecessors (so far as we know) were, however, men who wrote in Greek and not in Syriac; thus questions about John's bilingualism must be raised. What influence, if any, did these earlier works exert on John's collection? Is any cross-cultural borrowing apparent in John's choice of genre? Since John does not tell us anything specific in this regard, we can only assess circumstantial factors.

John was educated in a Syriac-speaking monastery known for its scholarly training.[30] At some stage he acquired a reasonable fluency in Greek, making possible his activities both as a Monophysite spokesman in the imperial court at Constantinople and as a missionary in Asia Minor where Syriac would not have been a language in use. Both Palladius' *Historia Lausiaca* and Theodoret's *Historia religiosa* would have been available to him on his travels in their original Greek.[31] Furthermore, at least parts of both of these collections were also available in Syr-

iac translation during John's lifetime.[32] But the question of heretical asso-
ciations damaged the reputations of both these works during John's day
and may have determined whether or not John was acquainted with either of them.

Palladius was hardly free of controversy during his career, and his
Evagrianism, in particular, led the Greek church to suspect his work of
harboring improper elements.[33] Nonetheless, these issues did not affect
the general popularity of the *Historia Lausiaca*, although tamperings at
the level of manuscript transmission reveal conflict between the love accorded this work and the anxiety caused to the church by its author's
spiritual loyalties.[34] But Evagrius was highly thought of in Syrian tradition; much of his teaching survives only in Syriac.[35] To a Syrian monk
such as John of Ephesus, Palladius' Evagrian spirit would have presented no problem.

About Theodoret, issues were sharper. Controversy concerning him
had been more extreme than for Palladius: the Second Council of Ephesus (the "Robber Synod") in 449 deposed him from his see at Cyrrhus.
The Council of Chalcedon in 451 reinstated him, but the vindication
of Theodoret's faith proved a major obstacle for the Monophysites as far
as the decisions of this council were concerned. To the Monophysites,
Theodoret remained categorically the enemy of Cyril of Alexandria.
Their obstinacy on this point enabled Justinian to resurrect the issue of
Theodoret's teachings during the Three Chapters controversy of 544–
554, and the Council of Constantinople in 553 reversed the reprieve of
Chalcedon, condemning Theodoret's anti-Cyrillian writings.[36] His very
name would have been anathema to the Monophysites, particularly during the years of John's novitiate and priesthood, as sentiments over
Chalcedon hardened.[37] Moreover, a number of Theodoret's more important subjects—Jacob of Nisibis, Julian Saba, and Simeon Stylites, for example—would have been known in the Syrian Orient through Syriac
writings about them. By John's time, a Syrian monk did not have to read
Theodoret's collection to study Syrian ascetic tradition.

But if John was familiar with either or both of these predecessors
(which seems likely at least in the case of Palladius), their works appear
to have exerted little influence on his *Lives* except, perhaps, by suggestion of genre. In contrast, Thomas of Marga in the mid-ninth century
made his imitation of Palladius both explicit, by frequent references to
him, and implicit, through an intentional parallelism in his stories with
those by the earlier Greek writer.[38] No such modeling is evident in John's
Lives. The astringent didacticism of Palladius' vignettes and the classi-
cism of Theodoret's accounts offer no parallel for John's rambling nar-

ratives. Similarly, their contents, both in emphases and in ascetic vision, differ distinctly from John's. The presence of a similar literary format does not seem to indicate a decision by John to follow precise models but rather to choose the hagiographical mode most comfortable for him.

John's literary choices, then, tell us certain things about him. His purpose here is found in story more than in history; his interest lies in what people experienced in the context of the events they lived through. So in this instance he writes hagiography and not a historical chronicle (as in his *Ecclesiastical History*), anecdotal portraits and not biography. Moreover, John's concern as hagiographer is not with the specific impact of a key individual on the world (e.g., the *Lives* of Severus of Antioch and John of Tella), but with the shared witness and experience of a given community, the Amidan ascetics, and with the meaning of that community's presence in the world of its time.

HAGIOGRAPHIC STYLE: ISSUES OF LANGUAGE AND CONTENT

The inhabitants of the Syrian Orient lived through a harrowing series of natural and political calamities during John's lifetime; at the same time they were caught in severe religious persecution. It is in fact the conditions of his day that prompt John to set these lives and events down in writing. He writes a collection because he has encountered many men and women who acted through devotion to the divine. The simplicity of that fact belies its profundity in this particular work and its particular historical setting. Again, he includes accounts of the great Monophysite leaders of his day—subjects for formal vitae by others[39]—but the majority of his chapters deal with a localized, geographically remote area and with people otherwise unknown to us.

With these choices, John declares his own understanding of the events of his times. The holy is not restricted to certain persons (nobles, leaders) nor to certain places (cities). It is found in the people and places of daily lives; it is found in the midst of the same events that would seem to deny God's presence. The *Lives of the Eastern Saints* are a restatement of one kind of world as another. So John's purpose determines his genre, hagiography, and also his hagiographical style, his use of the standard conventions of this literary form.

For John, action is the most important element of devotion to God. Hence writing is for him a functional task, an action he takes in response to an urgent situation. He sets for himself certain guidelines: the appearance of familiar hagiographical themes, the use of material of specifically monastic intent, and the occasional pause to preach to his audience. But, unlike Theodoret, he is not mindful of his labors as a craft in themselves. When John uses the tools of the hagiographer's trade, he is simply being practical by using a language common to Christendom in order to make his point.

John's hagiographical style, his use of standard themes and images, is also subordinated to his purpose of re-presenting the events of his times through the lives of his subjects. In the context of hagiography, the tragedy, the calamity, the apparent defeat of the Monophysites all become the means by which God's grace is revealed. Hagiography as a literary form and the language of its conventions enables John to accomplish his task succinctly.[40] But at a practical level, this also means that John makes no distinction between literary conventions and his own perceptions.

John's lack of artistic concern blurs the boundaries in his accounts between the topos as a literary device and the motifs common in a historical sense because they represent traits of the ascetic as a figure in religious and societal life. That is, John employs standard literary images to express the common understanding of a holy man or woman as a religious persona.

Thus, for example, John employs the topos of a hostile assailant suddenly frozen in midair,[41] or likewise blinded[42] or struck fatally ill,[43] by the power of a holy man or woman—the standard means of presenting a saint's spiritual authority in tangible fashion.[44] Elsewhere, John's solitaries do physical battle with demonic forces,[45] in scenes reminiscent of similar ones from the Lives of Antony, Simeon the Stylite, and Daniel the Stylite.[46] The scene is a common personification of the saint's battle against temptation and the test of fortitude that marks initiation into the ranks of God's chosen. However, John also enjoys telling us about the idiosyncracies of his subjects. He is committed, too, to portraying the cost in human terms of the tragedies around him. These interests conflict with the standardized nature of hagiographical formulae. Indeed, John seems unaware of the disjuncture in his narratives when a familiar formula clashes with the sensitivity of his portraits—as, for instance, in his chapters about holy women, where his stereotypic statements are at odds with the actual accounts he gives.[47]

Thus John uses common themes not to make his stories fit popular tastes but to present a particular understanding of the lives lived by his subjects. When the holy woman Euphemia dies, exhausted after a career of service to the needy, the reader cannot fail to see her story in terms of

an *imitatio Christi*.[48] But John has not molded her portrait to fit this ty-
pology; he tells us about so many quirks of Euphemia's personality that
her individuality dominates the chapter throughout. Nor does Euphemia herself choose to present her dying in this light: her determination
with regard to her vocation does not negate her humility. The parallel of
Euphemia's life with that of the Gospels arises because John intends his
audience to see what he himself has seen: Euphemia's life, and those like
hers, can only be understood in relation to the work of Christ.

Similarly, John's two accounts of holy fools remind us that motifs
might become popular, even standardized, and yet maintain their capacity to affect people's choices in their own lives.[49] His first story on this
theme is presented in terms familiar to hagiographic romance, so much
so that some have questioned the reliability of this chapter.[50] But the second story is clearly about a personal encounter that John has experienced. The text itself is awkward owing to John's memory of the incident. It is the task of the scholar to separate formulae from historic
elements in a saint's life, but in John of Ephesus we see the reverse process: a formula or formulaic theme could help the Christian community
to understand religious activity by expressing its meaning, and thematic
legends could inspire genuine emulation (imitation) by real people.

In fact, the motifs that occur most frequently in John's *Lives* are not
of a hagiographical character. They are traits that characterize the asceticism of the Syrian Orient. So John presents his ascetics as strangers
in this world, an image that rests at the core of the Syrian ascetic vocation.[51] He draws out, too, the concern for hospitality within the ascetic's
works.[52] Again, those monks or nuns truly blessed in John's eyes have
the gift of tears[53] and of foreseeing their own deaths.[54] These and other
features of the ascetic's activities have less to do with hagiographic portrayal than with describing what had become the trademarks of actual
asceticism in this area.[55]

In this vein, too, we can understand the repetitive features in John's
accounts of healings. In his stories barren women do conceive,[56] and sick
persons are cured,[57] in standard fashion: the vehicle for the miracle may
be a relic, such as a holy man's toenail (as in the case of Maro), or the
commonly employed *ḥnānā*, a mixture of consecrated oil, dust from a
holy place, and water used for liturgical as well as private devotional
purposes. The possessed are exorcised by the sign of the cross or by a
rebuke of the demon by the holy person.[58] But these methods are those
that the holy man or woman generally used in society and are not drawn
from hagiography alone.[59]

The use of familiar hagiographical language and tone provided John with a convenient shortcut. The unmistakable literary conventions placed his subjects in the company of saints. John does not have to justify, as Theodoret did, the religious choices his subjects made; by John's time, hagiography had grown to be so much a part of popular piety that its language alone was sufficient to justify its content. John writes without contrivance; if his style includes hagiographical clichés, the earnestness of his effort fills them with fresh meaning. They represent the language in which he thinks and sees the world; they are the means by which he can enable his audience to share the same perception.[60]

LITERARY STYLE: CLUE TO THE CULTURAL SETTING

True to his word,[61] John is no artist as a writer. The careless haste so prevalent in his *Ecclesiastical History* is seen more frequently in the *Lives*. The *History*, to be sure, was written in such adverse circumstances that John can easily be forgiven his lack of polish. But he wrote the collection of saints in considerably more comfort.[62]

Here John writes in a prose pompous, laborious, and enthusiastic. His bilingualism creates further problems. Lacing his sentences with frequent Greek words or phrases, he often uses syntax more Greek than Syriac. He tacks lines of participial clauses together, forming sentences of interminable length. Greek syntax can sustain a complex load such as this, but Syriac with its subtler syntactic structure does so with difficulty: the awkwardness comes through in translation. In fact, John is as careless in his thinking as he is in his use of language. He himself (like his readers) often forgets the point he is making, and he frequently changes subjects in midsentence.

The constant presence of Greek language in the *Lives* clearly indicates bilingual thinking rather than poor translation on the part of an intermediary. We might well presume that John could have written in Greek had he wished, though bilingual speakers tend to have a preferred writing language.[63] But John would have had no reason to use Greek for written work. From the time of Justin I's accession in 519, Chalcedonian orthodoxy had been the only imperially sanctioned Christian confession. Although persecution against the Monophysites was intermittent thereafter (but most serious in the eastern provinces), by the time that John of Ephesus was writing any serious possibility of reconciliation had long passed.[64] It was not John's intent to disseminate Monophysitism to a wider audience through hagiography: such an activity was neither practical in the given political climate, nor, by the

560s, a concern for the dissenters against Chalcedon. The work is written for a specifically Monophysite audience; John's use of Syriac, aside from being his natural choice of language (or so we must presume), also specified his chosen readership.[65]

The awkward use of Greek in John's written language also points to the cultural condition of his time, and so to the significance of his chosen hagiographic form. Greek language and culture had been intruding with increasing force into the world of the Syrian Orient. In John's day, however, Syriac literature still maintained its autonomous standards; a writer such as Elias in his *Life of John of Tella* could mold bilingualism into a creative literary form. John of Ephesus was not a craftsman. Nonetheless, he represents a kind of cultural syncretism that was at its peak in the sixth century: a fusion of the Hellenic and oriental thought-worlds and experience that still allowed an independent position for Syriac culture within the Roman Empire.

When John was writing, Syriac stood at a considerable distance from its later decline. To some degree, it held a higher position in terms of cultural respect than it had had at any earlier time, despite the fame, for example, of Ephrem Syrus. Learned Syrians were still not necessarily educated in Greek, as we know from the references to schooling in Mesopotamia that John makes in the *Lives*;[66] and the Syriac academies were thriving in Persia, though John would not report on these because of their Nestorian position.[67] Moreover, John's subjects reveal a genuine concern for the Syriac education of children, at least rudimentarily in the reading of Scripture and more strictly for those entering the monastic life; this determination for literacy, even if only at a basic level, is shown in John's *Lives* to be present in villages as well as in the more sophisticated cities.[68]

To be sure, the ethos of the later Roman Empire laid certain constraints on cultural interchange. The responsibility for bilingualism lay on the non-Greek; translations in both directions were invariably done by those who were native Syriac speakers.[69] Yet Syriac seems to have gained some respect from the elite world of Greek culture. For in the fifth century, sources tend to represent Syriac as a problem for the mainstream empire and those Syrians who could not speak Greek were cause for ridicule.[70] But by the sixth century, sources seem to be more judicious: for the Armenians, Syriac ranked with Greek in scholarly status,[71] and, indeed, respect was accorded even by Greeks to the educated person who was trained in Latin, Greek, and Syriac.[72] For the Greek cultural elite, Armenian was a language quite outside their interests;[73] but the serious Greek historian followed the example of Eusebius of Caesarea and employed a Syriac assistant who could provide access to Syriac archives and documents.[74] Again, the Syrian continuator who produced the Syriac version of Zachariah Rhetor's *Ecclesiastical History* showed enough initiative to epitomize rather than translate, and to continue the work, adding a significant and solid piece of historical writing to the original and producing in effect a "new" *History* in the process of re-rendering the old.[75] Despite the cultural imperialism of Greek, Syrians were proud of their language. John of Ephesus records the relief shown by a group of Amidan ascetics in Egypt who stumbled across one of their own kind: "and the blessed men . . . saw that he was an educated man and spoke their language."[76]

Although John of Ephesus writes of asceticism in a geographically remote area of the Roman Empire, the villages of Mesopotamia were not isolated from the context of the empire as a whole, any more than Syriac was an insulated provincial language. John's linguistically hybrid style in fact conveys his setting: a synthesis of cultural experience that characterized the world of late antiquity.[77]

John's *Lives of the Eastern Saints* are not a Syriac work in a Greek literary genre; they are part of a larger context. But they resemble the collections of his literary predecessors in form only, and it is in the concrete differences of content, both narrative and perceptual, that we can understand John's independence from what preceded him and, indeed, that we can find his worth as a hagiographer.[78]

· II ·

"LET YOUR LIGHT SO SHINE
BEFORE MEN": THE ASCETIC VISION

JOHN OF EPHESUS: THE ASCETIC MODEL

John portrays an asceticism clearly rooted in early Syrian tradition. His ascetics live within easy access of lay people and are actively involved in the affairs of the community. His ascetics also maintain a degree of individuality even when not living as hermits; the holy one may live in a monastic community, or as a master with one or two disciples; he or she may live in solitude most of the time, or in the heart of the city. Yet in each case, the holy one pursues a personal practice, a private as well as public religious discipline. By the sixth century, Syrian asceticism was a constant presence in the daily life of the eastern provinces of the empire. For John of Ephesus, this activity represents a reconciliation of the two poles of vocational life, service and contemplation, and that reconciliation takes place within the holy one's own person. He will not separate social and religious need.

Thus John's portrait indicates some developments in perspective by both the ascetic and the hagiographer. It is important to understand what holiness means for John; his subjects are inspired by love for the divine and are also themselves agents for divine activity in the world. But John does not set them outside the realm of the human, as other authors sometimes did.[1] These holy men and women are very human; John might say truly human.

In his first two chapters, on the lives of Habib and his disciple Zᶜura,

John lays out his map. We are faced with a venerable tradition of serious import for the functioning of society. Habib was a holy man from the district of Sophanene, near the territory of Amida.[2] From the age of ten, he received his training under the direction of a great solitary. He went on to become a politically efficacious figure, perhaps most noted for debt remission and causing the downfall of landowners and moneylenders. Whether for zeal or didacticism, John tells us that the wicked who opposed Habib suffered cruel fates for their acts of pride, so that even when Habib tried to intercede for them, divine retribution struck them down.

Nonetheless, John casts a particular light on Habib's work. In the first chapter, John in effect defines ascetic practice as public service:

> From his boyhood and through his old age he retained his humility
> and obedience which also distinguished him, so that [if] a widow or
> poor woman or poor man begged him to go with him on any business
> whatever, he did not, as a man of high reputation [would], refuse to go,
> but, in order to satisfy him, would go with him at once.[3]

Nor was there a task too menial for his attention. When a poor widow who taught drawing for a living was faced with two students who refused to pay their fee, she turned naturally to Habib, "because everyone who was defrauded whether of little or of much had recourse to the holy Habib as to a deliverer of those who were wronged."[4]

But for all his praise, John does not present Habib as the sole actor in the drama, or as the sole agent. A barren woman proved to be as essential as the holy man himself in effecting her own cure, just as Christ had demonstrated in the Gospels: she conceived because of Habib's prayers and because "she believed."[5]

John's account of Habib also indicates the way in which asceticism grew in the Syrian Orient: in depth it grew through the disciples who came after the holy one; in breadth it stretched as far as the holy one traveled. Hence, Habib was a holy man working through a wide area of Syria,[6] but his chief disciple was the monk Zʿura, who carried on after the old man's death to become a stylite and to spread his works far from his homeland.[7] Zʿura's story picks up where Habib's ends. He inherited his master's vision and his work. His change in the manner of his practice did not draw him away from the cares of society. Rather,

> thenceforth the deeds of power and healings of his master were per-
> formed through him. For, after he had gone up on the column, and it
> was accordingly no longer in his power to grasp paralysed persons with
> his hands and bend them and cure the sick, they used to give him water
> and he used to pronounce a blessing, and wherever it fell a cure was
> not long in following.[8]

Z'ura was forced down from his pillar by the Chalcedonian persecutors, yet he continued undeterred. Responding to the crisis, he traveled to Constantinople on behalf of the Monophysites and there took up
residence in a monastic community. His influence soon became widespread, and John would have it that even the imperial court paid him
great respect. Z'ura's ascetic labors had thus taken him away from his
roots but not from the teachings of Habib. In the trusted tradition of
spiritual father and disciple, John likens their relationship to that of the
Old Testament prophets Elijah and Elisha. They were men strictly and
carefully trained in their practice, but they did not question that certain
responsibilities were attendant upon their chosen vocation. Their asceticism was not a separation from the temporal world but a commitment to
work within it. The pattern John lays down in his "Life of Habib," and expands in his "Life of Z'ura," reechoes throughout his *Lives of the Eastern
Saints*. John's ascetics act out a life of service central to their ascetic vow,
and not an inadvertent result of it. A different tone predominates to that
which had come before. Service is inherent in, rather than a by-product
of, the ascetic's practice.

Such an emphasis raises other issues for John, especially with regard to other inherited traditions. In particular, the self-mortification
that characterized the asceticism of the Syrian Orient seemed to John
now less important. So much does he look to good works that he sees
extreme asceticism as a distraction from, rather than an aid for, the task
of devotion to God. John's concern here, as always, is pragmatic. He
urges time and again, as in the case of the holy woman Euphemia, that
one can better serve others if one does not punish oneself so cruelly.[9] In
a case such as Z'ura's, where the stylite's works of service are an integral
part of ascetic practice, John stands back. But in a situation where the
ascetic's practice seems confined to a contrived harshness, John inter-
venes. In his view, there are needs more pressing than the private mourn-
ing of such activities.

Such, for example, was the case of Harfat, from the district of
Anzetene.[10] Harfat had withdrawn to a life of solitude after a brush with
unsavory church politics. "Because he was very simple," Harfat hung
"great heavy irons" on his neck, hands, and feet and then settled on a
mountainside. He nearly died of exposure until a woman took pity on
him and built him a hut for protection. John of Ephesus came along soon
after and pressured the hermit.

> What regulation commands this matter of the irons to be carried out?
> . . . If we seek to humble our body to the earth, cannot we humble it
> without irons? . . . We wish you to throw off these irons, which are a

useless burden, and lade yourself instead of them with the burden of labours performed with knowledge, and thus you will please God.[11]

John defines asceticism as utter devotion to God, and so to God's commandments alone. Those who had defended Simeon the Stylite's choice of ascetic practice did so on the basis of Old Testament parallels.[12] John understands what he sees, too, in Old Testament terms, as he shows in the case of Habib and Z'ura. But for John of Ephesus, the model divinely ordained for prophet or for disciple also recalled a ministry among the needy, and, as Habib had demonstrated, one that answered to distress without concern for society's dictates or institutions. With a basic criterion of God-centered service, John finds his subjects in settings and circumstances of wide diversity.

HOLY CAREERS: VARIATIONS ON A THEME

Nowhere is John's admiration more apparent than when he writes of those persons who endure abstinence and self-mortification, and also channel that same zeal back into the "real world." In his eyes, the responsibility for commitment lies with the ascetic. Where Theodoret had portrayed holy men and women acting on behalf of those who approached them, John is clear that his ascetics act not only because an afflicted populace seeks them out but also because they hold themselves accountable for the society around them. They are not passive in their role as benefactors.

An example is John's "Life of Addai the Chorepiscopus."[13] Addai had been chorepiscopus in the territory of Anzetene on the Armenian frontier, responsible for the discipline of clergy and monastic communities in the region, at the same time caring for the poor, orphans, and widows. Evicted from his own monastery during the Monophysite persecutions, he decided to become an anchorite in the mountains to the east. For the next twenty-five years, Addai lived as a recluse in the wilderness, seeing only a few attendants and running from any other visitors who tried to approach him (as John himself unhappily discovered).

But Addai did not give up contact with his monastery, which he had enjoined to care for those in need. Over the first five years of his seclusion, however, the monastery was plundered repeatedly by the Chalcedonians and fell to ruin. Addai was beside himself:

> And the blessed man was grieved and distressed on account of the starving and distressed persons for whom there was no method of providing, and further, the inmates of his monastery also were pressed by

want, then he considered, "There is no longer any quarter from which
it is possible for me to provide for my brethren, except that the blessed
men should come and make a vineyard in these mountains, and it will
be a provision for them and for the needy."[14]

So the brothers planted a vineyard on Addai's mountain, and it soon
prospered—even the Cappadocians would travel there for wine.

> Thenceforth the anxieties of the holy Addai that had been troubling
> him because he had nothing in his possession wherewith to provide for
> the poor were much relieved, since he would send from forty and fifty
> *denarii,* and as many as came in from that vineyard, and buy clothes
> and distribute them to the needy, and similarly also corn and oil, and
> many articles.[15]

Thus Addai passed his years as a mountain recluse, withdrawn from human contact, yet shrewdly running a profitable business for the service
of others.

Often John indicates that his subjects lived as anchorites at an early
stage in their career—presented by John as a testing ground for the responsibilities to come—and then continued to lead a privately austere
life while conducting public business. For John, such a pattern is sufficiently ritualized to represent a rite of passage. Having withdrawn from
the world, the ascetic reemerges into it as a more potent force,[16] though
this is not necessarily the intent of the holy one. Abraham the Recluse
was an old man of sixty when he decided to take religious vows.[17] Leaving his wife and children, he sought tonsure at a monastery where he
was received despite his age.[18] Then to everyone's surprise, the newly
tonsured Abraham immured himself in a small oratory at the edge of his
village.

For eight years Abraham prayed and wept in solitude, receiving a
little food once each week. Many who at first had scorned his purpose
were in turn astonished by his perseverance. In his eighth year he received his reward, shortly before his death. It seemed that hail storms
had ruined the local villagers' crops for a number of years, but in this
year Abraham saw people weeping as the storm approached. Immediately he prayed, "My Lord, if thou hast been pleased with the sinner's
repentance, and thy mercy has declared of me that I shall not perish, let
not this cloud come within the boundaries of this village."[19] The storm
clouds passed on, leaving the village unharmed. The power of Abraham's prayer was acclaimed, and he died in peace soon after.

At times John's concern for the welfare of ordinary people determined his choice of subjects with surprising results. Perhaps most explicit in implication is the story of the two brothers Elijah and Theo-

dore.[20] These two men were traders and decided as their ascetic vow to run their business honestly, without deceit or contention (an interesting comment on sixth-century business). For their efforts they were generously rewarded; as John tells us, "When God saw their zeal, he caused everything to which they put their hand to increase abundantly. . . . And thus a blessing rested on everything that passed through their hands."[21] They used their copious earnings to establish hostels and monasteries, wherein they and their families took up residence and ministered to great numbers of people. Similarly, Elijah of Dara had practiced a rigorous asceticism privately, although a wealthy man; and he publicly served the poor and destitute, both before and after his banishment into exile during the persecutions.[22]

The public, in the meantime, was well aware of the advantages it gained from these holy works. The form of patronage that ascetics of the fourth and fifth centuries had made available to the common populace was now standard in practice.[23] Moreover, people had come to perceive the amplification of powers and possibilities made accessible to them by the summary temporal and spiritual authority of the ascetics as theirs by right as much as by need. John's subjects could not always choose to serve the world as they might wish.

The humble monk Jacob practiced asceticism in one of the Amidan monasteries and after a time was approached by persons possessed by demons. They demanded that he cure them.[24] Jacob did his best to avoid them, thinking that by calling for him, in particular, the demons were mocking him. Eventually, however, "under great pressure" he acted, revealing himself to be an authoritative exorcist. Soon crowds of possessed persons descended on the monastery crying out for Jacob, who tried to alleviate the suffering but soon found the situation out of all control. As the numbers of the afflicted increased, so too did the irritation of the monastic community. Jacob "wished to give up this business, and could not, on account of the multitude who used to come. And in consequence of such annoyances it became necessary for him to withdraw from the community."[25]

Jacob fled with another monk and together they established themselves as recluses in a different village. "But in a similar way again there also multitudes began to flock together to them."[26] Left with no choice, Jacob set up a private chapel for exorcism, a sort of clinic, in which he served his public well.

More amenably, John tells of Abraham and Addai, two monks who had trained together and decided to travel about setting up monasteries.[27] On their first attempt, "They asked for iron tools. . . . And, when the people of the district saw and heard it, they repaired to them from all quarters, providing money and wood and everything that was useful." [28] In time, over the course of twenty-five years, these two brothers erected and set underway twelve monasteries in various regions.[29] It was a happy case of mutual benefit to both populace and ascetic.

Thus John's basic model for the ascetic allowed any number of variations to its theme, true to Syrian tradition. But the vision remained constant in each case, and it was this constancy that John sought to glorify by presenting diverse ascetic forms of unified understanding. In similar manner, he presented a monastic organization that had evolved a means of containing within its structure the vision that devotion to God entailed public service, while still protecting the individual ascetic's vocational form.

MONASTICISM: AN INSTITUTION FOR THE INDIVIDUAL

By the sixth century, the ascetic's role in society had both expanded and become an orderly part of how society functioned. At the same time, asceticism itself had gained a greater sense of order. The responsibilities of discipline and work, which Theodoret portrayed as an individual's own concern, have in John of Ephesus' *Lives* become a shared affair between the ascetic and the larger monastic structure.

The monastic organization John describes and its provision for public services delineated clear patterns of authoritative response to social need. Temporal and spiritual tasks complemented each other without tarnish to the ascetic image—always a concern of the church. The monasteries ran soup kitchens and health clinics for their surrounding populace but did so in the context of an internal discipline that was both dignified and flexible. The entry process into a monastic order was long, arduous, and carefully ritualized, as John proudly describes.[30] Moreover, monasteries interacted through institutional canons that were respectful of each other's particular structures without creating competition.[31] Yet regulation did not deprive the monastic life of its moving force, or of its respect for individual vision. Hence, when Abraham the Recluse sought entry to the monastery order, his sense of purpose was allowed to override the canonical irregularities of his age and his decision to practice as a solitary outside the actual grounds of the monastery.[32]

Individual practice mingled with the tasks of running the monastery and its services.[33] The regime of the holy man Aaron, for example, involved working by day in the monastery's vineyard and gardens and receiving the visitors who called; standing through the long services; and passing his nights on a pillar rather than in bed.[34] Again, John the Nazirite devoted himself to hard work in the monastery's fields and eventually also to the tasks of exorcism and healing. At the same time, the brethren were distressed by the stringency of his diet, while he compounded his practice by laboring beyond the daily schedule, praying and weeping through the night, "insomuch that his eyelids shed their lashes from weeping, and the hair of his head fell off in front, from the number of times he used to knock [his head on the ground] before God in supplication."[35]

John's description of the Amidan monasteries by night, after their daytime ministries, is the more sobering for his admiration. In addition to those who spent the night singing psalms or practicing genuflexions,

> [there were] others ranged in rows and standing on standing-posts, and others who had fastened their bodies to the walls all night without standing-posts, and others who were tied to the ceiling of the room by ropes and vine branches, and were suspending themselves by them in a standing posture all night, having put them under their armpits, and others who were sitting on seats and never falling on their sides.[36]

Individual and community enhanced one another.

Regimentation of the ascetic life that included involvement with secular affairs was not new; Theodoret had described the schedule developed by Simeon the Stylite to cope with the demands placed on him by others, as well as the demands of his own religious vows.[37] What had changed was the perspective involved, and thus the manner of interaction between the ascetic and worldly realms.

Maro the Stylite provides a good example of how it all worked; his story illustrates the changes in asceticism, interaction with the world, and hagiography.[38] Maro came to his position of authority inadvertently, and although he did prove himself a worker of great deeds, neither he nor John—his spiritual son and biographer—ever forgot that this stylite was an ordinary human being. This is a homely portrait.

Maro had entered the monastery of Arʿa Rabtha together with his brother Abraham. Abraham became the monastery's leading stylite, and for years he served the crowds who came in need with many good works. Meantime, Maro had confined himself inside a nearby tree trunk, ignoring visitors and speaking only to his brother. But when Abraham died, Maro immediately took his place on the pillar, despite much trepidation and lack of confidence in his own position. Columns, too, had gained hereditary properties: when Maro himself passed away some years later, the column was next claimed by the presbyter who had served him.[39]

But when Maro ascended his brother's pillar, he faced the crowds below with difficulty.

> And when he had suppressed his own tears for a short time and restrained his weeping, he then said to them: "Brethren, pray for me, and leave me alone. I for my part did not desire this and my Lord knows, but, in order that my holy brother's place may not be vacant, I hope by his prayers that, until you bring me down as he came down, I shall henceforth not come down." . . . But the blessed man would in great affliction cry night and day to God, saying, "My Lord, let not this stone be to me a conductor to torment, but a conductor to life."[40]

John presents little mystery about this shy and awkward ascetic and his decision to become a stylite. Indeed, Maro's first miracle, saving John's life as a baby, was seen as a bumbling and clumsy effort by all concerned—Maro, his attendants, and John's parents.[41] But even further, John understood Maro's work in a frame that allowed humor: "God used to work acts of great and marvelous power through him in all the words that he spoke even when laughing."[42]

Uncomfortable with the responsibilities that came with standing on a pillar, this stylite did his best to dispel the mystique that hung about those of his profession. He sought to temper the cult of the individual virtuoso, both for the good of the monastic community and also out of respect for the common people. He dreaded the sick and possessed who came seeking miracles and pleaded to be left alone to his human failings. He cried out to the multitudes who supplicated him, "It was because of my sins that I came up here to ask mercy like every man, not because of my righteousness. To myself the madman and man of evil life why do you come?"[43] As for driving out demons, Maro mourned, "Would that I were driving out my own."[44]

Maro did, however, warily perform services for others, though sometimes threats were required to prompt him to action. When a husband once approached the stylite on behalf of his barren wife, he obtained Maro's aid only by means of an oath: "By God who chose you do not neglect me!" The effect was instantaneous.

> When [Maro] heard that [the man] adjured him by God, he was moved by two considerations, one that he did not wish to state of himself at all that he could do any such thing, and another that he heard God's name and his heart trembled; and he said to that man, "Why did you adjure me by God about a matter that is not my concern and is too hard for me?"[45]

But nonetheless he yielded. "And he took one of his toenails and wrapt it up and gave it to him. . . . And he said to him, 'See that no one undo and see it; . . . and next year you shall carry your son also and bring him to me."[46]

Like the barren woman who had petitioned Habib, this couple "believed" in Maro's words and in the blessing he sent through the tiny packet (not knowing it was his toenail). The wife conceived and a son was duly born. Maro in fact proved himself very good at healing the sick, curing sterility, saving the village from invading Huns, and other such deeds—including the supervision of young novices like John. But John presents him as a truly humble man, one who performed his duties as best he could, embarrassed by the fanfare, and concerned that neither the ascetic's integrity nor the common person's faith be abused. One needed no intermediary to approach this holy man, as had been the case with the stylites Simeon and Daniel. Maro did not view himself as the raison d'être of the monastery because he was its leading stylite; instead, he seems to have seen himself simply as another part of its structure. John makes no effort to present Maro in any other way.

The power of the ascetics, then, as shown in their practices and in their patronage, had become institutionalized to a large extent. While the individual continued to constitute the focal point of Syrian asceticism, a wider structure had evolved. This provided a coherent framework in which social responsibilities were shared and performed in an organized fashion; in which monastic groups stood in a canonically defined relationship to one another and to the lay community; in which the ascetic as solitary was permitted to pursue a chosen course of practice within the monastic establishment; and, above all, in which the common people were allowed an access to the ascetic's works that was more ordered in daily regimen and less awesome in approach. The ascetic still inhabited a realm outside the temporal world but also had become settled in the midst of its society.

Nonetheless, the accretion of established custom and familiarity in no way lessened asceticism's impact on society's functioning; the crowds alone would be sufficient evidence to the contrary. Nor was passion softened for the ascetics. Rather, John would have us see that the more clearly their place in society had been defined, the more keenly they felt their duty to it.[47]

But alongside the institutionalization of asceticism and its place in the world, there remained a tradition of the individual's choice to pursue religious vocation under private vows and to train outside the monastic structure, under tutorship by another self-disciplined solitary. The practices of the independent ascetics, and their informal gatherings in pairs or small groups, demonstrated that the vision John of Ephesus propagated was consonant with the heritage of Syrian asceticism. His model was found here, too, in those ascetic forms least refined yet nonetheless affected both by the position the holy man and woman had gained in society and by the understanding that the ascetic had become responsible for society. Moreover, it was this choice that prevented a loss of authority for the monastic communities, now well institutionalized; the two routes rendered each other viable.

The altered emphasis John reveals—a shift from disinterested work to work by decisive commitment—is shown in this context also to be a matter of individual resolution. The recluse Sergius illustrates this situation, as well as its ambiguous consequences. His is a blunt and ugly example of responsibility fulfilled by injustice, the hazard of self-righteousness carried to blind extremes.

Like the early anchorites, Sergius had trained under a holy man named Simeon, and the two dwelt together as hermits outside the village of Kalesh, in the territory of Amida.[48] Sergius eventually decided that he should immure himself as a solitary in a separate place, but he felt constrained first to leave the village in good order during his absence. To this end he set about waging a campaign against the sizable Jewish population in the area, determined to leave them entirely subjugated to the Christian locals when he departed:

> And every day he used to contend against them as with slayers of God, being fervent in the love of his Lord, and gnashing his teeth, and saying, "These crucifiers of the Son of God should not be allowed to live at all"; and he used to upbraid Christians who had dealings with them in the way of taking and giving.[49]

John portrays a ruthless campaign in which Sergius demolished the Jewish synagogue with all its sacred objects, books, and furniture and then violently opposed the Jews' efforts to rebuild their place of worship. He set up a watch through his disciples, so that even after his retreat to solitude the Jewish community would not be able to establish a gathering place for themselves. They, on their side, tried to stop the holy man's campaign, unsuccessfully appealing by right to the metropolitan church at Amida—to whom they paid dues for protection against such violence—and even resorting to revenge by burning the huts of Sergius' master Simeon, again a failed venture as Sergius soon rebuilt them. John would have us see Sergius' program as so thorough that the Jews remained a broken community long after the holy man had gone into seclusion, "so that during the days of his life the Jews could not raise their head there . . . and so they desisted from building all the days of his life."[50]

According to John, Sergius saw himself as acting in the interests of his community, to better ensure their welfare during his retreat. In fact, although the Jews were an oppressed minority in the Byzantine state, he had far overstepped the limits of civil law, which did provide protection for Jewish communities and their synagogues. But these laws were grudgingly granted, and Sergius was not only serving the more heartfelt prejudices of the Christian Empire but, further, doing so under the claim of a higher authority.[51] He was hardly the first ascetic to invoke this "higher right" when acting against the Jews; Simeon Stylites himself was said to have vehemently and successfully opposed protective efforts toward the Jews.[52]

Thus for Sergius the life of the recluse was not one of withdrawal from worldly concerns. Even in the solitude of his retreat he kept watch to control Jewish movement in the area; and when the Monophysite persecutions struck that region, he was not long in leaving his sanctuary to make a violent statement against the persecutors in the city of Amida itself.[53] John portrays Sergius as one for whom asceticism was a violent matter: both internally, in the austerity of his own practice, and outwardly, in the literal playing out of his vows. John of Ephesus sought to glorify an active ascetic understanding, which displayed its purpose openly and with resolution and whose impetus was in no way lessened either by its standing in the secular sphere or by its achieving an established institutional form.

THE MESSAGE IN THE MODEL

By glorifying the ascetic's use of spiritual power in the temporal world, John is not advocating a "secularization" of a mode of action originally seen as an act of grace. Rather, John's ascetics display an outward manifestation of their inward spirituality—and here the crucial issue is touched because John's *Lives* differ from those written by Palladius and Theodoret in a most fundamental way. For John writes at the time when the Chalcedonian-Monophysite dispute had reached its highest pitch. It is a time when the needs of the temporal world have become so pressing that the ascetic cannot afford the luxury of complete withdrawal. Moreover, it has become essential that ascetic involvement, as an act of grace, be revitalized beyond the complacency of asceticism as institution. There is rarely a chapter of John's collection that does not mention the Monophysite persecutions, the refugees, the exiled, or the martyred. Further, the anger of the persecuted ascetics was compounded all the more by their wider circumstances: for the Byzantine East, the sixth century brought its succession of famine, plague, and war. The ascetic response to these capricious natural and political crises was transformed with new meaning in the context of persecution.

John's *Lives* are charged with politics: the affairs of the empire are inescapable; responses to them are mandatory. Time after time John reiterates the rhetoric of martyrdom. This is not the language that praises a distant past, as in the tales of martyrdom that Palladius tells.[54] Nor is it the language spoken in the safely removed tone that Theodoret uses in his stories about the Arian persecutions.[55] John merges the symbols of the martyr who dies for the faith and the ascetic whose life manifests the same strength. Martyr and ascetic are here a physically fused presence.

These ascetics are not dead to the world, nor is such a state the goal of their religious practice. John takes care to point out that strangers could not be admitted to the Amidan monasteries without swearing the required oath to anathematize the "heresy" of Chalcedon.[56] And Elijah of Dara impressed John highly "as he stood and uttered anathemas and called the Chalcedonian bishops as well as those who wielded the authority of the crown, to their faces impious men, renegades, and new Jews."[57]

Palladius and Theodoret had both written their hagiographical collections in contexts of ecclesiastical battle. But Palladius deals in his writing with the issues of his day by denying that there is any disagreement; his *Historia Lausiaca* describes a peaceful picture that hardly indicates the state of the Egyptian church at the time.[58] Theodoret, for his part, wrote the *Historia religiosa* during a period of relative tranquility in his otherwise volatile career. His motives for writing it have been variously interpreted, but the work itself is calm and dignified and praises an asceticism of previously questionable validity in a literary format that grants it admirable respect.[59] In both these cases, the polemical interests of the authors play an understated part in their hagiographical stories and at times are barely discernible. Nor is there a sense of unified ascetic vision that speaks to personal vows, public suffering, and religious unrest such as that portrayed by John of Ephesus.

Similar contrasts are apparent in the kind of attention, or lack thereof, given to the matter of lapses in ascetic commitment. Theodoret presents a portrait of holy men and women who never fail, figures of seamless perfection, and hence removes us from any real contact with them. Palladius, from the opposite perspective, often recounts stories of fallen monks or nuns to counteract the sin of pride so prevalent among ascetics, and perhaps also to acknowledge (sometimes compassionately, albeit grudgingly so) how genuinely difficult the monastic vocation could be. John of Ephesus gives little time to such stories, but not because he presents a perfect picture, such as Theodoret depicts. For example, John tells the story of a monk who stole the books and relics of another solitary. However, remorse soon followed, and John himself was the mediator in the reconciliation.[60] It is a humane presentation, hardly a case of debauchery such as Palladius was prone to dwell upon; and it does not differ in tone from the rest of John's collection. He is too focused on the pragmatic needs of his world and the ascetic involvement in them for such distractions.

Nor does John express concern for the sin of *accidie*—the boredom one had always to fight in the Egyptian desert or Cappadocian monastery. Palladius knew the dangers of an asceticism so monotonous that this sin could lead to madness.[61] John's ascetic vision led to opposite results: Mare of Beth Urtaye "used to behave with great and measureless arrogance, and he was haughty";[62] but for Mare asceticism proved a cure. Not only did it redeem his disposition, it further enabled him to endure the persecutions courageously.

Again, the sometimes fantastic miracles recalled by Palladius and Theodoret have no place in John's work. Miracles there are, in abundance, but of a less histrionic kind: healings, or feats of endurance. John's holy men and women are as much victims of their times as the suppliants they serve; they, too, suffer from plague and famine, the destruction of invading troops, and above all the hardships of exile and imprisonment by persecutors. They have no wondrous solutions for the hardships at hand, except to work as best they can to meet the needs of their populace. Lust, boredom, and miracles, these are themes that do not concern John and for which he has no time. The imperatives of the present world are of too great an import.

John's *Lives* present an institutionalized form of the holy person's cult that resulted in an increased acceptability, accessibility, and range of activity for the ascetic. At the same time, he sets his subjects in the context of a church rent by persecutions and separatist activities, and of a society engulfed by tragic conditions. In such circumstances, the old rules and the old values no longer work. A different kind of ministry of service and of action is needed, and, in the midst of such chaos, a fluidity in the existing structures becomes possible.

John's arena is twofold: the intimate locality of Amida and its territory, and the vast size of the wider Byzantine Empire. His sense of purpose can in fact be seen to emanate from the microcosm of human experience and holy presence he witnessed in the small world of Amida. The vision John developed in Amida, and its extension outward in the larger empire, must be considered first, before turning to the implications involved.

· III ·

AMIDA:
THE MEASURE OF MADNESS

John of Ephesus presents to his readers the ascetic model (and its variations) by which he himself was trained. Although the *Lives of the Eastern
Saints* succeed in placing this model in a larger context, Amida's history
gave a specific shape to the asceticism that developed in its regions;
more pointedly, Amida's experiences during the sixth century provide
us with a measure for the urgency and compassion underlying John's
Lives.

ASCETIC ROOTS

From its inception, asceticism in Amida and its territory was en-
meshed in the volatile existence of the city itself. A metropolitan city in
the late Roman province of north Mesopotamia, Amida lay strategically
on the Tigris River, at the eastern frontiers of the empire, near to the
Persian borders.[1] Constantius embellished the city in the mid-fourth
century amidst frequent disruptions by the Sasanid monarchy. Soon
after, in 359/60, the Persians arrived, devastating Amida and its environs; insecurity was a given factor in the area. The desire for an ascetic
presence shared with the wider Christian realm by Amida was thus
tinged by concern for Amida's own fate.[2]

The growth of asceticism in Amida's territory concurred with that of
the Syrian Orient as a whole. By the early years of the fourth century

Amida's regions harbored individuals of noteworthy ascetic practice who pursued an anchoretic life in loosely gathered groups.[3] It was not long before the city itself could boast a growing monastic presence, and before the end of the century it was clear that asceticism and society had settled down to a coexistence. The monastery of Mar John Urtaya, to which John of Ephesus belonged, was founded during this period; John of Ephesus preserves the oral tradition of its community.[4] Mar John, called Urtaya because of his missionary work in Anzetene, chose to make a cell for ascetic seclusion outside Amida but near the city walls, around the year 389. He settled near a tiny site already known as a place of ascetic practice: a few huts belonging to a distinguished solitary named Mar 'fwrsm. John's spiritual labors soon won him a following and his first two disciples came from the monastery of the Edessenes, by this time relocated at Amida. When Mar John died, his community had "attained to a large increase in buildings and belongings and increase of brotherhood up to the number of fifty men."[5]

The early choice of an urban rather than a rural setting for the Amidan ascetics differs from that of their counterparts Jacob of Nisibis and Julian Saba, who chose to stay within reach of settled communities while dwelling apart in the wilderness. But Amida's practical problems were considerable. The threat of invasion was constant; an isolated recluse was not exempt from danger unless utterly remote, and proximity to the shelter of fortified walls and communal protection was a simpler alternative.

By the fifth century Amida's citizens and ascetics seem to have settled into a profitable coexistence. The tradition that John of Ephesus relates for Mar John Urtaya again presents the picture.[6] After the death of its founder, there followed a steady stream of leaders for the monastery right through the fifth century, all of whom are credited with expanding the community's size in numbers and in buildings. During the second half of the century, however, a dispute broke out among the brethren with regard to their abbot Abraham, himself a native of the city. After governing the monastery well for some time, "unfounded ill-feeling" arose, and Abraham was charged with embezzling the monastery's funds for the sake of his family.[7]

The ensuing clash led to Abraham's angry resignation, but he did not abandon his ascetic career; rather, he practiced it in seclusion at his home in the city, in accordance with the Syrian tradition of individual vocation. Apparently, urban connections with the monasteries had reached the stage where monks were prone to petty intrigues concerning the city's inhabitants—problems indicative of growing wealth and property for ascetic communities, and of growing integration with the social structure of the city.

Abraham's successor was another Abraham, under whom the monastery rose to its greatest fame and reached the size of four hundred monks. This Abraham, "being also formidable and severe and stern toward all the chief men and magnates of the city,"[8] became known even to the emperor Zeno, who summoned him to Constantinople. Received with honor at the imperial court, he was granted substantial gifts, including a village in Amida's neighboring district of Ingilene. Eventually, he was consecrated to a bishopric in Anzetene.

Although the monastery of Mar John Urtaya was perhaps the most acclaimed of Amida's ascetic communities, it by no means eclipsed all the others in reputation. With the advent of the sixth century, the city of Amida was known for the number of famous monastic communities it sheltered in and around its walls.[9] It was at this point that Amida's inhabitants were caught up in an acute crisis of circumstance, affecting local ascetic practice and its place in local urban society.

THE SIXTH CENTURY: THE SETTING

To read the Syrian chroniclers on the beginning of the sixth century is to see that they expected the worst: the turn of the century had hardly been auspicious. From 499 to 502, calamity repeatedly struck the Syrian Orient. Locusts came in masses, bringing famine and disease; earthquakes struck town and country; rivers overflowed their banks; city walls burst; twice, the sun was eclipsed; and burning signs appeared in the skies.[10] For Amida, disaster was imminent.

In the autumn of 502, the Persian army under the command of its ruler Kawad laid siege to Amida.[11] The siege lasted three months, with both sides suffering from the preexisting famine and the Persians suffering in particular from the onset of winter. Various devices were employed to no avail against Amida's impregnable walls, while those inside battled valiantly in return. Gradually the attackers grew disheartened, and the besieged overconfident. The Persians were on the brink of departing when Kawad gained new determination—attributed to a divine vision from Christ or to a premonition of the Persian Magi—indicating that success would soon follow. Indeed, a single lapse in Amida's night watch allowed the Persians sudden entry in January 503. Sources claim that eighty thousand people were slaughtered as the Persians sacked the city.[12]

Amida's fall was of serious consequence.[13] Claims were made that the defeat was an act of divine retribution for Amida's impiety. The accusation was raised, and became set in later tradition, that monks from the monastery of Mar John Urtaya betrayed the city: drinking too much wine one night, they fell asleep and failed to raise the alarm when the Persians scaled the walls.[14] However, the charges seem unlikely.

In the end, the monks of Mar John suffered a particularly gruesome fate.[15] Years later John of Ephesus met an old monk in Palestine, who wept when he heard that John was from Amida. He had been a brother in the community of Mar John Urtaya when the Persians took the city. He recalled for John how the brethren had sought refuge inside the city walls when the Persian army arrived; and how the conquerors upon entering the city had butchered the monks, killing ninety in succession before pausing for captives and booty—the point at which he had escaped, vowing never to return to Amida.[16] Nonetheless, the slanderous story of the monks serves to signify how visible they were in the city: it may well have been an attempt to explain why their holy presence had not protected Amida from the catastrophe.

The suggestion has been made that these accounts may indicate a changing political situation, that by the early sixth century anti-Chalcedonian dissidents of the east were prepared to turn anti-Roman in times of war.[17] But we have no contemporary evidence of disloyalty. On the contrary, the more trustworthy sources do not specify who was on guard duty that night. The account of "Joshua the Stylite" is sober but fair-minded: one cold January night, those on guard duty drank too much wine. Some fell asleep, and others went home because of the rain.

> Whether then through this remissness, as we think, or by an act of treachery, as people said, or as a chastisement from God, the Persians got possession of the walls of Amid by means of a ladder, without the gates being opened or the walls breached.[18]

The Roman army responded immediately; it was said that the emperor Anastasius was sick with grief when he learned of Amida's plight. By the summer of 503 the Romans were encamped against the city, but faced with its unbreachable walls, as well as their own internal problems, they shortly abandoned it. In 504 they returned, prepared for a drawn-out effort at recovery. The effects of this second siege on those inside the city walls, Persian or citizen, were merciless. Famine prevailed; charges of cannibalism and other desperate acts grew daily. The Amidan women suffered further: as food supplies decreased, the Persians imprisoned the city's men in order to keep available food for themselves; they left the women loose, however, to use as slaves and bed partners. Thus raped and abused–but not fed–the women especially were charged with cannibalism. As it is clear that men, too, were reduced to the same efforts for survival, the women's situation can only

have differed in this matter because of their relative freedom of movement in the city.

The Roman siege camp was also suffering, from weather as well as
from lack of supplies. At last, with both attackers and attacked in serious
straits, an agreement was reached in the winter of 505. Amida was returned to Roman hands, a shell of its former self.[19]

At this point, Procopius' narrative implies that the surviving Amidans forgot their misfortunes, a misleading impression, even on the
basis of his own account.[20] Before a generation had passed, war was renewed under Kawad's successor Khosroes, against Justin I and then
against Justinian; a final treaty was not to be signed until 562. Although
Amida was not again a specified battle site, it was garrisoned by the Romans; and with Mesopotamia repeatedly invaded in the course of these
campaigns, the area remained unsafe.[21]

Moreover, the Persian invasions brought an attendant and more diffused problem: in their wake followed the Hunnic tribes of Hephthalitae, who appear to have made continual, if sporadic, incursions into the
eastern Roman provinces during these years.[22] Whether for their own
purposes or in pursuit of the Persians, John of Ephesus depicts repeated
raids by the Hephthalitae.[23] Some stories surely were derived from the
Persian use of Hunnic mercenaries in their own armies; in this capacity
the Hephthalitae seem to have proved unruly and prone to unautho-
rized plundering.[24] And they carried out their own independent incursions, notably in 515 and 531/2, which wrought serious damage in
Roman territory and substantiated the common fear of invasion.[25]

While war against outsiders persisted, internal relations were rapidly breaking down. Religious persecution against the Monophysites
commenced with the accession of Justin I—"Justin the Terrible," as one
Monophysite source called him[26]—in 519. Justin shifted the imperial religious policy to impose the Chalcedonian faith by force;[27] this policy continued thereafter under his successors, despite occasional mitigation.
Amida in this instance, too, became the scene of particular suffering.

The persecutions themselves were uneven, in both place and duration, and depended largely on the patriarch or bishop at hand. Some
were perhaps more efficient than the emperor had envisioned.[28] But an
area so entrenched in Monophysite faith as Mesopotamia would provide
the most threatening resistance to the government's aims. The situation
might well seem to call for severe measures.

When the patriarch Severus of Antioch was deposed and banished
in 518, he was soon succeeded by Paul "the Jew," a staunch Chalcedonian.[29] In the course of the persecutions that Paul set in motion between

519 and 521, Abraham bar Kaili—the archvillain of Syrian tradition—
attained the metropolitan seat at Amida, which he then held for thirty
years.[30] Paul's excessive cruelty seems to have led to his replacement in
521 by Euphrasius, a Chalcedonian perhaps by fashion. Euphrasius may
have alleviated the persecutions somewhat, but his death during Antioch's earthquake of 526 was seen by Monophysites as a fitting end.[31] He
was succeeded immediately by Ephrem, a native of Amida and a government official of some power. It was the combination of Ephrem and
Abraham bar Kaili that unleashed suffering once more upon Amida.

The accession of Ephrem to the patriarchal seat of Antioch was
greeted by a menacing omen: the sun was obscured for eighteen months.
Reports indicate that it was not eclipsed, nor did it disappear; it simply
diminished in warmth for an unbroken year and a half.[32] Ephrem was
indeed a daunting figure. Although Syrian, he had received a Greek
education and gradually rose through the civil ranks to become *comes
orientis* around the year 522. While in this capacity, he was chosen to be
patriarch; as civil administrator he had proved himself competent and
efficient, and even his religious enemies would later attest his skills as an
official.[33] His consecration was thus significant on two accounts: first, as
an indication of the close interaction and shared responsibility between
high civil and ecclesiastical posts at this time;[34] and second, because his
secular offices enabled Ephrem to bring a military escort to his throne.
During his eighteen years as patriarch, Ephrem would use his forces
freely.

Ephrem promoted the Chalcedonian cause with such severity that
our sources are polarized on his behalf. He was influential within Chalcedonian ranks and could, when alarmed, carry out consultation with
Pope Agapetus of Rome.[35] Although trained in civil administration, he
was a respectable theologian.[36] Chalcedonian sources depict him as a
wise fatherly figure who sought to convert Monophysites by gentle persuasion.[37] Moreover, as patriarch he continued to embellish the city of
Antioch, looking after its affairs much as he had earlier.[38] But Monophysite sources viewed Ephrem in a different light, as one who encouraged
a thorough persecution throughout the East. These writers saw his support of the Chalcedonian faith as opportunism and were outraged by his
employment of civil troops.[39]

Ephrem's prime henchman was Abraham bar Kaili, a figure rarely
treated by scholars but whose role in the Monophysite persecutions was
felt all too keenly by his contemporaries. Although he held the bishopric
of Amida for thirty years,[40] Syrian tradition has woven his activity to-

gether with that of Ephrem. Abraham obviously conducted a harsher campaign than his superior, and while he acted at the patriarch's behest, he appears to have been more of an extremist. He may have been doing Ephrem's dirty work for him. Unfortunately, surviving evidence on Abraham is based almost entirely on John of Ephesus' *Ecclesiastical History*. One might wish for Chalcedonian accounts to balance the picture.[41] Their silence may be instructive, however, indicating a lack of information or interest. It is also evidence that the Chalcedonian presence in Mesopotamia was confined both to the upper echelons of the imperially sponsored civil and ecclesiastical administration and to the army, a case much like Egypt's. On the other hand, both Ephrem and Abraham were natives of Amida; further, if Abraham served as bishop for so many years, there must have been a sizeable Chalcedonian presence in Amida itself.

Abraham is charged with more than exiling the faithful and compelling Chalcedonian communion. Monophysite sources, based on John of Ephesus, report that he kept a census count on his citizens to ensure that not even a miscarried fetus or a stillborn child escaped Chalcedonian baptism; and that he invaded holy sanctuaries, tortured religious prisoners, crucified and burned dissidents, and was disrespectful of their corpses. The most sinister charge was that he employed a band of lepers; these he sent to pollute Monophysite property with their disease or to be prison companions for those disagreeing with him. Nonetheless, it was in concerted effort with Ephrem that Abraham's most brutal steps were taken, following Justinian's final banishment of Severus of Antioch in 536. Ephrem's "descent to the east" during 536–537 was considered the height of the persecutions in the Syrian Orient, but its worst crimes have been attributed to Abraham. As a parting shot, Michael the Syrian claims that Abraham was a gluttonous lover of wine, foppishly vain in dress, who conducted religious ceremonies with ostentatious pomp.[42]

The Persian campaigns compounded the persecutions and brought the return of famine as a chronic situation in Amida's territory. Local plagues broke out and were finally subsumed into the Great Bubonic Plague that struck in 542. Conditions were ripe for disease to flourish, and the Great Plague at its peak is reported by John of Ephesus to have killed thirty thousand people from Amida and its lands in the span of three months.[43] As elsewhere in the Byzantine East, famine followed the epidemic for those who survived, and outbreaks of the disease continued to recur for the remainder of the century. Our sources record an unbroken succession of natural and human calamities for Amida's regions as the wars and religious coercion continued also. Finally, in the year 560, the city of Amida went mad.

The accounts of the "plague of madness" are no less chilling for their confusion.[44] The sickness was called "dreadful, abominable, and hideous," and "maniacal and diabolical." Without exception, the madness was seen as an act of divine vengeance for the sins of the city. Later tradition also sought a divine cure for the "plague" and added the figure of Jacob Burdᶜaya to the event. Legend claimed that he predicted the suffering in advance, attributing it to those who had submitted to the pressures of persecution and joined the Chalcedonian ranks, and that the saint finally returned to exorcise the city.[45] But the primary version, on which the chronicles draw, is from John of Ephesus' *Ecclesiastical History*. John was a contemporary and, although not present in Amida at the time, well informed on events there.

John's account and those based on it show considerable insight when describing the context of the outbreak. They begin by summarizing the preceding forty years of war, persecution, plague, and famine, and the resulting persistent level of anxiety in the city. At last, on this occasion, a false report that the Persians were again attacking Amida and pillaging the countryside proved a sudden cause for panic.

It was then that the madness descended. People dashed around barking like dogs, bleating like sheep, clucking like hens; children ran crazed through the graveyards, throwing each other about, shouting obscenely, biting each other, hanging upside down, crying with trumpetlike wails; no one recognized his own home. Taken to the churches by the few who remained sane, the crowds foamed at the mouth and claimed with rage that only the intervention of the apostles and martyrs prevented them from massacring and plundering the entire city. The madness lasted some months, perhaps as long as a year. It struck elsewhere in the Orient, in Tella, Edessa, Charrhae, and Maipherqat; but no other place was reputed to have suffered like Amida.[46]

Despite its arresting scope in numbers and duration, the Amidan plague of madness is not without parallel. Other periods of history have witnessed similar outbreaks of protracted mass hysteria; significantly, these have occurred under similarly compounded conditions of famine, general want, disease, religious unrest, and natural calamity.[47] In Amida's case, the symptoms displayed all match the views of insanity prevalent during antiquity, both for the Oriental and Greco-Roman worlds.[48] Moreover, the other cities that suffered the same plague—Constantina/Tella, Edessa, Charrhae, and Martyropolis/Maipherqat—all experienced a succession of natural and political disasters nearly as unbroken as Amida's.[49] The account of Amida's plague of madness, then, stands as testimony to the fact that society, like the individual, does have a breaking point: the course of events that the sixth century brought to Amida could well have broached such a limit.[50]

The particular tragedy of Amida, and the horrors leading up to it, epitomized that of the Monophysite Syrian Orient as a whole during the sixth century. In Syrian tradition, the memory of those years did not lose the sense of trauma.[51] One would expect such times to raise the potency of the ascetic presence; but just as the lay populace would turn to the power of sanctity with particular urgency, so too would the ascetics be compelled to respond from their own suffering and involvement in the plight of the world. City and wilderness, the poles of ascetic experience, in these circumstances lost their distinctive boundaries and came to inhabit a realm of mutual crisis. It was this mutual realm that John of Ephesus elucidated in his accounts of the holy men and women of Amida.

AMIDA: THE DEVIL WITHOUT AND THE DEVIL WITHIN

The hermit of late antiquity had sought the holy by inhabiting a physical space—in desert or wilderness—as separate from the space of civilized society as the spiritual realm was from the physical. Even when society extended itself to include the holy, by incorporating the functional employment of the holy man or woman into its workings,[52] the space of the ascetic presence remained separate from the urban space of village or city, whether it was contained within a separate monastic complex or, more frequently, outside the city walls.[53] The populace came out to the holy presence, as they had to Simeon the Stylite.[54] Only the purest could achieve the estrangement from the world evidenced by the holy fool, living immersed in, yet untouched by, the debauchery of civilization.[55]

But the territory of Amida precluded the privacy of an external setting for ascetic practice, and even the inner space of the ascetic's spiritual life could not offer refuge for any length of time. The Persian invasions provide a concrete example. Procopius relates that in 503 during their command over Amida, they laid waste with fire the sanctuary of a holy man called Simeon, near to the city.[56]

The intermittent incursions by Huns as well as by Persians were as disturbing for the ascetics, even those living in seclusion, as they were for the village or town communities. Maro the Stylite had stood on his pillar near Amida for twenty years when he saw a vision foretelling the arrival of a raiding party of Huns. His horror, mirroring the reaction soon to be heard among the villagers, frightened the brethren of his community. Most of them fled with the townspeople to a nearby fortress—again, the proximity is instructive—while three loyal brothers stayed behind with Maro. Fortunately, they escaped the band's notice unharmed.[57]

However, such raids left behind a more insidious threat. In constant fear, the populace sought comfort in stories of divine protection. Thus Procopius tells of the anchorite Jacob, dwelling a day's journey from Amida, who was discovered by a group of marauding Hephthalitae but succeeded in rendering them motionless when they tried to attack him. They remained paralyzed until the Persian king himself came to beg their release, which Jacob worked with a prayer. Faced with such power, Kawad then offered the hermit any favor he wished, presuming money would be the request. But Jacob asked that he be allowed to shelter all who came to him as fugitives from war. We are told that the pledge was kept, and many sought refuge there as word went out of what had taken place.[58] Similarly, John of Ephesus tells how the young monk Z'ura (before his stylite days) had taken refuge in a fortress from an invading host of Huns. Sent out later to see if his monastery was still intact, he encountered the raiding band, and one of its members rushed upon him. Z'ura, too, rendered him motionless until his comrades had departed and then allowed him to go free without harm.[59]

Anxiety produced a fear both articulated and internalized. When Simeon the Mountaineer cursed the inhabitants of a remote village for willfully hindering his efforts on their behalf, they shouted at him, "If you think that your curses are so well heard, go and curse these Huns who are coming and making havoc of creation, and let them die."[60] More pointedly, ascetics now waged battle with demons appearing in the guise of marauders. Paul the Anchorite set out to exorcise a cave notorious for its demonic possession, located on a lonely stretch of the Tigris and needed as shelter for traders and travelers. For many days he stayed enclosed in the cave, waging battle against fiends of every shape and kind. At last, in an effort to drive the holy man out, the demons assailed him in the likeness of villagers fleeing in panic from approaching invaders; when Paul remained unmoved they put on their most fearful aspect, guised as the Huns themselves. It was the mark of Paul's sanctity that he was able to banish even these powerful forces.[61]

The sixth century, then, presented the Amidan ascetics with no separate "space," external or internal, and no escape or retreat. Their tradition had incorporated the physical dangers of Amida's territory into their ascetic practice by the custom of living cenobitically within close reach of local towns and villages.[62] But when wars and raiders drove the ascetics inside the city walls, they confronted a new danger. No privileged place awaited them as monastics, except the compounding of physical danger and an equally severe moral peril. For while the ascetics might suffer along with citizens the hardships of invasions, famine, and plague, it was the religious element, monks, nuns and clergy, who bore the brunt of the persecutions against the Monophysites.

The Amidan monasteries, fierce in their opposition to Chalcedonian persuasion and influential with the public, presented the most accessible targets for their Chalcedonian persecutors. Not surprisingly, the first step in any persecution campaign was directed at them and marked by the monks' banishment. The rhetoric their plight evoked was the language of martyrdom: John of Ephesus described them, "having all, small as well as great, been fired by zeal for the faith, and having been duly girded with the armour of truth, they also entered valiantly and heroically and courageously into the struggle against the defenders of the corrupt synod of Chalcedon."[63] And the experience of exile proved to be horrendous for the Amidan monastic community. They were "driven from place to place and from region to region,"[64] under circumstances that left no illusions as to the life suffered by refugees.

The first expulsion came soon after the accession of Justin I, around the year 520.[65] After much discouraging travel and effort, the exiled Amidan community finally halted in a remote area at a monastery called Mar Mama.[66] Despite unpleasant conditions, they stayed there five years before deciding to return to a district bordering on Amida in order to be near their former home. They passed several years in this new place at the monastery of the Poplars, under crowded and makeshift arrangements. Owing to Justinian's succession to the throne and to Theodora's subsequent efforts,[67] they were allowed to return, after nine and a half years, to their home city. "And they found their convents destroyed and demolished and knocked to pieces, and turned to earth." At once they set about rebuilding their former dwellings and reorganizing the religious assemblies of the Amidan populace, "so that few [of those who had gone over to the Chalcedonians] remained with the Synodites."[68]

Such behavior was obviously upsetting to the authorities; the monastic group was not long back before a new expulsion order was again issued against them.[69] They left, but the effort was wearing and their size had diminished.[70] Stopping first at the monastery of the Sycamores, they were pursued by Roman soldiers who tormented the surrounding villagers until they pleaded with the ascetics to leave their district so as to alleviate their suffering. Reestablishing themselves at the monastery of the Poplars, they were soon sought out by the vigilant Ephrem and his troops. This time their dispersion was frightening. For according to John of Ephesus, Ephrem "sent armed and armoured hosts of fighting men against them as if to fight against barbarians, and they expelled and ejected and scattered and dispersed them over the lands."[71] Moreover, it was winter; many were ill or old, and travel was dangerous. The Amidan community splintered over the East.

After some twenty years or more, the survivors gradually reassembled in Amida, once again finding their former homes razed. They were not long in the occupation of rebuilding before a third expulsion order drove them out again. When John of Ephesus completed his history of the Amidan monasteries at the death of Justinian, they had been living under the shadow of persecution for more than forty years.[72] Under these conditions, ascetic practice was not only compelled to bend to the circumstances—many a stylite was forced down from his pillar— but also to fulfill perceived obligations to the lay populace while under duress. Those obligations were only partially manifest in the social occupations of the ascetic as patron and healer; their greater import lay in ensuring that the Monophysite stance of the people did not lapse. The commitment to such a responsibility was clearly shown in the continuous efforts of the Amidan ascetics to return to the city, or to remain in close contact with it even when in exile. In the course of the crisis, the Amidan ascetics responded in two ways, retaining their practices as a body in exile while maintaining an "underground" presence in the city itself. But in either place, the space occupied by the holy had lost its separateness.

THE ASCETIC RESPONSE

The influence of the eastern monks on the attitudes and beliefs of common people is well attested by the sources for late antiquity.[73] Their constancy and zeal contributed to the Monophysite dispute an ingredient of popular faith, and not simply of theological debate.[74] For the Amidan ascetics, however, the immediacy of the religious crisis was matched by the cumulative impact of local natural disasters and political events. The ascetic ideal and motivation were thus profoundly affected by the state of the temporal world in a time of great need: the potency of ascetic actions rose.[75]

The desert had ceased to be a place of solitude. Pseudo-Zachariah Rhetor describes the communities that grew up in the wilderness during the persecutions:

> And so the desert was at peace, and was abundantly supplied with a population of believers who lived in it, and fresh ones who were every day added to them and aided in swelling the numbers of their brethren, some from a desire to visit their brethren out of Christian love, and others again because they were being driven from country to country by the bishops in the cities. And there grew up, as it were, a commonwealth of illustrious and believing priests, and a tranquil brotherhood with them; and they were united in love and abounded in mutual affection, and they were beloved and acceptable in the sight of everyone; and nothing was lacking, for the honoured heads of the corporation, which is composed of all the members of the body, accompanied them.[76]

Hence it was with pride that John of Ephesus stressed the continuity of tradition in ascetic practice for the Amidan monasteries, even while they lived in a present state of dispersal. The various communities continued, seemingly without interruption by their circumstances, the customary practices of fasting, vigils, genuflexions, weeping, and the use of standing poles and other aids. Further, they continued their role in society at large: admonishing and advising the local populace wherever they settled, healing the sick, and exorcising demons.[77] But they acted now, as pseudo-Zachariah indicates, in concert with the community that the wilderness fostered, bonded together by their common plight. Thus John of Ephesus praised the united body of Amidans, "the separate character of each convent being preserved in this only, the fact that its own brotherhood was separate, and its belongings and archimandrite and its priests, while all the affairs of them all were administered in common, together with all the spiritual labours of brotherly concord."[78]

The Amidan monasteries had for generations upheld a high-standing reputation for practice as well as for learning; their fame would spread on both accounts during their ordeal. In his history of the monastery of Mar John Urtaya, John of Ephesus records a faultless succession of abbots in the course of the persecutions.[79] Moreover, he reaffirms the monastery's ties to the city of Amida itself. Not only were the remains of the leaders who died in exile returned, when it became possible, to the monastery's own burial grounds; but further, the abbot appointed during the final period of persecution in which John wrote was born of a distinguished family of the city and had been in the monastery since he was a child.[80] Similarly, John saw fit, despite the disruptions of the times, to elaborate on the lengthy traditional method of gaining entry and serving as novice in another Amidan monastery, emphasizing the commitment to correct training.[81] Nor was the image of the Amidan monasteries enhanced by John alone. John of Tella had immediately welcomed the Amidan exiles he encountered, knowing their place of origin and its high standards in ascetic practices and religious education.[82] Above all, wandering ascetics continued, with confidence, to join Amida's communities in exile, just as they had previously, so constant was the reputation they upheld.[83]

In the *Lives of the Eastern Saints*, the few accounts John offers of ascetics devoted purely to the pursuit of private worship are presented in this context. They are people who came to the Amidan communities before and during the periods of persecution: Abbi, who wore rags and passed his days reading the Gospels in ecstasy, speaking and eating rarely and always with tears; a poor stranger who would not reveal his name or anything of his travels, who meditated with mournful humility throughout the nights and allowed no morsel of food or drop of water to pass his lips without a prayer of thanksgiving, thus taking one hundred sips to drink a cup; and Zacharias, who shunned all contact with others, secretly carrying a pebble in his mouth to impede speech and mortifying his flesh with knots of rope to prevent unworthy thoughts from finding their way into his mind.[84]

These accounts stand in seeming contrast to John's emphasis on asceticism practiced within an urban setting or in close contact with village populations, for his usual ideal is that of an asceticism ministering to a crisis-ridden society. But the contrast becomes less when one realizes where he makes room for the virtuosi of private ascetic practice. For the exiled communities, these holy individuals ensured the validity of their tradition and of their spiritual authority, as much in time of peace as in trial, under the strongly politicizing pressures that beset the Monophysite population.

It is with this intent that John relates the story of a monk who joined the Amidan monasteries while they were settled at Mar Mama.[85] Since it was uncanonical for a monk to leave his monastery to enter another without an official release, the Amidan archimandrite carefully examined this monk as to his previous training and present status. In fact he had not been released and had lied in order to join their community. Then a local plague broke out, and in the cramped living quarters of the exiles it raged freely, killing eighty-four of the Amidan brethren as well as some of their guests. The newly received monk, too, fell ill and was divinely punished for his perjury by hovering paralyzed just outside death. The brethren finally guessed his situation and stood themselves

surety to gain his release, sending a deacon to petition his former archimandrite. As soon as this was done, the man died. Such an account un-
derscored the Amidans' authoritative status, illustrating their care with
canons was no less than that with faith.[86]

In the same way, John stresses an unbroken pattern in the Amidan
ascetics' social involvement, despite their flight to unfamiliar territory.
The personal trial of exile, with its hazards and discomforts, was not
considered a release from an ascetic's obligation to others. Hala, a monk
at the monastery of the Edessenes in Amida, had devoted himself for
some years to caring for the destitute and strangers in the city.[87] When
the monastery was expelled and its property confiscated or hidden, Hala
was beside himself, having nothing with which to comfort those in
need. At once he set about finding new ways of continuing his ministry,
paying no heed to the affliction of his own monastic community or to
their mockery of his efforts. Rather, he collected old coats and rags from
dung heaps and then cleaned and sewed them together into cushions
and rugs for the poor visitors who came. "And so he found this method
of carrying out his own employment, not giving up this strenuous pursuit in peace or in persecution, in the city or in exile."[88]

In fact, the Amidan communities could in many respects conduct
their life in exile just as they had previously, if they could find a safe
place to stay. Their ministry during times of famine was both moving
and familiar; they had dealt with such circumstances before.[89] However,
exile was at times relentless. When they sought refuge in the monastery
of the Sycamores, Abraham bar Kaili sent Roman soldiers under his command to expel them again. Upon their arrival the soldiers were stunned at
the sight of hundreds of ascetics engaged in worship, standing row
upon row without fear. Unnerved, the troops turned upon the nearby
villagers, plundering their land, killing their animals, eating their food,
and taking over their houses; the soldiers told the inhabitants that they
would leave only if the monks were persuaded to depart as well. Oppressed beyond their means, the villagers collectively begged the monks
to relieve them of their burden. The ascetics saw their grief, and wishing
to cause ordinary people no harm they left at once.[90] The Amidan community and the laity they met seem to have aided each other wherever
possible.[91]

But in such a context, the wilderness and its solitude bore fruit very
much intended for the temporal world; it did not serve as a place of retreat for its own sake, or of refuge from the plight of the eastern cities. In
their continuity of practice, of spiritual tradition and of social involvement, the Amidan ascetics in exile acquired an ever-increasing prestige.

And the potency of that authority was fully concentrated on the persons and events of their own time.

The expulsion of the Amidan monasteries carried further implications. Their absence left a burden on those who remained in Amida and its territory, that their services for the populace be continued. Thus a local recluse, who had chosen a separate life outside the city and its monastic complexes, found himself forced to leave his retreat and return. Simeon the Solitary had once been renowned for his labors in an Amidan monastery, both in private ascetic practice and in his ministry to the poor and strangers in the city.[92] When he chose to take up life as a hermit in the mountains nearby, he was "supplied by many persons with all that he needed" and served residents and travelers from his huts, while his fame spread throughout the region. Finally, however, the situation in Amida—the loss of its spiritual community—called him back:

> But afterwards the storm of persecution was stirred up against [Simeon] together with all the rest of the church; and he bravely and heroically contended in the conflicts. . . . But he himself held firm; and thus he persevered and maintained a heroic contest, and he used to go around in the city itself at the very height of the persecution, and give absolution and baptise by night and by day.[93]

The persecuting Chalcedonians, on the other hand, had not allowed the city walls to restrict their efforts. Under Abraham bar Kaili, the local anchoretic sanctuaries were violated now for a different kind of booty. Local celebrities such as Maro the Stylite were coaxed for an unwitting slip of the tongue so that Chalcedonians could claim, "Behold, even Maro on his pillar agrees with us!"[94] The authorities were well aware of the ascetics' influence and knew that even apparent verbal capitulation on the part of such figures could draw many people to their communion.[95]

These solitaries and their disciples, no longer left to their business of serving community needs from their retreats, were forced into the social arena. Not only were their sanctuaries invaded but the strength of their religious commitment would not allow them to continue a life apart from the events around them. When the hermit Sergius was dragged from his hut, beaten by physical and by verbal blows, he could not continue his anchoretic existence.[96] His reentry into the city of Amida demonstrated in no uncertain terms the solitary's response to Amida's situation:

> But the blessed Sergius went out, and arrived at the city on the holy day of Sunday, at dawn. He then went straight to the church, and as the whole city was sitting there after the morning hymns . . . suddenly at the door of the church there appeared a strange and shocking sight, and all were stunned, seeing an appearance not their own: a hermit was

entering, wearing rags patched together from sackcloth and carrying his cross on his shoulder. And he went right in, going straight to the middle of the church without a question, neither speaking nor turning to either side; and as the preacher was standing and speaking, he stopped, while astonishment fell upon the crowd, and they looked to see what was the matter. But the holy man, as soon as he reached the chancel, struck his cross upon the steps and began to mount. And when he had climbed one or two steps in silence, everyone thought that he was getting ready either to say something or to make a petition to the city or to the bishop [Abraham bar Kaili]. But when he reached the third step where the preacher stood, he flung out his hand, grabbed him by the neck, held him fast, and said to him, "Wicked evil man, our Lord commands, 'Do not give what is holy to dogs nor pearls before swine'; why do you speak the words of God before those who deny Him?" And he swung his hand round, punched him, twisted his mouth awry, seized him and threw him down.[97]

Sergius succeeded in rousing the congregation into full riot before he himself was beaten unconscious and carried off to an Armenian prison camp reserved for Monophysites. He was not long held, however, and soon escaped back to his own cell.[98]

Thus the city of Amida became a battleground against the forces of evil that had once been sought in the harshness of the wilderness. For there were those ascetics who chose to remain in Amida rather than go into exile with the majority of the monks, and these intensified their ascetic practice by the danger of their situation. Abraham was both cruel and thorough in the campaign he waged through the city.

Nonetheless, city life afforded some protection through the possibility of anonymity, and John of Ephesus speaks with admiration of the "underground" communities, the secret groups of ascetics exiled from their own monasteries or convents who remained in the city, residing in housing ostensibly rented for tenancy by others. Many of the exiled, as well as their various communications and business matters, passed through such groups, aided by sympathetic townspeople. For in order to ensure a presence eluding the authorities but efficacious for the populace, it was imperative that the Monophysite leaders inside the city depend upon the efforts of individuals and avoid the visibility of actions as a body.[99]

Such a person was the holy Euphemia, who had for many years lived an ascetic career in Amida with her daughter Maria.[100] She followed a private rule of austerity in her own life (John of Ephesus and others would beg her to show herself some of the kindness she so liberally bestowed on others) and, at the same time, with Maria's aid devoted herself day and night to ministering to the city's poor, sick, homeless, and afflicted. There seemed no corner of the city or its environs unknown to her, and no one person, rich or destitute, citizen or stranger, whose life had not been touched by her grace and charity.

When the persecutions struck, a steady stream of exiled monks, singly or in company, began to appear at Euphemia's door for refuge. In no time she had organized accommodations for both housing and worship, setting up a substantial network through which they could stay in the city pursuing their habitual monastic practices or, if traveling, could have the assurance of lodging and hospitable company (no small gift when suffering flight). But it was not long, only a few years, before the Chalcedonian authorities became suspicious of the doctrinal leanings of the holy woman and her daughter and imprisoned them with the intent of forcing their submission to Chalcedonian communion. However, the officials had not reckoned on the support of Euphemia's followers, and the entire city, small and great alike, demanded the release of the two women. Faced with a public uprising, the authorities quietly banished Euphemia and Maria from the city.

Euphemia's life is a particularly instructive one, for her personal career well reflects the fortune of Amida in the sixth century. Thirty years of her life were passed in service to those in the city who suffered famine, invasion, and plague. The appearance of the persecutions at first seemed yet one more trial with which to contend. But her story reveals the cost that Amida's calamities were to exact from its citizens and ascetics, and if her end was less histrionic than the memory of a city driven mad with suffering, it was no less indicative of the times.

After their banishment from the city, Euphemia and her daughter went to Jerusalem, passing some time in pilgrimage. John of Ephesus then tells us,

> imagining that perhaps the anger against them had abated, they returned to Amida and entered it secretly; and they stayed at the house of a certain nobleman. But when it began to be noticed, and their opponents began to speak about them, the people with whom they were staying became anxious, begging them to depart lest their house be plundered. But the blessed Euphemia was weary, and she wept aloud to God, saying, "My Lord, your mercy knows that I have grown weak, and I have no more strength. It is enough for me." And on that very night, the request of her prayer was answered.[101]

Within a week Euphemia had died of illness, having attained, John assures us, the crown of martyrdom. But hers was a death not caused by suffering under persecution so much as by the gradually wearing effects of the calamity that buffeted her time and place.

In this way Euphemia's story typifies the ascetic's experience in sixth-century Amida. The commitment of the ascetic to the temporal world was as pressing as that to the eternal; the space of the holy was not inviolable for either secular or religious forces, nor could it remain aloof from the events surrounding or involving it. The space of the holy was found nowhere separate for the Amidan ascetics or populace. On the contrary, it was everywhere present.

· IV ·

PURPOSE AND PLACES

When the Amidan ascetics were expelled, some journeyed widely. John himself traveled through Palestine, down into Egypt, across the Anatolian provinces, and on to Constantinople; his journeys provided much of the material for his *Lives of the Eastern Saints*. John's accounts of the ascetics who stayed in and around Amida are combined with his narratives of the Mesopotamian ascetics working in larger arenas of Christendom, especially in Egypt and in Constantinople. The combination provides a powerful medium for his ascetic vision, a vision as unified as his subjects and locations are diverse.

EGYPT: THE COMMUNITY WITNESS

Following the lead of Severus of Antioch, Monophysite bishops by choice began to gather in Egypt even before the order of banishment reached their sees; for others, it was the nearest point of refuge.[1] It was not surprising that exiled ascetics should arrive also, drawn as much by the tradition of Egypt's deserts as by the hope for safety.[2] The first arrivals set the tone: a community was formed, noted for its discipline in faith and in practice. When John of Ephesus set out for Egypt in the early 530s, it was to visit this exiled community.[3]

The community that interested John was from Palestine, but its roots were Syrian and its fame in John's time rested largely on its identity as a Syrian group. Its founder was the holy woman Susan, by birth from the Persian territory of Arzanene, an area with strong ties to Syriac Christianity.[4] Susan had turned to asceticism as a child. At the age of eight she left home, first in pilgrimage to Jerusalem and then to enter a convent in Palestine between Ascalon and Gaza. Some ten years later the persecutions began. Palestine was a major target, and Susan's convent, "since it was large and celebrated," was soon attacked. Facing the alternatives of confrontation or flight, Susan decided to leave for the desert outside Alexandria. Her choice distressed the sisters, who held her in high regard; five chose to follow her, despite her admonitions to the contrary.

From Alexandria the women soon found a suitable place to settle: an area in the desert, not far from the village of Mendis, with an abandoned fortress for shelter.[5] Removed from the pressure of harassment and with Susan as spiritual guide, the nuns resumed their routine of prayer and labor. The village provided handiwork by which they could earn their keep and also looked after their general welfare.

Susan, however, had longed for solitude, and a nearby cave offered seclusion.[6] But her testing of her vocation as a hermit brought panic to the sisters, for the nuns looked to her for leadership: "Don't you know that we came out to the desert trusting in you after our Lord? . . . Don't you know that without you we cannot exist?"[7] At last a compromise had to be reached, and Susan agreed to a split routine, divided between solitude and interludes with her nuns. Susan's contemplative labors provided the embryonic community with a testimony to spiritual authority that did not go unnoticed; the community began to grow. At the same time, its reputation spread. The nuns' story reached a small community of monks, also of Mesopotamian origin, who had lived near to their convent in Palestine but were now suffering pursuit by the Chalcedonian authorities. Hearing of "the quietude and sweetness of that desert," the men soon found their way to the nuns and established themselves in the same area. Numbers in both communities increased as the persecutions elsewhere wore on. Still, the safety of Egypt did not provide an escape from the responsibilities of the religious crisis. Susan desired the anchoretic life, but the congregation outside Mendis required strong leadership because of the circumstances that had brought them together. In the eyes of both the men and the women, Susan alone was capable of this role. For her part, Susan understood that times of crisis demand critical action; although unhappy to assume the role of director for the community of men and women, Susan did so—and she did so very well.[8]

But Susan's community and others like it were more than resettlement camps for refugees. They were places in which the Monophysite faith was nourished and practiced, providing a steady witness in the midst of persecution. Their impact was strengthened by the parallel activity of Severus himself,[9] a situation John of Ephesus emphasizes specifically in his *Lives of the Eastern Saints*.[10] Fleeing Antioch in 518, Severus had gone first to Alexandria and the hospitality of the patriarch Timothy IV.[11] From there he went on to the desert, where he "carried out to the full" the monastic vocation of his youth.[12] As in the case of others with similar experience, Severus' standing as church leader had been reinforced by his early ascetic training at the hands of Peter the Iberian in the monastery of Maïouma outside Gaza.[13] The return to the ascetic life enhanced his status in the broader world, all the more since withdrawal did not lighten his workload. Severus continued to conduct affairs internal and external for the Monophysite body.[14] There were, however, some who took the patriarch's retreat as an excuse to slacken their ecclesiastical discipline.[15] Severus' fear, unhappily prophetic, was that internal problems were diverting the believers' energy from the real battle at hand.[16] By the nature of his presence and activity in Egypt, Severus enacted the model that John of Ephesus propagated: under persecution the Monophysites witnessed the soundness of their faith, and that witness was grounded in an ascetic practice responsive to times of crisis. John himself praised the religious vehicle Egypt had become in its position as Monophysite base. His account of Thomas the Armenian, for example, relates how this ascetic, while founding a monastic community in his homeland, came to Alexandria both to obtain books and to converse with the leaders and the religious who were gathered there.[17]

Elsewhere John offers praise for the Egyptian Monophysite body itself.[18] But in his *Lives* he hints that Egypt's spiritual authority was heightened by the presence of those who brought to it the particular witness of his own ascetic roots; so it is that John includes the story of the two deacons Thomas and Stephen.[19] When the persecutions reached Mesopotamia, Amida's episcopal throne suffered from a crisis in leadership. The bishop Thomas, who had guided Amida since 504/5, died upon the arrival of an imperial order for his banishment in 519. He was succeeded by Nonnus, who survived only three months. The distinguished Mare was then consecrated and expelled, probably in 521. Finally the seat was taken over by the Chalcedonian Abraham bar Kaili, who held it for the next thirty years.[20]

Mare was banished to Petra; with him there went a small retinue that included the deacons Thomas and Stephen.[21] Petra proved a harsh place for the Amidans. In desperation, Mare sent Stephen to Constantinople for help.[22] There Stephen encountered the future empress Theodora, at the time a newly married patrician. In the peculiar pattern that later became their standard, the royal couple intervened: the place of exile was changed to Alexandria.[23] Soon after, when Mare and his followers were resettled in Egypt, they heard of other Amidans in the region and of Susan's community in the desert of Mendis.[24] It did not take long for Thomas and Stephen to find their way there. Thomas in particular was inspired and longed to partake of their spiritual discipline. In a "pit" not far from the community—possibly the "cave" that Susan herself had used for solitary practice—the deacon undertook the hermit's vocation.

But Thomas' story is joined to that of his comrade Stephen, and their partnership, as John writes it, is essential.[25] Stephen himself was no less fervent than Thomas, but chronic infirmity had modified his own asceticism. At the time of Thomas' decision, Stephen, showing a sentiment near to John's, begged his friend not to seek so rigorous a practice: "For ourselves, this is too great a thing to live in the desert on account of our feebleness; but, my brother, let us look after our soul, and gain a desert by our manner of life and our heart, and always entreat the Lord to cause his grace to shine upon us."[26] Thomas was undeterred; after one brief trip home to sort out his affairs, he labored in his pit for many years until his death. But John leaves no doubt in the reader's mind as to Stephen's own excellence: the gentler deacon went on to achieve great works as a leader in the refugee community of Constantinople and as an adviser to the empress Theodora, so touched by her first meeting with the Amidan. As elsewhere in John's *Lives*, these two men and their respective works are shown as two halves of the same whole; each completed the other.

However, it was the likes of Thomas that made Monophysite Egypt more than a cauldron of discontent, a point that John does not fail to underscore. Eventually Egypt had to be dealt with as the haven it had become. A Chalcedonian government could not allow the continued nourishment of a dissenting church. Justinian's efforts towards Chalcedonian restoration in Egypt began in 536, following the final breakdown that year of religious negotiations in Constantinople. His measures led to bloodshed that was to last decades and in Alexandria in particular was to flare up at every excuse.[27] It was not until John the Almsgiver assumed the patriarchal seat in 611 that serious attempts were made to win over the Egyptian Monophysites, rather than to force submission.[28] In fact, John's eight years on the throne were spent pacifying memories of Chalcedonian atrocities committed at a level "unknown even among the pagans."[29]

Still, Egypt's deserts were vast, its ascetic communities numerous and remote. Imperial officials could not compete with the loyal monastic networks; Egypt continued to offer escape for the persecuted. In the *Lives of the Eastern Saints,* John of Ephesus speaks of Severus' exile after his final banishment by imperial decree in 536; at the same time, he points to the nature of the authority that the Monophysites gained by practice in Egypt, such as that of Thomas or, indeed, such as that found in Susan's community.[30] Working for the Monophysite faithful—and in irreproachable company—Severus completed his days. But the kind of refuge Egypt now offered gradually transformed the haven into a house prison.

CONSTANTINOPLE: INDIVIDUALS IN COMMUNITY

Monophysite refugees had one other base at which to gather during Justinian's reign: the imperial city itself.[31] Severus had paved the way by his presence there during the early years of the sixth century, under sponsorship of the emperor Anastasius. As the story of Thomas and Stephen indicates, another powerful source of influence was now had in the empress Theodora. Through her, favors could be sought and, in Constantinople, safe shelter found.

The curious bipartisan religious loyalties of Justinian and Theodora played a fundamental role during their reign. Justinian's commitment to Chalcedonian faith and Theodora's to the Monophysites seemed odder for the fact that theirs was truly an imperial partnership.[32]

Traditionally, the key to their religious differences has been sought in the writings of Procopius.[33] Procopius insists that the antithetical loyalties of the pair were in fact an illusion, that they purposely cultivated this appearance as part of a larger policy to divide and rule. "They set the Christians at variance with one another, and by pretending to go opposite ways from each other in the matters under dispute, they succeeded in rending them all asunder."[34] A similar view is offered by Evagrius Scholasticus,[35] a more cautious historian, who claims that the ecclesiastical policy of Justinian and Theodora was one that allowed them to divide the empire between themselves: by dividing their religious loyalties they gave way to neither, while ensuring that both sides were cared for financially as well as politically. But Evagrius indicates the complexity of the situation by adding that in matters of faith, fathers were opposed to sons, sons to parents, wives to husbands, and husbands to wives.[36]

Monophysite sources offer ample tribute to Theodora and her works on their behalf. It was Theodora who brought relief from the persecutions, whether by influencing Justinian to relent even briefly or by providing safe refuge; it was she, too, who sheltered and protected the Monophysite patriarchs while they visited the royal city, and she who gave money for the relief of the ascetic refugees; and it was her death that marked the end to Monophysite hopes, according to some sources.[37] Syrian tradition went so far as to rewrite altogether the history of the empress's notorious youth. The child of a circus family who grew up on stage as a sexual acrobat became the chaste daughter of a Monophysite priest in the eastern provinces, with whom the young Justinian fell in love while on a military campaign. Her parents, this story went, were alarmed by Justinian's Chalcedonian views and agreed to a betrothal only on the grounds that he would leave her faith unchanged.[38]

Theodora was undoubtedly as loyal to the Monophysite cause as she appeared. Her conversion to this theological stance apparently happened while she was in Egypt, long before her marriage to Justinian,[39] and Chalcedonian sources also attest the money and effort she expended on their opponents.[40] Less clear is the exact nature of Justinian's religious convictions. Monophysite sources present a confused memory of the matter. Even some of the sources that record the persecutions offer praise for Justinian's religious activities.[41]

In fact, our subtlest picture of Justinian, and of the perhaps more elusive Theodora, emerges from the pen of John of Ephesus, who knew the royal family well. It is apparent in the *Lives of the Eastern Saints* that John holds a heartfelt respect for both, regardless of official imperial policies—a situation the more profound for its circumstances.[42]

In the *Lives*, John praises Theodora's works and mentions her activities apart from Monophysite affairs; he neither shuns nor exploits her rise from prostitution to the imperial throne.[43] Yet, John also indicates that the empress's efforts on behalf of the Monophysites were successful only to a certain degree: she was able to intercede for mercy on behalf of her supplicants and to sponsor the maintenance of the many refugees who came to Constantinople. Nonetheless, these measures amounted to little more than providing immediate comfort for those in need. Constantinople, like Egypt, became a convenient house prison by which the government could curtail the activities of its dissidents; similarly, Theodora's protection for the vulnerable Monophysite patriarchs, though allowing for their safe concealment, did not permit them freedom of movement.

It is in relation to Theodora that John offers information on Justinian's nature. Not only did the empress act with the emperor's knowledge, but he himself sometimes patronized the Monophysites in the
capital.[44] He accompanied her on visits to the Monophysite holy men for
religious instruction and, even after her death, continued to show concern for the welfare of the Monophysite community, especially in Constantinople, because of his love for her and devotion to her memory.[45]

Then, too, this Chalcedonian emperor chose John to perform extensive missionary work against pagans and heretics (primarily Montanists)
in Asia, Phrygia, Caria, and Lydia.[46] Few have doubted that John used
the opportunity to spread Monophysitism; although Michael the Syrian
reports that John propagated Chalcedonian faith because he was acting
at the emperor's behest, and that he judged it a lesser evil than paganism
or Montanism.[47] John clearly had the privilege of forthright speech with
Justinian.[48]

But the emperor's position was understandably affected by diverse
concerns.[49] His aspirations to regain the lost western provinces necessi-
tated courting the papacy by advancing an official pro-Chalcedonian
policy. At the same time, he took this crisis seriously as a theological
problem. He rejected what he saw as the too easily categorized pro- and
anti-Chalcedonian positions and sought a solution that could reconcile
the language of Chalcedon with that of Cyril of Alexandria. He marked
this idea with "conversations" he sponsored between Chalcedonians
and Monophysites. Over the course of his reign his own theological
writings progressed significantly towards this goal. Ironically, his final
lapse into aphthartodocetic heresy gave witness to deeply Monophysite
leanings in his personal theology.[50]

The imperial conversations were sporadically convened from the
time of Justinian's accession but were regarded by the Monophysite
leaders, at least, as less than serious efforts. Nonetheless, the failure of
these dialogues to reach satisfactory results did not daunt the spirit of
the Monophysite community for a surprisingly long time but instead
seemed to spark their optimism. Perhaps the simple fact that these dialogues took place sustained their confidence as to their own strength.

However, the designated spokesmen for the conversations did not
share such a view. Severus of Antioch, for one, was convinced from the
start that a peaceful resolution was impossible.[51] For a time he continued
to refuse numerous imperial summonses, so the first large-scale attempt
at discussions held in 532 took place without him.[52] Even so the Monophysite cause was impressively represented by John of Tella, John of
Beith-Aphthonia, and others. The three-way interchange, between Jus-

tinian, the pro-Chalcedonian bishops, and the Monophysites was exhausting and hazardous. It did not work, and the telling point was its failure on what amounted to practical rather than theological grounds: although Justinian granted generous theological concessions, he would not suspend the policy that bishops had to sign a document accepting the Chalcedonian definition in order to hold their sees.[53] In other words, while gaining their right to dissent, the Monophysites would not be allowed to resume their ecclesiastical positions without actually accepting the Chalcedonian definition they had rejected. Politics ruled the event. Severus' absence bothered Justinian, as it should have.[54] The gathering dissolved without achieving a compromise.

Repeated summonses to Severus, prompted by Theodora, produced no result, for he argued that if he came to Constantinople, public opinion would be dangerously provoked.[55] Finally, in 534/5 Severus conceded, pressured from all sides about the urgency of what was taking place in the capital.[56] For a year and a half after that, efforts were made on all parts to reach an understanding. Alarmed, the Roman papacy intervened, a move that culminated in a renewed proclamation of Chalcedon and a final condemnation in 536 of Severus and the other Monophysite bishops.[57] When Theodora died in 548, a lukewarm attempt was made to bully the Monophysites, now without their imperial advocate, into an agreement. It showed itself as markedly ill judged: the extreme measures had served only to harden the Monophysites' convictions.[58] The General Synod of Constantinople in 553 with its condemnation of the "Three Chapters," and the renewed initiative in 571 of Justinian's successor, Justin II, to seek theologial resolution through imperially sponsored dialogues, proved futile.[59] John of Ephesus wrote of these times, describing the Monophysite spokesmen who came repeatedly to the imperial city, "seething, burning with zeal for unity" on each occasion, each time leaving with nothing at all accomplished.[60]

In his *Lives* John of Ephesus indicates that the Monophysite community in Constantinople grew up during the early years of Justinian's reign for two basic reasons. First, some came to the imperial city out of anger to protest against the anti-Monophysite policies. This was not a foolhardy act. When Constantine I convened the Council of Nicea in 325, he sanctioned imperial accountability on religious issues. Matters of dispute could be, and frequently were, brought before an imperial audience by holy men or women whose spiritual authority superseded their often unimpressive civil statuses.[61] Second, some of the Monophysite body were drawn to the capital by the patronage of Theodora, whose thirst for spiritual direction was great. Despite the violence of popular opinion against Monophysite thought in Constantinople,[62] it was a natural gathering place: the sheer concentration of life in the New Rome somehow gave space for all who came.[63] While Egypt offered a stabilizing center for the persecuted Monophysite movement, in the overall circumstances attention inevitably shifted to Constantinople once Justinian and Theodora ascended the throne. Dependent on those who stayed behind to care for the faithful, the Monophysite community in the imperial city presented a pattern of activity that profoundly substantiated the moral force of their position.

John of Ephesus presents the Constantinopolitan community during the years of Justinian's reign with a particular tone of confidence. Here his stories are heroic, filled with forceful acts by the Monophysites and cowering humility by the Chalcedonians. John's tone in these stories is distinct, presenting a picture of far greater impact than can possibly have been the case. But since the solution to the religious conflict within the Byzantine Empire lay in the hands of the imperial court, these stories suggested to the wider Monophysite audience that their position with the authorities remained strong. The stories offer, too, the comforting picture of the Monophysite holy men interceding effectively on their behalf in the presence of their earthly rulers no less than with those above.

The stylite Z'ura was one of the first to come.[64] Forced down from his pillar near Amida by Chalcedonian zealots, he had set off at once for Constantinople in order to protest the state of religious affairs, accompanied by a band of trusted disciples, perhaps in the year 535.[65] But Z'ura was more than a disgruntled stylite; he was a holy man whose career had set him in a position of authority for the eastern Monophysites. His impact on the imperial city is attested elsewhere than in John's account,[66] a point that lends weight to John's claim that Chalcedonian informers had warned Justinian to watch out for Z'ura's arrival.[67]

In John's story, Justinian prepared himself for the encounter. But Z'ura arrived with such presence and spoke so bluntly that Justinian's only response was a temper tantrum. John tells us that Z'ura left the court "in violent rage" and returned to his holy works, now in the confines of the royal city. John portrays the entire sequence as one continuous and valiant action: Z'ura's ascetic practice, his labors on the pillar, and his foray into Constantinople and perhaps into the palace itself, all in fulfillment of the holy man's vows. There was neither hesitation in the stylite's actions nor faltering in his ascetic practice, despite the dangers of persecution.[68]

In earlier days, Daniel the Stylite had prefigured this action, also with extravagant drama, when he descended his pillar during the brief reign of the usurper Basiliscus; but in Daniel's case, the stylite had acted in support of the opposing cause of Chalcedonian faith and (by default) that of the emperor Zeno.[69] In Zʿura's case, John describes a scene of sharp positions, tinged with a biblical flavor that recalls the meetings between Moses and the Pharaoh of Egypt. Divine intervention led, John tells us, to Justinian falling seriously ill, as if in chastisement for his treatment of the little holy man. Theodora, "who was very cunning," concealed the emperor's condition but summoned Zʿura who, John claims, effected a cure immediately. "And thenceforth the dread of the blessed man fell upon Justinian."[70] Since Justinian suffered near-fatal illness more than once during his reign, John may well be conflating a group of events in attributing one of these occasions to Zʿura's encounter with the emperor.[71] But more importantly for John, the story enables him to present a chastened emperor, whether because Theodora had put pressure on him or because Zʿura himself had proved so commanding. According to John, Justinian recanted and paid due homage to the stylite, "but only the state of the church he did not set right."[72]

But John could turn even this ambivalent victory to Zʿura's advantage. He tells us that the stylite and his disciples proceeded to undertake a ministry within Constantinople, working with the poor and strangers and becoming very popular as a result. Theodora herself provided his place of residence, a villa at Sycae across the Golden Horn.

John further relates that Zʿura's reputation had reached Rome, worrying the pope who later humiliated himself in a vain effort to confront the stylite.[73] Eventually, Zʿura's standing in the public eye grew large enough to warrant a response from the palace. The empress sent him to a camp in Thrace that she provided for Monophysites, lest he bring about "sedition and evil in the city [of Constantinople]."[74] By this time, Theodosius, the patriarch of Alexandria, had also settled there in exile, and John tells us, "thereafter the blessed men dwelt there together, while that camp thundered praise."[75]

John portrays the Monophysite ascetics who came to Constantinople, whether to protest or to seek shelter, as persons of serious consequence to the life of the city and to the imperial couple. For example, he tells the story of Mare the Solitary, an Amidan ascetic who had pursued his vocation in Egypt. When the persecutions struck there, he too responded by hastening to Constantinople and forcing his way into the court.[76] Mare's behavior was so extreme that even John was shocked, and while praising his motives, he could not bring himself to present the details of Mare's encounter with Justinian and Theodora.[77]

Mare settled in Constantinople's environs, though his desire for solitude led him also to Sycae across the water. John presents Mare's ascetic discipline as if it were as forceful a weapon as his assault on the imperial court. People marveled, Justinian and Theodora no less than others. Indeed, John claims that Theodora pursued the solitary, begging his personal guidance; but when she flooded him with messages, gifts, money, and requests, the Amidan holy man scorned them all.[78] Instead, after some time as a recluse, Mare used money earned from his own labors to found a monastery that served as a hospice for the poor. Thus, Mare's days were passed "practicing mighty spiritual labours . . . and stoutly always reproving the king and queen with great freedom and without fear, and everyone marvelled at his teaching and at his deeds and at his words."[79]

Ascetics like Z'ura and Mare continued the Syrian tradition of religious vocation as an individual action beyond the confines of church or monastic institution. John understood the import of their presence in Constantinople in specific terms. When the Great Plague struck the city, Mare was to be one of its victims. John offers the story of Mare's life in much the same way as the solitary offered himself in sacrifice during the scourge. Thus, while the populace suffered the dreadful destruction, Mare "passed his time in affliction and great sorrow, and occupied himself with constant prayer and petition to God . . . kneeling and praying on behalf of the whole world."[80] At his death, John claims, Justinian and Theodora commanded a magnificent procession in honor of the blessed man. The words John speaks for another ascetic are also meaningful here: Mare died, "nothing whatever having been found to weaken him, or to make him remit what he had originally undertaken, not sickness nor persecutions nor any other distresses."[81]

CONSTANTINOPLE: THE COMMUNITY WITNESS

In contrast to the negotiations and the theological dialogues, and as if to provide a practical defense for Monophysite theology, Theodora took the occasion of the persecutions to gather an impressive flock of ascetics to the imperial city.[82] Thus when John narrated the "Lives of Thomas and Stephen,"[83] he specified Theodora's reasons for bringing Stephen to the imperial city: "because of his eloquence and his conversation and his wisdom, and moreover because he also lived a pure life and after the manner of a solitary."[84]

In John's view, the ascetics brought at the empress's request were no less worthy than those, such as Z'ura or Mare, who came of their own volition. For his part, Stephen had not been happy to receive the imperial summons to a far more public life than he would have wished, but he chose to accept it. Like John's other subjects, Stephen pursued his ascetic practices in Constantinople with the same humility that he had shown elsewhere. John found him there,

> a great harbour of rest for all the afflicted who used to repair to him from all quarters . . . so that even the king and queen themselves stood in awe of his venerable mode of life.[85]

Comprised of such figures, the Constantinopolitan community appeared to the Monophysite body as a witness to their faith in the midst of the very city that produced their trials. So John paid homage to those "gathered together in the royal city by the believing queen," where

> the congregation of persecuted saints was so widely extended that it shone with many who had under the constraint of the persecution come down from columns and been ejected from places of seclusion, and been expelled from districts, and their congregation was rendered illustrious by great and distinguished heads of convents from all quarters of the east and of the west, and Syria and Armenia, Cappadocia and Cilicia, Isauria and Lycaonia, and Asia and Alexandria and Byzantium, countries which beyond others burned with zeal for the faith.[86]

This company settled in the city under the empress's aegis at the palace of Hormisdas; some, such as Stephen, settled in the imperial residence itself.[87] With Theodora's generosity, they transformed their quarters into monastic dwellings. One could enter Hormisdas "as into a great and marvellous desert of solitaries and marvel at their numbers, and wonder at their venerable appearance."[88] Their impact on the imperial city was, John tells us, disconcerting:

> Many of the supporters of the synod of Chalcedon . . . when they saw this marvellous community, and learned the causes of the persecution of it, had their mind filled with affliction and contrition, and renounced the Chalcedonian communion, and asked for communion with them.[89]

To this body Theodora came frequently, "going round among them and making obeisance to them and being regularly blessed by each one of them." Justinian, too, "who was ranged against them on account of the synod of Chalcedon," came and "was attached to many of them and trusted them, and was constantly received and blessed by them."[90] One can allow for considerable exaggeration by John with regard to the actual impact of the Monophysite community on the Constantinopolitans, but the spirit he portrays among the Monophysites themselves must lie close to the mark, for it was this spirit that provided the strength to build their own independent tradition. John would have it that the exiled community had turned a "foreign" land into their own; they had transformed a place of persecution into one of worship.

John heightened his emphasis on the role of the Constantinopolitan community by placing his account of it alongside a brief chapter commemorating the Monophysite patriarchs "who distinguished themselves in exile in the time of persecution."[91] This chapter primarily praises the leadership team of Severus of Antioch, Theodosius of Alexandria, and Anthimus of Constantinople, who became the main target for the final banishment orders in 536. Anthimus, formerly bishop of Trebizond, had participated in the imperial conversations of 532 as a Chalcedonian delegate. But he had been deeply moved by the Monophysite arguments and came to develop a close friendship with Severus when the latter arrived at the imperial city. His consecration to Constantinople in 535, like that of Theodosius to Alexandria in the same year, owed much to Theodora's efforts. Once he had been won over to the Monophysite cause, Anthimus remained steadfast despite the hardships involved.[92] Severus, Anthimus, and Theodosius together and individually served the Monophysite movement with spirit and skill during the persecutions, almost entirely while suffering their own hardships in exile.[93] Their concerted energies were crucial for stabilizing the Monophysite movement as a whole; the lack of such unified effort by their successors contributed to the disintegration of the Monophysites into bickering factions toward the end of the sixth century.[94]

The Monophysite refugees in Constantinople made their impact largely because the Monophysite leadership was articulate and cohesive in providing a theological basis for their witness of faith. In turn, the leadership was strengthened by having this disciplined ascetic following prominently in view.[95] But John did not allow his readers to forget the realities of the situation. Thus he includes the "Life of Tribunus," a layman who accompanied the expelled Amidan monks to Constantinople and whose story offers a different shading to John's portrait of life in the refugee community.[96]

Tribunus was from Sophanene, near Amida, born of a wealthy and well-educated family. He became a frequent visitor at the monastery where Habib and Zᶜura dwelt, and he continued to follow Zᶜura's guidance when the holy man ascended his pillar after Habib's death. When the persecutions forced the stylite down, Z'ura chose Tribunus to accompany him to the imperial city, "as an interpreter of the Greek tongue." But the pious layman did more than that; he settled in Constantinople with Z'ura and his disciples, "imitating their practices and occupied in spiritual employment." Soon he asked permission to take monastic vows. Suddenly, vision and necessity collided.

> For the blessed men would not allow him, saying "It is better both for you and for us that you should go in and out of the city and the palace as a layman, and carry communications for us." . . . And so he performed the service . . . insomuch that he gained easier entry and more freedom, and they even thrust the office of a count on him under constraint by [Z'ura's] command saying, "This will be no impediment to your practices; and when you wish, it is easy for you to give up the office." [97]

"Count" Tribunus obeyed (though, as a secular appointment, the office had to have come from Justinian), acquiring the worldly title and means he had always scorned when pushed in that direction by his family. Finally, Z'ura died; the layman was now free to answer his calling. He did so, "accomplishing the labor of his practices on a great scale, having also added to his spiritual labours the extra labour of hospitality and the relief of the poor, living and delighting also in voluntary poverty." [98]

As an ascetic, Tribunus fit precisely the model John praised. His withdrawal from the temporal world was in no way the abandonment of those who were in the world; his turning to the spiritual life was a turn to the life of service. Yet Tribunus was for many years denied his full vocation by those who were its greatest exponents, this for reasons of simple expediency.

John's account of Tribunus makes two points. First, whatever triumphs might be claimed for the exiles, their position remained insoluble. Tribunus, "who in habit was a layman and a count, but in the performance of excellence complete and perfect," [99] was proof that when the Monophysite ascetics were forced into the methods of the temporal world, their faith was not necessarily belied. But second, and perhaps more decisively as John again puts forth his view, holy presence, or divine agency, cannot be confined to a space separated from the temporal realm and its needs. Rather, a layman, as much as a stylite, might be the occasion of God's presence in the world. Thus, John tells us, the gathering grew, gradually gaining its own reputation for ascetic excellence. [100]

But John does not imply that the imperial city was devoid of its own authoritative witness. A telling example is his account of Theodore, who was chamberlain and *castrensis* in the imperial court. [101] Theodore conducted his work in the royal palace while "living in fasting and constant prayers, and sorrow and tears and works of charity." In fact, he had found a model for this double-edged career in an old man who had served the court before him as *praepositus sacri cubiculi*.[102] But after a time, Theodore longed for undistracted pursuit of the divine. He asked permission from Justinian to leave "the turmoil of the palace" and to "devote himself to the practice of religion only."[103]

The emperor granted the request and Theodore turned to serving the city's poor and needy; the wealth he brought with him was rapidly spent. John describes Theodore, whom he often saw, as "intoxicated with the fervour of divine love," but many in the ascetic community felt concerned because he had soon reduced himself to destitution. Unexpectedly, John says, Justinian himself intervened, granting the ascetic a substantial annual stipend, enough both for Theodore and for much work with the poor.[104]

John presents the Constantinopolitan Monophysite community honestly. The witness displayed by its members did not conceal the reality that this shelter from persecution was little more than a house prison for dissidents. The community was compelled to make compromises even to maintain its own ascetic integrity, as in the case of Tribunus, in order to remain active; indeed, the more prominent leaders had to be kept virtual prisoners by the empress, so great was the care required to keep them safe.[105] Moreover, as Theodore's story implies, much of the Monophysites' freedom in the capital was possible because of Justinian's beneficence rather than Theodora's activities. The emperor was sensitive to expressions of genuine faith, and he found among the Monophysites an element of religious spirit that truly did move him, despite his official policies against Monophysites elsewhere and despite his harsh treatment of heretics, pagans, and Jews.[106]

But if John was honest in describing the life of the exiled community in the capital, his enthusiasm was unimpaired. The refugees arrived, he tells us, to find the means for resuming their vocations. Here too there was work to be done. So it was for John's compatriot Hala, who reached the imperial city ill from the hardships endured en route.[107] But the sight of the ascetic gathering in the palace of Hormisdas, and of the many suffering people of the city itself, was for him like manna from heaven:

> Like a poor man who loses one of his great possessions, and decides in his mind that it will never be found again, and suddenly sees it and is astonished and glad, so it was with this blessed man also . . . and so he perfectly carried out all the ministry to the needy. . . . [And he] sought that one object, to relieve persons in trouble, till everyone was astonished at him and they gave thanks to God.[108]

In the face of so many individuals carrying out such activities, it was no surprise that Justinian's successor, Justin II, felt it necessary to persecute the Monophysite gathering in the capital with a severity previously reserved for the provinces.[109]

The accounts John offers of ascetics in Egypt and Constantinople are not separable from his narrations of the Amidan community. The *Lives* tell us why the Monophysite ascetics of the East played such a critically complementary role to that of the movement's leaders, solidifying the cause at a popular level. In Amida's villages, in Egypt's deserts, and in the imperial city itself, Monophysite spiritual life was pursued in the midst of temporal turmoil and in the midst of secular society.

EPILOGUE. AMIDA AND CONSTANTINOPLE: HOLY PRESENCE

Private contemplation of the divine and personal ascetic pursuits do have their place in John's presentation, but their purpose is specifically allotted and not portrayed as self-justifying. John does not disapprove of those who follow such practices, but the infrequency and the brevity of his accounts on such subjects indicate their secondary position in his scheme; they are congruous with his overall portrait only when their wider context is established. So, for example, with Thomas and Stephen, the single-minded seclusion of the first and the selfless labors of the second are juxtaposed in such a way that each is validated by the other. But an impressive statement of John's perspective on solitary practice can be found in his two accounts of holy fools.

The holy fool represented an ultimate severance from the temporal world, one so complete as to be completely internalized. Consequently, it was displayed by disguised immersion in the most debauched and cruel aspects of urban society.[110] Where the ascetic ideal focused on life in a space apart from urban society—in desert, wilderness, monastery, or convent—the holy fool achieved the ideal condition wherever he or she might be in utter estrangement. Dead to the world, no worldly space existed for them: they inhabited only the realm of divine contemplation.

John's most elaborate account is of two holy fools, a man and a woman living in spiritual marriage, who stayed for a time in Amida.[111] Their story is unique in the *Lives* for it is told secondhand, although John does claim to have seen the couple in Tella.[112] The literary incongruity of the story has led to the view that it may be fiction, a story within a story, which John included in his *Lives* for its edifying value.[113] Such a piece is wholly uncharacteristic of John in this collection; however, the chapter's function in light of John's views remains the same in either case.

The couple masqueraded by day as mime actors, hence as harlot and pimp; they received daily abuse and humiliation. Yet by night they could not be found by those who wished to buy the woman's favors. While they were in Amida, a monk had noticed the strange matter and followed the couple secretly, only to discover that under shield of darkness their profession was not what it had seemed. By night, they prayed in a remote spot on the city walls until dawn threatened their privacy; the air around them shone with radiance. Distressed at having been discovered, and unable to convince the monk that he must publicly abuse them as the crowds did each day, they left for another city to retain their anonymous practice.

The story's actual setting and the couple's perfection offset one another. The couple had been drawn in particular to Amida: "We like being in this city which is a city of Christians." [114] Further, their religious practices were exercised on Amida's city walls. [115] But as John himself had recounted elsewhere, Amida's experience of tragedy in the sixth century had been overwhelming. [116] Its walls had been the scene of treachery and slaughter; its citizens had endured a religious war within their own ranks. Yet this couple had found the city good, "a city of Christians," and had blessed by their acts of prayer the very walls that once had brought destruction.

True or not, the story provides John with a moving statement of redemption and divine favor for the city and its people, themes that are most often his central focus. The Amidan ascetics are affirmed and legitimized here by this outside witness: divine grace was thus made manifest in Amida. The ascetics' own authority could only be strengthened by such testimony.

John recounts one other appearance of a holy fool, this one taking place in Constantinople. [117] In contrast to the romantic tones surrounding the couple in Amida, this encounter is clearly genuine; but the contextual parallels are striking. John himself had observed a certain beggar who fearfully fled any offer of charity. Thinking this poor man must in reality be "a spiritual person," John sent one of the monks from his monastery at Sycae to follow him. The monk discovered the man in the act of prayer and, finding the spectacle so powerful, fell into a state of hysteria lasting the entire day despite John's efforts to calm him. When they finally achieved a dialogue with the beggar, he expressed the same loathing of public recognition that the couple in Amida had.

He told John's monk that he was one of seven men leading a life of poverty, anonymity, and ascetic labor in Constantinople; and that the group of them met once each week for the Eucharist and for encouragement. He, too, begged to be left alone and nameless in his labors.

> I have given you the information; see that you do not make yourself the cause of my moving from this city, in which I have much peacefulness, and especially the fact that I am reckoned a madman by them, and there is no one who speaks with me. And beg the abbot [John of Ephesus] that though these things are known to him, he will leave me as I am, and not show any difference toward me.[118]

As discussed earlier, like Amida, Constantinople was caught in the hardships of war, political unrest, and Bubonic Plague. Themselves refugees from the tragedy of the Byzantine East, John and the Monophysite community labored among Constantinople's populace just as they and their comrades had done in the city of Amida. The encounter with the holy fool once again served to offer hope for salvation; grace was present even in Constantinople despite the times. Once more, John's ascetics are granted authority by contact with a practice of single-minded contemplation of God; likewise, this man could pursue his solitary practice with integrity because of its complement in the labors of John's ascetics.

In the course of his *Lives,* John presents several portraits of virtuous solitaries, set in the various locales of his stories. Thus he reminds his readers that he is writing in praise of lives devoted to the divine. They serve to emphasize that spiritual authority and its temporal extension are grounded in a vision of holy presence and divine grace in society's world. And nowhere does John say this more clearly than in his tributes to these holy fools.

· V ·

SPIRITUALITY AND ACCOUNTABILITY: CONSEQUENCES OF THE ASCETIC VOW

The works of the exiled community that John of Ephesus records in his *Lives of the Eastern Saints* are presented as a logical extension of the ascetic's practice. But the context of these works is larger than the immediate situation of religious persecution. Indeed, John extends the context by the juxtaposition of these narratives to his accounts of missionary activity undertaken by the Monophysites, whether spontaneously by individuals or in accordance with the authority of the collective Monophysite body. John unites the experience of service, exile, and mission in his chapters devoted to the major endeavor of the sixth-century Monophysites: the ordination of those who were to become a new church order. In so doing, he raises the issue of the ascetic's accountability, both for the nonbelieving world and for the believing congregation.

MISSION: INDIVIDUAL RESPONSIBILITY AND COLLECTIVE AUTHORITY

Expansion is not the act of a demoralized church. But the *Lives of the Eastern Saints* record Monophysite missions undertaken both inside and outside Roman borders and, eventually, in direct opposition to the imperially proclaimed "orthodoxy." By the end of the sixth century, Monophysite missions were to produce a substantial church body, whose confines bore little relation to the empire's physical boundaries and whose members would feel little loyalty to an emperor upholding a faith opposed to their own.[1] If this situation did not directly facilitate the Persian and Arab conquests of the Byzantine East in the seventh and eighth centuries, it certainly undermined basic political assumptions in the East regarding the significance of Byzantium's theocratic imperial authority.

John's *Lives* indicate that missionary activity might come about simply as a result of circumstance. In this context, missionary work is part and parcel of the ascetic vision John offers. Such was the case presented in his "Life of Simeon the Mountaineer."[2]

Simeon was a hermit who wandered the territories along the upper Euphrates; he "used to go about the mountains like the wild beasts, and . . . had no intercourse except with God."[3] Conditions in these regions were such that the ascetic could live in this manner only eight months of the year: the snowy season drove him annually to lower areas. One year, Simeon chanced upon a settled people of the remote mountain summits, whose villages—with their inhabitants loosely scattered over wide distances—were unlike those of the other communities he knew. Surprised at finding domesticated life in such rugged countryside, the hermit inquired about their general livelihood and customs. To his dismay, he discovered that these people were apparently "godless," having no religious practices and acquainted with Christianity only by name. As the situation was made known to him, Simeon's "bones shook from his fright and his tears gushed out."[4] The hermit was beside himself:

> Perhaps it was indeed for this reason that God's grace led me to the mountains here, in order that there may be salvation for these souls that are in the darkness of error. . . . What pagan is there, or what other worshippers of creation, who for so long a period of time would neglect to pay honour to the object of his worship, and would not always worship that which is reckoned by him as God? These men neither worship God like Christians, nor honour something else like pagans and they are apostates against the one and against the other.[5]

Simeon set to work. A little church was found in the district, unused in living memory. Helped by the local inhabitants, Simeon cleaned the chapel, summoned the people of the area, and began to preach. It was as if he spoke to "irrational animals," for the people "looked at him in astonishment, and they had nothing to say." Undaunted, the holy man went on to lay down strict injunctions for their religious conduct, so that they might offer penance for their years of neglect and render fitting worship to God. For Simeon discovered matters to be worse than he had thought. Asking why none of the children had been dedicated to the religious life of the Sons and Daughters of the Covenant, he was told, "Sir, they have not time to leave the goats and learn anything," upon which "the blessed man marvelled at the people's simpleness and carelessness."[6]

Nor did Simeon's intervention stop there. He imposed further injunctions on the chastened populace against blasphemy, fornication, and murder. Those transgressing his orders Simeon promptly punished; few seemed to question his right to authority. On the contrary, "then [the people] began to feel a little fear, both of God and of the blessed man himself, while he continued sending and fetching all who were on the mountains to the house, and converting them afresh, as if from paganism."[7]

But greater plans were afoot. Simeon gathered the children of the district together and shut them in the church, explaining to their parents that he had a gift for them. Then he separated one-third of the ninety children—eighteen boys and twelve girls—closed the remainder in another room, and with his helper quickly tonsured the chosen thirty, "soothing them with blandishments; and of them some wept, and some were silent." Thus were set apart the foundations of a monastic community and school. An outcry followed, but Simeon persuaded the parents of the virtue of his act, except for two families who refused to part with their children. Within three days the two youngsters had died. "Then the terror of the blessed man fell upon everyone, when the power of his word and of his prayer upon those men was seen; and they also repented."[8] Simeon's will was never tested again.

The holy man continued his own ascetic practices and, once order had been established, again returned to solitude during the summer season. After twenty-six years of such labor, Simeon grew feeble; and thereafter he stayed in the village, in his cell, and practiced with an equal severity.

> And accordingly the blessed man's name had gone out over all that country, and he was a law and a judge of the country; and every matter that was in need of reform was referred to him.[9]

An anchorite in the oldest tradition of the Syrian Orient, Simeon had offered the whole of his existence to God in worship. Having sought the divine in the purity of natural creation, he found it where he least expected it: in the imperfection of human society. John pays tribute to Simeon as one who reveals the unsought possibilities of life dedicated to holy pursuit. For here was a region too remote to be reached by matters afflicting the greater part of the East; indeed, Simeon's story contains none of the calamities so visible in John's other accounts.[10] Simeon is not drawn or forced out of seclusion by the urgency of crisis. Rather, he is confronted by a "godless" existence, and his reaction is as spontaneous as it is thorough. Set on saving the mountain people, this holy man was not satisfied with offering a church tradition of ritual and preaching; he imposed upon this isolated society the fruits of his ascetic discipline. He was law, judge, and spiritual father to them, far more than priest or abbot.

Simeon had in fact fulfilled an aspect of Syrian ascetic tradition that many had followed before him. Spontaneous missionary activity had long been part of the ascetic's responsibilities in the Syrian Orient, both in Roman and in Persian territory.[11] But Simeon was not consciously taking up this role and was thus all the more in accordance with his own heritage: precisely because the Syrian ascetic had of necessity to stay within reach of society, conditions ripe for evangelization arose. As in Simeon's experience, it was more often than not a case of responding by instinct to religious need. But Simeon when instituting his rules of conduct for the villagers did show an intentional awareness of his role; for example, by the early fifth century, it was canonically ruled by the Syrian Church that chorepiscopi should set apart certain sons and daughters of each family, in each village, for the Sons and Daughters of the Covenant.[12]

The story of Simeon the Mountaineer underscores the tie between John's subjects and those ascetics who preceded them. Responsiveness was inherent to the tradition of the Syrian ascetic's vocation. But Simeon's case is one among several John presents that is concerned with mission, and each adds a different dimension to his portrayal of activity in this sphere as a collective act of grace. Comparison highlights the contrasting nuances involved; the case of Simeon the Debater, who became bishop of Beth Arsham in Persia, is one example.[13]

John refers to Simeon the Debater as "the brave warrior on behalf of the true faith." Indeed, this Simeon did more warring than episcopal administering. Something of a legend in his own time, Simeon's story lent itself to melodrama; John played on this with narrative styled as romance. Thus in John's telling of the story, Persia is a land steeped in the hated traditions of Marcion, Bardaisan, and Mani as much as in those of the Nestorians resettled from Roman territory, who were then the majority of the Christian populace.[14] Further, when Simeon debated with the Nestorians on doctrine, the Magi invariably awarded the victory to Simeon and sometimes even converted.[15] As a debater Simeon "put everyone to shame," and was even more skilled "than the ancients."[16]

Nestorians trembled at his name. As spokesman for the "orthodox" minority, Simeon traveled with the help of an underground network over vast distances at tremendous speed. Wherever a dialogue on faith was taking place Simeon appeared:

> As if God had made him ready and as if the earth had vomited him up, Simeon would suddenly spring up and be present there, since from the greatness of his zeal and fervour of his will he did not rest and sit still in one district.[17]

But John's story of Simeon also contains the historical reasons behind his daring and intrigue. By Simeon's time, it was the Nestorians, based at Nisibis in particular, who held sway among the Persian Christians; against these "the blessed Simeon was always strongly armed and ceaselessly contending"[18] in the regions beyond the eastern Roman frontiers, in Persia, and among the Arab tribes. Although John paints Simeon as so impressive that almost everyone who heard him converted, Simeon himself seems to have seen his main task as one within the church body. This was a different matter from that of Simeon the Mountaineer's confrontation with heathenism, or of John of Ephesus' own battle against paganism. "Deeply versed in scripture," Simeon "debated" misguided doctrinal positions, a method of discipline by persuasion.

Simeon's reputation was not unfounded. The Monophysite minority in Persia was periodically harassed by the Magian imperial cult, John claims at the promptings of the Nestorians. On different occasions in the course of his career, Simeon called upon the respective authorities of the emperor Anastasius, the Aethiopian king, and the empress Theodora, each of whom successfully interceded with the Persian king on behalf of that minority.[19] Eventually, Simeon was consecrated against his will and by force to the metropolitan see of Beth Arsham. This added responsibility apparently did not hinder Simeon: "And so he would go about in the interior countries beyond the Persians and make disciples, and convert men from paganism and Magism, and return again to the same country, and strenuously meet those who held the impious doctrine of Nestorius in the same contests."[20] Thus Simeon passed his life until he died of old age while on a visit to Constantinople, where he was staying with John of Ephesus.

If the story of Simeon the Mountaineer illustrates the range of responsibilities for the ascetic, that of Simeon the Persian Debater indicates the scope of care needed within the church's own confines. Both accounts are focused on activity outside the mainstream social and political sphere that provides the major context for most of John's *Lives*. But the particular emphases found in these two narratives illuminate John's other, and considerably briefer, accounts of missionary activity. John was too self-conscious to speak at length of his own role in the missions to the pagans, but his *Lives* offer tribute to the deacons, presbyters, and bishops who aided this undertaking.[21] Of the campaign itself, John here tells us only that

> eighty thousand were converted and rescued from paganism, and ninety-eight churches and twelve monasteries, and seven other churches transformed from Jewish synagogues were founded in these four provinces, Asia, Caria, Phrygia, and Lydia.[22]

Elsewhere, in his *Ecclesiastical History,* John writes of these missions performed under imperial aegis and carried out not only in the provinces but in the capital city itself. Pagans were turned from their ways or, failing this, tragically put to death. So too were many heretics: Manichees, Montanists, and others.[23] If Justinian's patronage of the campaign prompted confused speculation about its purpose, John's *Lives* dispelled doubts about the theological tenor of the undertaking.

The ascetics who accompanied John were "strenuous workers."[24] These holy men "gained a blessed end" not, John assures us, for any reason other than their own witness in mission.

> Each one of them . . . was strengthened to abolish paganism, and overthrow idolatry, and uproot altars and destroy shrines and cut down trees in ardent religious zeal; and . . . all of them also toiled and laboured with us with joy and great earnestness.[25]

In his *Lives* John names some of his coworkers; but he tells us they were part of an entourage altogether deserving of the same homage. That he should include his helpers in his collection of holy men and women is sufficient statement of their spiritual integrity, whatever the political impetus of the missions themselves; he does not discuss the doctrinal positions of these coworkers, leaving us without knowledge of the group's makeup in this respect. Again, the complexity of Justinian's religious policy comes to view.

To a large extent, the value of John's *Lives* lies in their orientation toward the events and crises of their times, a vantage point often lacking in hagiographical works. It is in his accounts of mission that John merges critical situations in time into the timeless realm of divine activity worked through human agency. The service missions in various cities of Paul of Antioch,[26] or the salvific campaigns led by John himself, express an urgency offset by the measure of the two Simeons. For through his tales of the Mountaineer and the Debater, John declares that mission is a labor intrinsic to asceticism, that times of crisis are inherently those in which the ascetic moves, and that political boundaries offer no barriers to ascetic endeavors.

John portrays mission as an extension of the ascetic vocation and its responsibilities. But such individual autonomy carried inadvertent consequences: it contributed to the development of the Monophysite body into a separate church.

ORDINATION: INDIVIDUAL RESPONSIBILITY AND COLLECTIVE ACCOUNTABILITY

While John presents better examples of specific activities elsewhere in the *Lives of the Eastern Saints*, nowhere in John's writings can the critical juncture of his ascetic vision and its implications be seen more clearly than in his account of the bishop John of Tella.[27]

John of Tella exemplified all that John of Ephesus admired: he was ascetic, priest, hero, and martyr. He distinguished himself early in his career as a solitary[28] but was raised to the bishopric of Constantina/Tella in 519. John of Ephesus tells us that John of Tella conducted his ecclesiastical affairs while continuing his severe ascetic labors. When the persecutions reached Osrhoene in 521, he was expelled along with the other bishops and ascetics of his area; he took his place in the desert with the rest of the exiled community, providing a steadying presence.[29]

The desert, as we have seen, did not serve as a place of dissociated retreat for the expelled Monophysites; rather, for those like John of Tella, it nourished their spiritual resources. The persecutions were succeeding, even if differently from the way their instigators had hoped.

In the wake of the expulsions the faithful body as a whole was forced by circumstances to reassess its religious situation. For John of Ephesus, the Monophysite believers showed remarkable determination, refusing the poison of "false" shepherding by the Chalcedonians. Instead, pressuring those in exile to provide them with the guidance they required, they asked that new pastors be ordained to meet their needs.

> But the blessed men, inasmuch as they were troubled by fear of lighting the furnace of persecution more hotly against them, refused to practice this openly, though they did a few things in secret; and a murmuring on the part of those among the believers who had been banished from every quarter began to be stirred up against the blessed men [the bishops], since they had been reduced to great difficulties. . . . Then all the bishops assembled together, and considered what to do. . . . Finally, out of fear, they refused the thing.[30]

As the bishops knew, the issue of ordination was not an innocent one; it involved more than avoiding further wrath from the imperial court. The greater issue at stake was the question of orthodoxy and the church. In the history of the dispute over the Council of Chalcedon, despite its lurching from side to side, no rival clerical or ecclesiastical structure had been discussed. The dispute had been played out within the existing church structure and body; despite vehemence on all sides, the opposing groups had resembled political parties that, although based on apparently divergent principles, worked within the same system. Severus of Antioch and the other leaders were more aware of the dangers of moving towards the ordination of a separate clergy than the rank and file of the anti-Chalcedonians. These latter feared for their personal salvation, which might be irreparably damaged in the event of receiving the Eucharist at the wrong hands; salvation to them was far more important than the welfare of the ecclesiastical structure.[31]

Severus did his best to impart an appropriate sobriety to the Monophysite body, strictly adhering to canon law, scripture, and patristic teaching. In exile, he continued to fulfill his responsibilities as patriarch of Antioch in the context of patriarchal jurisdiction, rather than as the leader of an "outside" group. He continually drew upon the precedents, and to his mind parallel experiences, of Basil of Caesarea and Gregory of Nazianzus during the fourth-century Arian controversies. To ordain a "private" clergy for the Monophysite body, instead of healing the diseased church from within, should only be a last resort.[32]

But the presence of a Chalcedonian clergy in charge of the lay populace was a danger of more tangible proportions for many of the faithful.[33] Finally, John of Tella took their cause before the bishops.

> And henceforth whither shall the persecuted and distressed believers who are with us go? Do you wish, pray, that we should send them to those who are every day killing them? For God knows that I for my part was ready for a life of quietude by myself, but that I should leave God's people and church in distress and need, and serve my own self, far be it from me in the Lord's name.[34]

So sometime before 527, John of Tella having passed his exile thus far in retreat, the Monophysite bishops, apparently sanctioned by Severus himself, granted him special permission to ordain clergy to meet the needs of the faithful. This authority was recognized as an emergency power, since John received the authority to ordain all who came to him if the candidates met the disciplinary standards of the church. The results, as has been said, were sensational.[35] Even if John exaggerates the numbers (as he did), the response was great enough to warrant attention.

Multitudes "rushed in crowds to come to the blessed man freely without impediment like a flood that is produced in a river by thick clouds." [36] John traveled about, receiving candidates for the priesthood and diaconate in monasteries or makeshift hideaways. While John of Ephesus was quick to glorify the situation, he took care to point out that the bishop's choices did not lack quality for the quantity.

> [He was] receiving and dismissing companies of fifty and of a hundred in a day, and even now and again as many as two and three hundred a day, giving expositions and injunctions and caution and instruction, and performing the ordinations after careful investigation and many testimonies given, subjecting every man to a careful examination and test in reading the Scriptures and repeating the psalms, and ability to write their names and signatures. [37]

Candidates came from "every city as far as the frontier, and as far as Armenia and Arzanene, and the land of the Cappadocians and the seacoasts." [38] Among them in 529 came the young John of Ephesus, to be admitted to the diaconate, while John of Tella was based in Marde. He arrived with a group of brethren from the Amidan monasteries, then in exile as well; they were warmly received by John of Tella, who knew of their communities by reputation and was impressed by their learning and discipline. The pioneer bishop left his mark on the young monk John, who "remembered always" the impact of his presence. [39]

For a time John of Tella performed his ordinations from the city of Marde, in the company of Philoxenus of Mabbog and others. Severus wrote to them, praising them both for the excellence of their ascetic practices and for their labors on behalf of the Monophysite body. [40] The importance of John of Tella's ascetic training and prowess was not to be underestimated, as Severus knew. Not only must there be no charges of canonical misconduct, but John himself had to be above reproach. [41] His ascetic training and vocation provided the necessary assurance and, as in the case of Severus himself, must have been genuinely formidable. But in the eyes of John of Ephesus, John of Tella was inspired to the work of ordination because of the nature of his religious calling. When he received official orders from the government to halt his subversive work, he gave the reply,

> I for my part have received a gift from God, and with it I am trading and am not negligent; and know this, that, as long as I am in the bodily life, and a hand is given me to extend to anyone that is in need, not you nor any earthly king shall hinder me from performing the service that the heavenly king has given me. [42]

The imperial authorities were understandably alarmed. It fell to Ephrem of Antioch, "the executioner of the believers" (as John of Ephesus calls him), to take on John of Tella.[43] John's eventual death in prison in 538 was as powerful as an act of martyrdom as his career was impressive throughout. It thus heralded disaster for pro-Chalcedonian hopes. John of Tella had been decidedly efficacious; if John of Ephesus exaggerates hopelessly in claiming that John ordained 170,000 men into the clergy,[44] it is of little concern. Two irrevocable steps had been taken: first, a network of ecclesiastical leaders had been established, ensuring the renewed care of the Monophysite congregations; second, the precedent of an independently ordained Monophysite structure had been established. If the founding of the "Jacobite" church has traditionally been attributed to Jacob Burdʿaya, it was in fact John of Tella who laid the necessary groundwork.

From the "Life of John of Tella," John of Ephesus continues his collection with the story of John's spiritual brother and successor, John of Hephaestopolis.[45] Following a pattern similar to that of his predecessor, this John began his career as an ascetic. He was promoted to the episcopacy by the patriarch Theodosius of Alexandria, with whom he journeyed to Constantinople when the persecutions were launched in Egypt in 536. Not long thereafter, while living with the refugees in the imperial city, John of Hephaestopolis took up the task left by John of Tella to continue the ordination of Monophysite clergy.

Recognizing that he seemed to be straying from his professed intentions, and covering territory more appropriate for his *Ecclesiastical History*, John of Ephesus felt the need to defend his choice of bishops as subjects in this collection; he prefaced his "Life of John of Hephaestopolis" with this apologia:

> [John of Tella and John of Hephaestopolis] were complete and perfect in both forms of beauty [pastoral and ascetic]; and for this reason, though we seem to be passing from one subject to another, we did not think it alien to the excellent purpose to describe and hand down to remembrance for the glory of God that life which was practised by these men also.[46]

By granting these select bishops a place in his *Lives*, John strengthened their authority at a time when their activities involved a canonical and theological risk. Furthermore, the decision was both a declaration about Monophysite asceticism and a statement about Monophysite leadership. In the schema of John's *Lives* and in the ascetic vision they reflect, the campaign for ordinations set underway by John of Tella and

John of Hephaestopolis was in effect obligatory for men of their spiritual standing.

The imperial decree on the church in 536 had effectively confined the Monophysite bishops and clergy to the refugee camps in Thrace and Constantinople; Egypt was no longer safe territory, and John of Tella was soon imprisoned in Antioch. The need for pastoral care was acute. Crowds began to arrive in the imperial city, not only seeking solace from the Monophysite community but, even more, seeking ordination "as there was absolutely no man to extend a hand of ordination to any believer in the whole Roman territory as far as the Persian frontier." [47] Yet, even with Theodora's protective presence, those with authority refused to ordain the candidates, "as it was indeed truly impossible for them to live if an ordination were performed there, if the adversaries heard of it." [48]

To John of Hephaestopolis, it seemed the bishops were no longer fulfilling their episcopal duties: "We for our part have been named pastors of God's church to no purpose, since we have suffered her lambs to be torn by wolves. . . . What is the benefit that we are now doing for God's church?" On his own authority, he acquired separate quarters in the capital with Theodora's help and began to ordain the "companies of those who were in distress, and had been for a long time beaten and buffeted and had none to relieve them." [49]

An immediate and angry clamor arose from inside the Monophysite ranks, from those concerned about simple safety. But the patriarch Theodosius of Alexandria, now head of the Monophysite community in Constantinople, granted tacit blessing to the renegade's activities by disclaiming responsibility but not censuring John; Theodora herself begged John to "remain still and keep quiet like your companions and do not make priests in this city." [50] But John contrived to escape the imperial house prison and took his authority where it was needed. He traversed the islands and territories of the eastern provinces, receiving candidates for the priesthood, performing ordinations, and ministering to the congregations. The Chalcedonians complained to Justinian that "one of the bishops [from Constantinople] has come out, and has thrown the whole church into confusion." [51] John's actions, indeed, bordered on the outrageous. In Tralles, John of Ephesus served wide-eyed as deacon while fifty men were ordained secretly in the upper-level women's gallery of a church, with a Chalcedonian service in full progress below; he tells us, "I was amazed at the man's courage and fortitude." [52]

But John of Ephesus could look upon the ordinations only as an act of grace; in his eyes the two Johns were God given:

> In this time of [the church's] distress also [God] set up these two pillars
> of light in it to comfort it; by whose holy prayers may schisms and
> strifes be done away from within it until the end, Amen![53]

John of Ephesus could not see that the process was irreversible. The
ordinations were charged with the awareness of resistance. The momentum would neither be diverted nor reabsorbed into a "mainstream"
church. By the time Jacob Burd'aya and Theodore of Arabia were consecrated to the task of replenishing a shrunken Monophysite hierarchy,
the way was clearly set. Even without Jacob's energy, an equally decisive
act would surely have taken place.

The death of John of Tella had left a gap partially filled by John
of Hephaestopolis; but age and the hardships of enforced exile took
their toll on the other leaders of the Monophysite body. Philoxenus of
Mabbog had died in 523, and Severus himself died in 538 almost immediately after John of Tella. Most of the episcopal hierarchy marshaled by
Severus had disappeared or been rendered ineffectual.[54] Then, in 542,
matters changed. Harith bar Gabala, king of the Saracens and a Monophysite sympathizer, approached the empress Theodora because "a
lack of priests had . . . arisen in the countries of the east and of the west,
and especially of bishops."[55] He asked that she direct two or three bishops to be consecrated for Syria to ensure the welfare of his own tribes
and fellow believers.

> And, since the believing queen was desirous of furthering everything
> that would assist the opponents of the synod of Chalcedon, she gave
> orders and two blessed men, well-tried and divine persons, whose
> names were Jacob and Theodore, were chosen and instituted, one for
> Hirtha of the Saracens, that is Theodore, and Jacob for the city of
> Edessa.[56]

Jacob began, John tells us, by sharing a cell in a Constantinopolitan
monastery with another monk named Sergius.[57] Together they practiced
arduous and severe ascetic labors, yet Sergius seemed to emerge second
best in John's eyes. John explains that although Sergius practiced in the
same manner as Jacob, he would also speak to those who approached
their cell on matters of business and hence fell short of Jacob, who "entirely refused to take part in these things, and refused also to appear
during the day outside his cell."[58] This was, of course, but a preparatory
process.

Jacob and Theodore were not to be ordinary bishops; their jurisdiction was governed by the state of emergency in which the Monophysites
found themselves. Their task was to restore the depleted ranks of the
ecclesiastical hierarchy and, specifically, to refill the sorely wanting

higher echelons. In Theodore the faithful had chosen a diligent worker; but with Jacob, the movement came into its own.

> And, while the blessed Theodore exercised authority in the southern and western [Syrian] countries, and the whole of the desert and Arabia and Palestine, as far as Jerusalem, the blessed Jacob, having armed himself with religion, and clothed himself in the zeal of heroism, extended his course over all the countries not only of Syria and the whole of Armenia and Cappadocia . . . but also of Cilicia and the whole of Isauria and of Pamphylia and Lycaonia and Lycia and Phrygia and Caria and Asia, and in the islands of the sea Cyprus and Rhodes, and Chios and Mitylene, and as far as the royal city of Constantinople.[59]

Once again, John's narrative turns to romance embellished with legend: the Monophysite movement was transformed, as if at once. Jacob "accomplished his ministry, causing the priesthood to flow like great rivers over the whole world of the Roman dominions."[60] He traveled over distances and at speeds that defied human strength: his disguises were impenetrable, his movements untraceable.

But the practicalities lie close by in John's story. Charged with so awesome a task, Jacob engineered the ordination of two other bishops to travel with him to ensure the canonicity of his ordinations and consecrations.[61] John claims he ordained more than 100,000 clergy, as well as twenty-seven bishops and two patriarchs.[62] Among these was John himself, whom Jacob consecrated to the titular see of Ephesus around the year 559. Before Jacob's efforts, it was possible to claim that the Monophysites did not constitute a separate church in their own right. But despite John's impossibly high numbers, Jacob did turn a de facto situation that had long been hardening, into an institutional one. The Jacobite Syrian Orthodox Church had been founded.

The tracing of Jacob's activities—of exactly what he did and how he did it—is a sensitive operation.[63] As legends grew, his work was entwined with that of Severus of Antioch. Later tradition claimed that Jacob was consecrated to his task by the great patriarch himself.[64] These two have been glorified above all, yet neither would have accomplished their work without substantial efforts by their comrades. Jacob, for his part, ended his career a puppet in the factionalism of his own movement, far from the glory of his ecclesiastical conquests.[65]

In fact, what had happened to the Monophysites in the sixth century, and what is unwittingly chronicled in John of Ephesus' *Lives of the Eastern Saints*, was a transformation of structure, as much in their thought as in the governance of their movement. Once an ecclesiastical hierarchy was in existence, specifically in opposition to another system holding different bonds for communion (loyalty to the Council of Chalcedon), then the subsequent dialogues ceased to offer any real solutions to end the division. Refined theological definitions, even outright concessions, could not measure up to the concrete obstacle of two separate systems.[66]

The pivotal point goes back to John of Tella. For wherever Jacob went, he found ranks of candidates, deacons or priests such as John of Ephesus himself, prepared for the priesthood; they had received their ordination at the hand of a Monophysite and aspired to fulfill their vocation within a Monophysite hierarchy. And he found, too, the receptivity of a laity pastored by such leadership.

But John of Tella had not sought such a consequence to his efforts, and it is here that one must look again to his inclusion, and indeed Jacob's, in the *Lives* of John of Ephesus. John of Ephesus was raised from his childhood within the Amidan ascetic community; he was ordained deacon by John of Tella, blessed by John of Hephaestopolis, and consecrated bishop by Jacob Burd'aya. The degree to which his ascetic views were shaped by the spiritual mentors he encountered, is the degree to which his *Lives* display a vision not his alone but shared by a significant part of the Monophysite body.

For John of Ephesus the particularities of the ascetic's situation are overridden by the ultimate responsibility of the ascetic's vow. Maro the Stylite had climbed his brother's pillar with fear but without hesitation. Z'ura the Stylite had responded to persecution by descending his pillar in order to protest at the imperial court of Constantinople. Susan had forfeited her devotion to solitude to guide an exiled community in Egypt. Simeon the Mountaineer had embraced the lost flocks of the Lord in their unwitting error; John of Tella had taken on the burden of ordaining shepherds for the faithful.

These holy men and women lived out a personal relationship with their God; ultimately, they were bound by neither canon nor ecclesiastical rank. John of Tella badgered his fellow bishops and superiors for official sanction to perform his ordinations; John of Hephaestopolis did not and took his authority and justification from the legacy of his predecessor. The official charge to Jacob Burd'aya was a virtual fait accompli, but he fulfilled it to an extent probably greater than his superiors had intended him to. Like the local ascetics of Amida, these men responded to the crises of their times according to their understanding of their vows.

· VI ·

SOME IMPLICATIONS:
THE CASE OF WOMEN

Thus far our focus has been on John's own understanding of what he was doing in the *Lives*, from inside the ethos pervading the Mesopotamian communities whether in their own country or elsewhere. By the same token, John enables us to assess his own ascetic vision and the conditions contributing to it. The women in the *Lives of the Eastern Saints* provide material by which to look at these points from a different perspective. John's presentation of women raises the issue of how far he is willing to depart from convention when confronting the Monophysite crisis of his day and, further, what the implications of his concern for expediency in such circumstances might be. Because the case of women is specific in its own right, it requires its own treatment.

WOMEN, THE EARLY CHURCH, AND THE SYRIAN ORIENT

It is clear from our sources that earliest Christianity granted women an unusual scope for religious activity. Women were part of the group that traveled with Jesus and provided much of the financial support for his band of followers.[1] They participated in the Jesus movement as disciples rather than as serving women.[2] There is evidence both inside the canonical New Testament and outside of it that women held leadership positions in the earliest Christian communities and were also teaching, prophesying, and sometimes even baptizing converts.[3]

But our sources also indicate a strain imposed by this fact. The Deutero-Pauline writings, for example, with their injunctions that women be silent and submissive,[4] are strident to the point that they can only be reacting to a situation quite different from what they demand. Although the church insisted from the start that women and men stood equal before the Lord—citing Paul's statement that in Christ there is neither male nor female[5]—this view was not used to question the existing social order.[6]

Some of the dilemma was expediency. The early church needed both missionaries and martyrs and was quick to glorify the work of women in these situations. But social tension was apparent. In the "Acts of Thecla," for example, Paul appreciates Thecla's work but attempts time and again to restrict her activity, "fearing lest some greater temptation had come upon her."[7] Precisely because of social dictates, women were often effective missionaries in their roles as wives and mothers, converting their non-Christian husbands or raising their children as Christians whether or not their spouse might approve. Indeed, this kind of behind-the-scenes evangelism helped Christianity to succeed.[8]

The early Christian ideal of celibacy also held important implications for women. In practical terms it physically freed them from the bearing and raising of children and allowed women the possibility of travel for the church, as missionaries or pilgrims, and of work for the church community of their own locale. At the same time, virginity bestowed considerable honor on its adherents; here too women benefited from an increase in status.

The earliest Christian communities developed defined positions for women, first as widows and virgins, and later as canonicae and nuns. These positions granted women a recognized status in the larger church structure but also substantially restricted their range of activity.[9] As the church began to settle into place during the fourth century, women with social power—the wealthy patronesses of Rome, or the empresses—could sometimes follow their own decisions, but most women found themselves in seriously limited circumstances.[10]

The particular experience of women in the Syrian Orient both reflects and illuminates the larger picture. The ancient Near East evidences religious traditions remarkable for their receptivity toward feminine aspects of the divine, thus differing greatly from the classical realm.[11] From its polytheistic past came the heritage of the Syrian Goddess, in the forms of Ishtar, Ashtoreth, Astarte, and the Aramaic Atargatis. The cult of the Syrian Goddess was pervasive across the Mediterranean cities, enduring through Hellenistic and Roman times and into the early Christian Era. In the pagan cosmology of the Syrian Orient, she functioned as part of a triad, a "holy trinity," of Mother, Father, and Son; such a configuration frequently characterized religious beliefs of the ancient Near East. Her worshippers recognized her as a universal divine presence, identifying her with Isis, the Phrygian Cybele, and Greek Hera, as the Great Mother of creation.[12]

On the other hand, the Syrian Orient was primarily Christianized through Judaism.[13] Judaism offered a practical heritage in which women often played an important role in the salvation history of the Israelites, despite the cultic restrictions imposed on them.[14] Here too the aggressively masculine imagery of the God of Israel constituted a consciously contrived imagery, working in reaction against neighboring religious concepts and deities. An undercurrent of female imagery is also found in the Old Testament: God as midwife (Ps. 22:9–10), God as comforting mother (Isa. 49:15, 66:13), and God travailing in the throes of divine labor pains (Isa. 42:14b).[15]

The complementary strains of thought fostered within Jewish monotheism are striking. Most notable is the female personification of Holy Wisdom—Hokhma, "Wisdom," is a feminine noun in Hebrew—as she who sits at the Lord's right hand, the force through whom God creates and acts. When the prevalence of Gnosticism threatened mainstream Wisdom speculation, there followed a rabbinical development of another female image, that of the holy Shekinah—also a feminine noun in Hebrew—the female personification of God's divine presence, she who is His daughter and His bride.[16]

Neither Wisdom nor the Syrian Goddess represented the dominant theological focus of their respective religions. Yet both, and in particular the Goddess, were more powerful than comparable female deities of the Greek or Roman pantheons.[17] It is perhaps not surprising, then, that early Syriac Christianity developed a tradition of feminine symbols for aspects of the divine. Syriac tradition at its earliest, and for centuries thereafter, saw the Holy Spirit as female, following both the instinct of grammar (ruhā is a feminine noun in Syriac) and the inherited pattern of a divine triad.[18] The second-century Odes of Solomon offer profound feminine imagery. Not only is the Holy Spirit portrayed in the feminine, as the Mother Spirit, but so too at times is Christ clothed in feminine images and terms; and the striking Ode 19 hymns God in female form.[19]

Ode 19 points to a further contribution in the Syrian appreciation for the feminine. In this ode, the Virgin Mary is hailed as the "Mother with many Mercies," who "bore . . . without pain"; she who "loved with redemption," "guarded with kindness," and "declared with grandeur."[20] The confidence of this passage exceeds the reserved picture of Marian devotion in the second century that we draw from more Western sources, and it appears somewhat precocious: the themes touched upon prefigure major Marian doctrinal developments, rarely pursued before the fifth century elsewhere, and some not until the tenth century.[21]

There is a spiritual kinship bridging Ode 19 to the highly developed Marian hymns of Ephrem Syrus in the fourth century.[22] Although Ephrem marks the artistic and theological flowering of Syrian veneration for Mary, without this background he could not have introduced Marian devotion in so mature a form to the Syrian Orient. This kindred sense may add weight to the theory that the *Protevangelion of James*, the influential second-century apocryphal account of the Virgin, is of Syrian origin.[23] The Syrian version of the *Protevangelion* is our oldest translation of the work, and its immediate and long-lasting popularity in the Syrian Orient is well attested. An independent but related Syriac *Life of the Virgin* was also in circulation, again probably as early as the mid-second century.[24] Certainly, Mary's place in early Syriac Christianity contrasts with that of the Western church until the rise of mainstream Marian devotion during the fifth century.[25]

Again, not unconnected is the emphasis in early Syriac tradition on birth imagery in relation to baptism.[26] The imagery popular in the Greco-Latin churches was that of resurrection, of baptism as a "dying and rising," and the baptismal water as a "grave," following on the Pauline teachings of Rom. 6:4–6 especially. In early Syriac tradition, baptism was above all a rebirth, following John 3:3–7, and the baptismal water was the womb that bore true sons and daughters for the Heavenly Kingdom. Baptism became the "Mother of Christianity," as Mary had been the Mother of Christ. Womb imagery embellished Syriac theology further: Syriac writers saw the three major events of Christ's life—the Nativity, Baptism in the Jordan, and the Descent to Hell—as three "wombs." And birth imagery revealed the progression of cosmic order: the virgin earth "gave birth" to humanity, Mary to Christ, and Christ to Christians through the womb of the baptismal waters.[27] The image of baptism as a new birth, from the womb of the font, continues to this day in the liturgies of the various Syriac churches.[28]

Religious experience in the Syrian Orient had thus long resonated with an understanding of the divine that deeply embraced feminine aspects, both in its imagery and in its symbols. This experience was not easily shared with Greco-Latin culture, despite its fervent reception in Hellenistic times of the oriental goddess cults. These cults had remained external borrowings even when "Hellenized" or "Romanized" and, as such, were in fundamental tension with the adopting society.[29] They point to what was lacking in classical spirituality, rather than to what was inherent in it. Thus, for example, the Western church banned the *Protevangelion* as a heretical work almost as soon as it was published; again, female imagery on a par with the *Odes of Solomon* would not appear in the West until medieval times. So it was not unexpected that Syriac Christianity should eventually find its "wings clipped," under pressure to conform to the mainstream Greco-Latin churches.

By the year 400, Syriac writers were presenting the concept of the Holy Spirit in closer conformity with that of the "orthodox" church. This involved a dramatic change on their part. When used to signify the third element of the Trinity, *ruhā* ("Spirit") was treated grammatically as a masculine noun, although the word itself remained unaltered. The change governed only that particular usage of the word. After 400, Syriac writers no longer followed the tradition found uniformly in earlier works but referred to the Spirit in masculine terms and imagery (although an occasional hymn writer followed the older practice, apparently for metrical reasons).

In similar manner, the otherwise feminine *melthā*, "Word," became masculine when used to translate the Greek *logos*, as found in the Peshitta. The case of *melthā* is not necessarily as provocative as that of *ruhā*, where a clear theological concern prompted the change: the Holy Spirit was not female and that was that. The transformation of *melthā*, on the other hand, may reflect the translation techniques of the time, whereby such an alteration could happen simply in the attempt to render important terminology from one language to another more faithfully. We do not have cases in the early Syriac Fathers of a female imagery for the Word as we do for the Spirit. But the indisputable motivation with regard to the Spirit would suggest that the parallel experience of the Word is too close for coincidence.[30]

On the other hand, it has been suggested that devotion to the Virgin flowered in concert with the decline of the Spirit as a "motherly" presence.[31] But Syrian veneration for Mary is clearly well established long before the fifth century, and the two feminine objects of reverence coexisted easily, for example, in the hymns of Ephrem.[32]

Spirituality can permeate various aspects of a culture, but the question here is whether or not the feminine symbolism of the Syrian churches brought any practical results for the Christian community.

As was generally the case for the Roman Empire as a whole, Syrian society before its Christianization provided women with a relative degree of freedom and respect, at least for those of the upper class, resulting from the advantages of an affluent society.[33] Again, as was the general experience of the Greco-Roman world, the basic Christian precepts of equal worth and responsibility for the sexes were received by this society with some ambivalence. There was, however, an important difference in nuance: the Syrian Orient received these teachings in a religious context that instinctively comprehended them, harboring an inherent sense of feminine presence in the experience and perception of the divine. That this was indeed a matter of nuance rather than precept must be stressed. Nonetheless, religious and societal concepts gave substance to one another when they coincided; to this extent, the society of the Syrian Orient would have been more vulnerable to the consequences of the Christian injunctions toward equality than the less sensitive societies in which classical presuppositions held sway. A greater strain on familiar Syrian social structures would perhaps have resulted. The changes in the religious culture, from earliest Syriac Christianity in the second century to that established as "orthodox" in the fourth and fifth centuries, charts the development from a Christian society that initially granted women new choices to one that seriously curtailed their place.

Marcionism was probably the most pervasive form of early Christianity in the Syrian Orient.[34] Significantly, it offered an understanding of the Gospel message that was essentially egalitarian. Its practitioners lived and worshiped according to a literal interpretation of the Pauline injunction that in Christ there is neither male nor female. Its women were granted the exceptional rights to teach, exorcise, and baptize. The practical consequences of Marcion's preachings against marriage meant that women were not restricted to producing children and serving a family; they had more freedom of activity.[35] The Marcionites offered women leadership roles important for the social rendering of their religion, as much as for its theology. In the Syrian Orient, these ideas would fall on especially fertile soil, as an extension into the temporal realm of religious concepts already deeply rooted.[36]

Asceticism also flavored the overall development of Christianity in the Syrian Orient, heretical or orthodox, for many centuries. Much as Marcionism had done, the general glorification of celibacy as part of popular Syrian Christianity raised new prospects for women.[37] As widows or virgins, in spiritual marriage or through the office of the Daughters of the Covenant, the *bnath qyāmā*, women held a venerated place within the social community. These practices continued to be popular forms of Christian life even after the rise of the monastic movement offered a further option, separation from the lay society. Nor did the limitations of existing social patterns restrict women's spiritual ambitions: convents became common, but women, too, undertook the rigors of the anchoretic life and even stylitism.[38]

But the overall situation was double-edged, and it was ultimately the negative image of women that prevailed. By the late third century, pressure to conform to the Greco-Latin churches was growing. A major target was the curtailment of ascetic activities in lay society. Spiritual marriage, in particular, was attacked, a battle that proved difficult for the mainstream authorities.

By the fifth century in the Syrian Orient feminine imagery of the divine was eliminated, leaving only the Virgin Mary as an exalted feminine symbol. During the fifth century women's place in Syrian Christian society became rigidly restricted. By that time, even ascetic women were viewed as a source of danger to men. Monks took vows never to speak with a woman or to lay eyes on one; it was canonically forbidden for monks to eat with any woman, including their mothers. Monks without beards were despised for resembling women, yet self-castration maintained its popularity in some circles. Nuns were treated as simply less bothersome and easier to control than ordinary women: a greater stress was laid on cenobitic communities for them, rather than eremitic pursuits, and it was felt that they should have a "master" (rabā) placed over them. Furthermore, it was widely held that nuns should not see the priest during the communion service; thus, abbesses were also deaconesses, able to distribute the Eucharist themselves, a practice that was not shared by their Greek or Latin counterparts and that lasted into the sixth century.[39]

Despite ample testimony in writings from the Syrian Orient that women exercised spiritual leadership, writers rarely acknowledged that women had this capacity. The Syrian church did not encourage autonomy for women. Theodoret's Historia religiosa pays little attention to women, and those few he does see fit to mention are confined to the last two chapters.[40] His women subjects practiced a penitential asceticism: they were veiled from head to toe; their eyes were ever downcast; they never spoke; they were enclosed; they wore iron chains; they wept continually; they were supervised by men. These women fit an acceptable social pattern, despite the physical strength and the very real suffering their practices involved. For their manner, paradoxically, fit mainstream views on the social position of women. Unlike the aggressive and exhibitionist asceticism of their male comrades in the Historia religiosa, Theodoret presents us with women who labor at a passive, inward practice.[41]

Two women saints important to Syriac tradition illustrate where the boundaries lay at the turn of the sixth century, the time when their hagiographies were probably written, and roughly the time that John of Ephesus was born. The first is Saint Febronia, martyred by Roman officials around the year 300.[42] Whether of legendary or historical character (and we can assume a small kernel of truth, around which the *Life* was built), the *Life of Febronia* is an extraordinary text.[43] It tells the story of a woman raised from birth in a convent near Nisibis, especially renowned for her ascetic discipline and her capacity to teach. But the mark of her sanctity lay in the fact that Febronia had never seen a man or been seen by one. The arrival of Roman soldiers, however, led to her imprisonment and death by slow torture, much of it sexual, as a warning to other Christians in the area.

A primary aspect of Febronia's *Life* lies in the tension between Christian purity (symbolized by Febronia's physical and social virginity), and pagan lust (in the form of the Romans' alternative offer that she could live if she would marry one of their officials). The sexual torture displays this symbolism sharply. So great is Febronia's purity that the use of her body as a sexual object does not convey sin, as women's sexuality was commonly seen to do. Rather, in this martyrdom it was specifically her body in its sexual identification that brought her salvation—and the early church always understood a martyr's death to bear upon the salvation of all believers. Thus, in this text, we have a rarely heard sentiment in early Christian writings when Febronia declares that she is not ashamed of her naked body.[44] In fitting homage, this text claims to have been written by a woman—an event remarkable in itself in antiquity—Thomaïs, a nun of Febronia's convent who later became its abbess. Literarily, the female authorship underscores the story's central theme of purity and defilement, but it also results in an unusual characterization of women. In this text, great emphasis is placed on women's friendships with other women. Moreover, the women in the story are depicted as well educated, intellectually sophisticated, and courageous in the largest sense. The common hagiographical practice, Syrian or otherwise, is to present women saints as individuals who are exceptions to the rule of their kind; convents are generally treated as groups of women and thus derided for harboring institutionally the worst traits of their constituents. By contrast, Febronia is presented as a special woman among many fine women.

An altogether different view of women and their sexuality is presented in the story of Pelagia, Antioch's notorious courtesan. Converted suddenly and in spectacular manner, she then disappeared and secretly lived out her life in Jerusalem in the guise of a eunuch hermit. Pelagia thus left behind not only her former life but also her former self: her former gender. Her real identity was discovered at her death.[45] Pelagia's tale was captivating and, unlike Febronia's story, inspired numerous other saints' lives along the same line. The transvestite saint was a hagiographical motif that flourished across the Christian Roman Empire between the fifth and ninth centuries, having started in the Syrian milieu. The transvestite saints were women who chose to pursue their Christian vocations disguised as monks, and whose sanctity hence derived from living literally as men.[46] Their ruse was inevitably discovered, at their death if not before, and always accompanied by exclamations of praise and wonder: here, truly, were women who had risen to glory.

The roots of this theme date back to the apocryphal "Acts of Thecla," in which Thecla had begged Paul's permission to dress as a man for her missionary efforts, much to his distress.[47] But the starting point for popular literature was Pelagia's story. The related variations on the transvestite motif were often blatantly allegorical: these women chose to disguise themselves as men, to "become" men, because they could not serve God adequately as women. Nor was this theme found only in legend; real women followed Pelagia's example.[48] Although the motif was of questionable orthodoxy—Deut. 22:5 expressly forbids either sex to assume the dress of the other, and church fathers debated this matter with reference to Thecla, at least[49]—the extremity of the Syrian method here clearly tapped an incisive and widespread sentiment; the image crystallized the misogynism that had become an integral part of Syrian Christianity, as of the larger church.[50]

The tendencies and concepts underlying the development of Christianity in the Syrian Orient are consonant with those displayed throughout the Greco-Roman world. What marks the Syrian Orient as peculiar in relation to the wider church are the extremes to which it played out ideas common to the whole, whether in religious behavior or in religious literature. Consequently, although the larger Christian body might decry the excesses of Syrian practices, often, as with the popular practice of celibacy, the mainstream church exhibited a similar predilection; or, as with stylitism, it adapted the practice to its own circumstances. So too the literal enactment of images and symbols in the Syrian Orient, as in the case of the transvestite saint, reflected the wider consensus, but with a more specific articulation.

Such, then, was the tradition inherited by the women in John of Ephesus' *Lives of the Eastern Saints*, and it is against this heritage that their cases must be considered. In some instances, John contributes directly to the societal edifice the broader church was then constructing for women.. To that extent, he reveals a Syrian Christian society that has aligned itself, or considers itself aligned, with a wider church body. The various directions that had been fostered by earlier Christianity had settled into the marked confines of an institution imposed over the whole of the Christian community, however diverse its members.

But John shows something akin to a naive innocence in his response to the holy women he meets as individuals. He seems unaware of the conflict between his language and their actions, between what he says about them and what he tells us they actually do. Ever mindful of the afflictions suffered in the Byzantine East, he is keen to offer his female saints as proof of the strength with which the church could handle times of crisis. Hence he delights in presenting these women as empowered by and responsive to the Christian message. But he also preserves a safety valve, by looking at their activities as part of the "emergency" operations of the Monophysites. John's women indeed reveal many of his ideals, but his manner of presentation at times, as we shall see, reflects contrary social values.

JOHN'S *LIVES:* SIXTH-CENTURY PATTERNS

John's treatment of women in the *Lives of the Eastern Saints* was typical of his day. He devotes only a few of his chapters to female rather than male ascetics; and although he mentions numerous cases of deeply religious laywomen, he brushes over these without detailing them. Elsewhere in his *Lives,* womankind appears in her more familiar guise: weak, feeble minded, and sister to Eve.

Women in general fall outside the scope of John's collection. But he does provide us with occasional glimpses of women's experiences, and these are not without insight: the grief of the barren women who seek help from his holy men and the equally desperate joy when a child is born to them.[51] John veers in these instances between the specific and the universal: motherhood in marriage was the only socially acceptable occupation by which a woman could justify her existence, apart from asceticism. But the social stigma of barrenness was a paradoxical one. In the ascetically minded view of John's day, the blessing of children was a dubious gift, if not futile. Celibacy was the higher achievement. Motherhood might be necessary, but it brought women only grudging praise. The connection John misses is that between these childless women with their frightened prayers and the extraordinary number of possessed women who turn to his holy men for exorcism. Instead, he simply takes for granted, without seeking a cause, that women and girls are the ones most susceptible to demonic madness.[52] Childbearing and insanity are the two main reasons John presents for women's recourse to holy intercession; these are the contexts in which they are seen.

John does not portray women as intrinsically evil, corruptive, or destructive. But as if to echo Tertullian's sentiments, John presents women as passive, even unwitting, instruments of Satan's wiles: they are literally the devil's gateway, the path by which evil can most effectively cause the downfall of holy men. The blessed Tribunus was sorely endangered when a landlady attacked him "with all the lasciviousness and violence of impurity and adultery." His victory in the situation gave proof of his spiritual fortitude.[53] Not without reason did the stylite Maro forbid women to enter the enclosure of his column, demanding instead that they shout to him from beyond the enclosure wall if they desired counsel.[54]

John highlights the ambiguity found in the views of the wider church. He is quick to honor women of virtue, but these are presented as particular individuals for him; women in general are ready tools for the Adversary. He sets the two views side by side and yet misses the irony of doing so. Thus he dedicates an entire chapter of his *Lives* to the "believing queen" Theodora.[55] Here and in other chapters, John praises Theodora for her aid to the Constantinopolitan refugees,[56] her perseverance in seeking counsel from holy men, and her piety. Laywoman and empress, with a Chalcedonian husband and the obvious disadvantages of her past, Theodora is yet presented by John as a model Christian. And when later, after her death, the Chalcedonians tried to desecrate her good works, it is no coincidence that they chose to do so by polluting the palace of Hormisdas, sending into it "some women with their husbands, and others who were not chaste, and filled the place where the blessed men lived, where the sacrament and service of God used to be performed."[57] A sudden fire turned the tables, "purifying" the holy place and killing some of the women. John does not hesitate to call this divine justice.

Such incidents in John's *Lives* are relatively few when compared, for example, with John Moschus' *Pratum spirituale*. Nonetheless, in his most bizarre account of temptation by the devil, John plainly states that seeing the image of the Blessed Virgin in any woman is folly. John's story of two monks who encounter Satan in the guise of Mary's image is an unusual one,[58] and not least because he so rarely discusses fallen monks or nuns.

Jacob and his spiritual brother, the same two monks who had been forced to establish a sanctuary for exorcism, roused the jealousy of the Evil One, who then contrived an ingenious downfall for them.[59] One night from among the crowds of possessed persons who slept in the sanctuary awaiting a cure, Satan chose a young woman "of worldly appearance."

> Her accordingly the demons took, and they clothed her in awe-striking forms of phantasmal rays; and they led her up and seated her on the bishops' throne. . . . Then they filled the whole martyr's chapel again with phantasmal forms, as if forsooth they were angels of God.[60]

Meanwhile, some of the demons entered where the holy men were sleeping. "Emitting rays with the appearance of light," they roused the two monks and exhorted them to make haste for the chapel, explaining, "the holy Mary the God-bearer has been sent to you, with a great host of angels." Seizing some incense they flew to the chapel, where they found demons in the likeness of "angels of brilliant light," and the woman en-throned with "a semblance of light flashing from her." Fear and awe stole their wits, and commanded by the demons the monks prostrated themselves in obeisance before the unholy sight. Worse sacrilege, how-ever, was yet to come. The young woman proclaimed her identity as Mary the Mother of God, claiming that Christ had sent her to ordain them presbyters. The two monks thought this vision had come to them as an act of special grace, and they knelt before her as she performed the ordinations.[61]

At once, the demons filled the air with laughter; and the phantasmal vision faded, revealing not the Blessed Virgin but a simple Greek girl seated on the bishops' throne. Jacob and his brother were mortified. They fled to John of Tella, who heard their confession (with suitable as-tonishment) and laid three years penance on them. Thenceforth the two monks "led even more severe lives than before, with sorrow and tears," until at last they were absolved of their guilt in the strange affair.[62]

John has no blame for the woman herself. She is already possessed by demons before the episode takes place; she is "unaware even herself" of what is happening; and she is not responsible for what is said, since "the fiend spoke in her."[63] She is a mute puppet, instrument for but not party to the wiles of Satan. The arresting point, however, is that these monks do not fall into sexual sin, as so often happens in hagiography; they sin theologically, an altogether different theme of women as the source of evil. That the Virgin Mary should command her own worship, as if she were not exalted but divine; that she should further dare to con-secrate men to the priesthood, an authority granted to no woman, not even herself (as Epiphanius of Salamis and others enjoyed recalling): such ideas could only be the work of the devil.

John's account of the feigned image of Mary is his most lurid statement regarding the potential dangers of women. Fittingly, it pinpoints the church's paradoxical attitude towards women. For the guilty woman here is very much a sister to the crowds of women John leaves undifferentiated elsewhere. She is nameless; she comes to the holy men because she is possessed; she is a source of evil to these monks through no fault of her own, no will of her own, and no knowledge of her own.

In his portrayal of women as instruments of Satan, John did occasionally, as in the case of Tribunus' would-be landlady, evoke woman in the image of Eve. Yet, what John tells us of women's actual involvement in the Christian community more often directly contradicts this portrayal. Thus we learn from John's *Lives*, apart from the chapters about holy women, that women in all ranks of society were involved in the religious affairs of the community. In the cases of Peter[64] and the traders Elijah and Theodore,[65] pious sisters living private religious lives brought them to their conversions. From "young girls" to "old women," John's cities and towns did not lack in good works by Christian women. Indeed, as if not seeing his own contradictions, John writes about pious wives who are crucial for the holy work of their husbands. At times, it is women specifically in their roles as wives and mothers who surpass all others in the quality of their religious practices.[66] One such woman was Maria, wife of Thomas the Armenian.[67] John tells us little about her other than to mention her work setting up a convent in tandem with Thomas' monastery, to which she brought her daughter and the other women of the household as companions in the monastic life.

Maria is named by John; otherwise the women in these brief citations are not. He mentions them in passing in the course of his accounts of their brothers or their husbands or their sons. Their individual identities are not important to him, although he clearly affirms their importance to the life of the church community. Further, unlike the few he presents in the image of Eve, John tells us that these devout women act by their own choice. They know their vocations and they carry them out.

John's account, then, of Satan at work through the image of Mary is not so outlandish as it might appear. In a work such as the *Lives of the Eastern Saints*, a work whose basis lies in experience rather than in stereotype or didacticism, the use of Mary's image rather than Eve's for admonitory purposes is surprisingly appropriate. John's encounters would suggest that if women represented a threat to the Christian community of his times, they did so under Mary's aegis, by their capacity for worthiness, and not through the inheritance of Eve. By their competence and fortitude, women themselves belied the church's stance against them.

JOHN'S HOLY WOMEN: WOMEN OF SPIRIT

John feels compelled to justify his inclusion of holy women[68] by citing the apostolic injunction that in Christ there is neither male nor female (Gal. 3:28). He further insisted that the lives of these women in no way detracted from, or fell short of, the standard set by his other subjects.[69] Of the holy woman Susan he says, "Not only is the mighty strength of Christ God apt to show its activity in men who are powerful in appearance and mighty and forceful, but also in weak, feeble, frail women."[70] The highest praise he could offer the anchorite Mary was to honor her as "a woman who by nature only bore the form of females but in herself also bore the character and soul and will not only of ordinary men, but of mighty and valiant men."[71] The frequency of such statements in hagiography pertaining to women indicates that John writes formulaically in this respect.[72] But the significance was not lost in the formula; for where John expresses the common sentiments of his church and society, he tells us, too, something of the actual conditions of women's lives.

Yet despite this, John's holy women emerge from his text in their own right. Their decisions and courses of action suggest a sense of self-determination not generally found in ascetic women as it was in men— such autonomy being even rarer for laywomen—but to some extent made possible through the fluid and often chaotic sixth-century Monophysite struggle. These are women who chose to define themselves not in relation to father, husband, or child but only in relation to God; sometimes they acted autonomously rather than through a convent. But it is important to remember their cultural context: these women were not acting out of a sense of self (as we might see it). They acted because they believed God had called them to this action. Their sense of self was altogether absent; indeed, in their minds, irrelevant. In each case, public reaction to them was the standard applied to any holy man. Whatever inhibitions the church may have had, ordinary people seem to have measured sanctity by effective action rather than by gender.

John selects only a handful of women for special attention. Culturally, they cross the spectrum of social strata that characterizes the sixth-century Byzantine Empire; ascetically, they represent a diversity of experience. Taken as individuals, these women fit well into John of Ephesus' overall schema: his vision of the Monophysite cause as lived out through an interlocking relationship of asceticism and society. But seen as a group—and, as we may gather from the references treated above, as part of a much larger community of women within the Monophysite body—they provide us with significant insight, both toward John himself (and thus the leadership he offered the Monophysite movement) and toward the ideals he sought to nurture.

These women are seen in the *Lives* as playing roles critical to the needs of the stricken Monophysite cause; further, they are seen to provide encouraging and inspiring leadership to the Monophysite community. Although none of them sought this status, it emerged as a consequence of their own religious commitment.

John begins with Mary the Pilgrim, who, like her namesake, chose the "better way" of life devoted to faith rather than to works in the world.[73] An ascetic from childhood, Mary eventually decided to go on a pilgrimage to Jerusalem. There she spent three years on Golgotha, practicing a severe asceticism and passing much time in ecstatic trances. Those who saw her reckoned her a feeble-minded beggar, mad or senile. Mary herself cherished her anonymity: nothing and no one distracted her from her chosen course.

But it happened that some men came who knew her, and seeing her in prayer they made obeisance to her. Mary was "greatly upset" because she did not want people to know about her labor, but the men had soon told her story throughout the community.

> Then those in whose eyes she had been reckoned a foolish old woman— one who sat there because of charity, so that she might sustain her body's needs—now began to honour her as a great and holy woman, begging her to pray for them.[74]

But Mary did not want to be a holy woman, "lest she lose the fruits of her ascetic labour." She fled, "deeply saddened."[75] Making her abode in Tella, Mary made a vow to return to Jerusalem each year to pray in the sacred places. This she fulfilled, traveling always in the hottest season; at the same time, she continued to shun worldly affairs while making her annual pilgrimages. Yet, John tells us, so holy was this woman that "many powerful miracles were worked by her presence, and not by her will or her word."[76]

In some respects, Mary, having chosen a form of asceticism taken up most often by men and only rarely by women (at least as far as we know), reminds us of the early Syrian anchorites. Moreover, not only did she choose to reject the standard course taken by women who desired the religious life—the convent community—but she further refused to be bound by the institutionalized aspects that overtook so many male ascetics over time. Her strength of character in this regard contrasts with the timidity of Maro the Stylite, unhappily and unwillingly drawn into the worldly responsibilities attending his profession.[77] The occurrence of miracles wrought simply by Mary's presence was but an affirmation of the authority gained by such a life-style, and, in John's view, ultimately its validation. Mary may have separated herself from the world, but the power of her sanctity remained at work within it.

John's enthusiasm, however, is even greater for Mary's younger sister Euphemia, although Euphemia was, in worldly terms, a more obvious threat to the existing social and religious order.[78] Euphemia's remarkable career and the leadership and service she gave to the city of Amida in its time of need have already been discussed in chapter 3. What concerns us here are the particular traits that characterized Euphemia's asceticism and ministry.

Unlike her pilgrim sister, Euphemia had married but was widowed shortly thereafter and left with one child, a daughter Maria. Watching the work of her sister, Euphemia turned to the religious life with Maria, regulating their life together according to a rigid devotional plan. Euphemia also educated her daughter in psalmody, Scripture, and writing. "But while observing her sister Mary's abstinence and other practices, at the same time Euphemia was fulfilling another sublime and exalted role, since she served two orders together—asceticism and relief for the afflicted."[79]

Euphemia's distinct way of life was soon known throughout the city of Amida. Rejecting even her role as mother, she drew her daughter into the same service as sister rather than child, and Maria wove yarn that Euphemia sold in order to supply a meager fare for themselves, as well as to purchase the necessities to care for the sick and destitute. Such disregard for social convention unsettled Amida's more conservative inhabitants, who admonished Maria about her "working mother."[80] Others sought to support these activities with donations and urged Euphemia to accept food for herself and Maria. The holy woman, however, would not have it.

> God forbid that I should . . . satisfy my body from the toils of others while it has strength to work, or receive the stains of their sins upon my soul! . . . Do you want to soil me with the mud of your sins? I am blemished enough as I am.[81]

But with the onslaught of the Monophysite persecutions, and the exile of the Amidan monasteries, Euphemia found herself laboring further to care for refugees and other victims. Unable to support such ministry by the earnings of her own and her daughter's handiwork, she was forced to take greater contributions from others. Nonetheless, she would not allow those of the city who were well off, and thus able to give her aid, to feel that they were benefiting their own souls through her charity.

For as it is written that the righteous shall be as confident as a lion, so this woman confidently upbraided everyone regardless of their rank until the noblemen and women of the city were full of trepidation because of her. When she entered their thresholds and they heard that Euphemia was coming, they would say, "Alas for us, [Euphemia] has come to give us a good thrashing!" Then she would boldly take whatever she wanted to give to whoever was in need. . . . And so she passed judgment on them until those of the secular life were somewhat peeved with her.[82]

Many urged a less strenuous life upon Euphemia, to her consternation: John himself would jokingly plead with her, "Don't kill yourself so violently!"[83] But Euphemia's life fulfilled John's own ascetic ideals, especially her pragmatic change in ministry once the persecutions began. While acclaiming the contemplative life practiced by those such as her sister Mary, he clearly empathized with those who, akin to Euphemia, sought God amidst suffering. John juxtaposed the two ways of perfection as complementary to one another and so suggested that together these women rendered perfect worship to the divine. "So the report of these two sisters was told throughout the east, and wonder seized everyone that each of them in a way of life without equal bravely exerted herself, acquiring righteousness."[84]

Euphemia's activities were more gregarious than those of her sister, but her determination to define her life through her relationship with God was similar in impact. In refusing to allow others to control or even influence her ministry, even when they contributed goods to it—refusing, as she said, to take their sins upon herself—Euphemia like her sister appeared indifferent to social mores, not simply in terms of what was acceptable for women but also in terms of what were the established patterns for asceticism. Theirs was an activity perhaps more possible under conditions of cultural instability and religious anxiety, the confines of sixth-century society in the Byzantine East.

John's account of the holy woman Susan has also been treated elsewhere in the present work.[85] As he portrays her, she seems a less abrasive figure than Mary or Euphemia. Also an ascetic since childhood, Susan chose exile in Egypt with a handful of her sisters rather than oppression at the hands of Chalcedonian authorities; further, although she desired the solitary life and accordingly labored as a hermit in the inner desert of Mendis, she was persuaded to remain with the "establishment," by the pleas of an uprooted community, and to take on the supervision of an ascetic institution of both women and men. For the Monophysite refugees, Susan was a holy woman adept at healing, exorcism, and instruction. Her leadership calmed a distressed people. The conditions of persecution thus demanded from her a role otherwise unthinkable for her.

But there were more factors at work. Susan's life as a holy woman arose out of the course of her ascetic career: her authority was the result of its excellence and single-mindedness. Her inheritance of secular wealth was renounced before she entered her first convent; she did not translate a secular title or a position of influence into the ascetic community.[86] Although she ultimately agreed to follow an institutional role, she did so in an effort to stabilize in some way a community fraught with trauma.

Unlike Mary or Euphemia, Susan expressed a self-consciousness of her limitations as a woman. Although at no point did she allow such thoughts to hinder her actions, she was continually concerned about relations between the monks and the nuns.[87] She impressed John because she kept her head veiled and her glance cast downwards so that no man ever saw her face. He learned that she had taken this vow upon entering the ascetic life, and that through her many years as a nun had not looked upon a man's face, fearing, she said, both the harm her sight could cause men and the harm their sight could cause her.

The men under Susan's guidance supported her leadership. John, too, when he visited her community, came away "in great wonder at her words"; it had, indeed, been her reputation that originally led him to visit the community. But despite his praise for her, John found her position as leader for both the male and the female communities uncomfortable and was himself taken aback when he witnessed her authoritative response to a monk suffering temptation.[88]

But the importance of Susan was that she and her kind were precisely what was needed by the Monophysite body in exile. Like Mary the Pilgrim, she ensured spiritual quality; like Euphemia, she led valiantly. Not surprisingly, John left her community, "praising God" as he went.

Mary the Anchorite represented another example for John.[89] Daughter of a noble family, Mary was brought as a child into contact with a holy man in a neighboring district. The meeting transfixed her. Pondering what she had seen, and also the luxurious life that lay ahead of her, she made a categorical decision: "For what reason do we not become as this holy man? Is not this a human being?"[90] and she turned to the ascetic life at once.

Mary's family sought to stop her. With haste, they began wedding preparations, fearing "lest she run away and go to a monastery, and

[they] lose the [rich] man who was to take her to wife." But Mary left and, entering a convent, took the tonsure and the habit. In John's eyes, the course she then followed was the fulfillment of her calling.

> And from that time she took that holy old man as her model in all things. . . . And she also distinguished herself in the conflict of persecution for fifteen years, no longer passing night vigils but vigils lasting even a week, and then days, and then she would taste something. And, when she had walked strongly and heroically in the road of righteousness for thirty years, she finished her course and received the crown earned by her life, and fell asleep in peace.[91]

Mary the Anchorite chose for herself a male model. But having taken it, she made it her own and it gave her the means for freedom. When the persecutions struck, Mary turned upon them the power of her prayer. Like the solitaries John describes in relation to the Amidan ascetic community, particularly during its time of exile,[92] Mary's withdrawal from the temporal world is neither an abandonment of it nor a denial of its needs in the crisis at hand. Rather, her spiritual battle serves to anchor the Monophysite cause in its true context: a holy war.

Mary's initial use of a male model does not involve the negation of herself, or of her being, as it does for those women of the "transvestite saint" motif. The model is a means to an end. John praises Mary, in accordance with the theme of her adopted model, in terms that measure sanctity by degrees of maleness: "she only bore the form of females," she was not simply equal in strength and will to "ordinary men" but to "mighty and valiant men."[93] But John's *Life* makes it clear that Mary does not "become male," as Pelagia's successors did; she is glorified for what she does.

Mary's aversion to marriage was, of course, a common feature in the popular religion of the day.[94] Nor was it women alone who sought freedom from what was often a social straitjacket. John tells us, for example, that the holy man Tribunus, too, had fought off the plans and hopes his wealthy family had held for the marriage he could make.[95] But for the women John portrays, there is more at stake than a cultural embrace of the celibate ideal. The ascetic life offered a real alternative to society's structure. John's holy women proved how independent a woman's life could be despite social constraints. The two Marys, Euphemia, and Susan exercised an enviable degree of choice. The contrast of their lives to those of married women—even when a husband shares his wife's religious orientation—is enhanced by John's final two accounts of women of God.

In choosing to write about Caesaria the Patrician, John took on a daunting task.[96] Famous, influential, and wealthy, Caesaria was a holy woman more effective in some respects than an unmarried woman could have been.[97] In the secular society, she had been recognized, as the Roman matron of earlier times, in the role of wealthy patroness; and in that role, had she remained in it, she would have stood in its distinguished Christian ranks, with the likes of Melania the Elder, her granddaughter Melania the Younger, Paula, Olympias, and others.[98] But Caesaria did not, as these women had, translate a role born from the social-class structure into a "Christianized" society of the same nature. Her encounter with the divine called for a different response.

Caesaria had long wished to leave her husband and devote her life to God, but Severus of Antioch had forbidden her, reminding her that a woman's body was not her own.[99] By the time John of Ephesus met her in Alexandria (previously she had lived in Constantinople), however, she had succeeded in gaining control of her life, whether by her own decision, mutual consent with her husband, or widowhood (as seems most likely) we do not know.[100] In any event, here was a woman "who had been reared in endless luxuries, and had grown accustomed to royal habits, who suddenly came to be cut off from all these things, and subjected herself to asceticism beyond measure."[101] So formidable was the ascetic regime Caesaria had undertaken that John was at once beside himself:

> So that having found her living in all this asceticism and hardship, we continued blaming her and advising her to give up high things and embrace moderate things, lest being unable to endure she might either lose her strength or fall into severe illness and be forced from necessity to give it all up.[102]

It was characteristic of John's own inclination to advise a softening of ascetic extremes for the sake of channeling such zeal into the needs of the church community as a whole. In Caesaria's case, however, his motives may not have been so altruistic. He appears to have been uncomfortable with her capacity for rigorous practice. Again, although she begged his instruction in spiritual matters, John found she conversed with him as comrade rather than as pupil: "The blessed woman condescended to make confession and say, 'I have here more than seven hundred volumes in number of all the Fathers, to which my intellect and my attention have been devoted for many years.'"[103]

Caesaria's own commitment had inspired many of those who were part of her "secular" household; and like herself, many of them turned to a life of religious devotion, for the most part accompanying her as their mistress in faith as well as in society, and practicing asceticism with her in her changing places of residence.[104] But to this woman, such continuation of her worldly role was intolerable; she pleaded with John to assist her in severing herself from this vestige of her former existence, so that she might go in the company of two others alone and live as an anchorite in the desert. John would not agree,

> because we saw that these plans were unnecessary, and they were beyond her capacity and strength and condition; and besides many [other] arguments . . . we were afraid lest this ardour and the plans came from the evil one.[105]

John's protest, curiously distrustful of Caesaria's vocation, then brought in another point: his fear that if she were to go off to the desert, the members of her household who had followed her to Egypt would be in "danger of destruction." When Caesaria pointed out that it was exactly this worldly responsibility she longed to leave, John was scandalized. "Know that you are an old and feeble woman, and your nature is not strong enough to hold out against these thoughts of yours and endure and struggle.'"[106]

Caesaria was "vexed and annoyed" at John's overruling of her decision. But her determination did not wane. Founding a monastery for men and a convent for women, "in grand and admirable style," and having endowed them both generously, she herself withdrew into the convent as a recluse, "performing severe and sublime labours." Further,

> she declined the headship of the same monastery, but sent to another monastery, and took thence a certain blessed woman great in her modes of life whose name was Cosmiana, and her she appointed archimandritess, she herself submitting to her like an insignificant and poor sister. And so she continued to labour till the end of her life, which happened after fifteen years.[107]

Far, then, from being a feeble woman of frail nature as John had called her, Caesaria surmounted her obstacles without abandoning her obligations and without compromising her spiritual integrity. John could allow for this kind of decision by an ascetic such as Susan or Mary the Anchorite, who had renounced wealth and influence before inheriting them; or, for example, by a figure such as Thomas the Armenian, who had translated his worldly position and means into the monastic setup he established. Furthermore, John vehemently opposed Caesaria taking on the spiritual battle for the cause that he praised so highly in recluses such as Mary the Pilgrim or Mary the Anchorite. Caesaria's founding of the monastic communities assisted the cause and probably, like Susan's community, helped to absorb some of the refugee problems. But she refused to use her religious vocation as a springboard for activities of patronage or political influence, as John seems to have wanted. The Monophysite cause may have needed her for work in the temporal world, but Caesaria would not carry her worldly position into her ascetic life.[108]

Marriage for Caesaria had proved to be her cross to bear. While her husband had been with her, marriage encumbered her spiritual aspirations; afterward, its residue, the people dependent upon her and the demands placed on her as one high in the social structure, inhibited her activities. In similar manner, Caesaria's chamberwoman Sosiana endured restrictions on her religious hopes because of the confinement in marriage. Although her husband, Caesaria's chamberlain, shared her high-minded faith and practice, it was not until his death that Sosiana had the liberty to pursue her vocation as she truly desired.

Sosiana and her husband John had been married by law for thirty years; but theirs was a spiritual marriage in the fullest sense:[109]

> Never holding carnal intercourse with one another, but living in devoutness and honour and holiness, occupying themselves in fasting and prayer, and genuflexion and recitation of service and watching by night, while hairmats were laid down for them each apart, and in this way they passed the whole length of the night hours, kneeling and lying on their faces, and weeping in prayer and mighty crying to God, without this becoming known to many.[110]

Her husband's death and Caesaria's withdrawal into the convent freed Sosiana at last to fulfill "the vow she had made to God." Delivering to John of Ephesus the accumulated riches from her household— embroidered silk clothes, tapestried linens, garments encrusted with woven gold thread, precious articles of silver—she ordered that the clothes and linens be cut and sewn into altar cloths and veils, and the goods melted to mold chalices and crosses. These she then gave John for the adornment of the churches he founded in the course of his missionary work in Asia Minor. For herself she kept only a few "cheap, ordinary clothes." John was alarmed by Sosiana's sudden self-imposed poverty, and also by the nagging concern that these goods might better be sold for the poor. But the blessed woman insisted on the importance of her vow "made before God"; and John himself was "frightened by our Lord's expression in the gospel about the fine ointment of great price which the woman poured on his head" (John 12:7–8).[111]

Sosiana, then, enclosed in the confines of marriage and secular occupation, achieved a pure religious life. Nor was her vow an irresponsible one. Just as her ascetic devotion served to adorn the Monophysite body, her material gifts were to adorn the churches.

Mary, Euphemia, Susan, Mary the Anchorite, Caesaria, and Sosiana, these are the women John singles out for honor. They serve his cause well, and they do it by a variety of vocations and paths. Even among John's select gathering of Eastern saints, they are an arresting group. John tells us about them; what, in turn, do they tell us about John?

JOHN AND WOMEN: IMPLICATIONS OF A VISION

In John's stories of these women, we can see not only the perspective of his presentation and its circumstances, but also its consequent meanings. The contrasts between his treatment of women and those in other works of this same genre of hagiographical collections are marked.[112]

Palladius would apparently urge women to lead separate lives for the good of all rather than by reason of devotion to God. Separated into groups, as convent communities, his female ascetics quarrel constantly and require male supervision; but they are prone to vainglory whether alone or in a cenobitic practice.[113] Those women in Palladius who seem most successful in their ascetic pursuits lived anchoretic, enclosed lives.[114] Palladius is willing to praise an active role only among women of high social standing and wealth, advantages of serious import at a time when asceticism was just becoming established within the sociopolitical structure of the empire.[115] His praise for the dignity of Amma Talis and for the convent she governed appears in his collection as if it were a concession to an unstereotyped reality. It is the exception to his rule.[116] Palladius keeps his readers ever-mindful that women, ascetic or otherwise, are a continuous source of sin.[117]

Theodoret's women ascetics are unobtrusive to the degree that they barely figure in his work, except in affirmation of a passive presence.[118] Enclosed, they intrude neither into the temporal world nor into the workings of the church within the world. Their devotional presence is their only acknowledged role. Theodoret does tell us that holy women deserve higher praise than holy men, since theirs is the feebler gender;[119] yet the brief glimpses he provides reveal that in fact these women underwent grave feats of endurance, both physical and spiritual. One finds here a "chosen type" of holy woman, well tailored to suit the interests of an authoritarian ecclesiastical structure.

The treatment by John Moschus is the most stereotyped of these authors. His women characters, whether ascetics or not, are presented almost invariably in relation to the sin of fornication. Sometimes they bring it about through their own intrigues;[120] most of the time, however, they are inadvertent, unwilling objects of lust, who seek to prevent or escape the foul crime.[121] Although Moschus plants the guilt firmly on womankind, it is in fact his male characters who weaken in the face of temptation, or who find themselves tormented beyond endurance by their sinful thoughts. Female victims frequently labor to save the souls of their would-be rapists. At the same time, Moschus laces his tales with adoration for the Virgin Mary, whose place in popular religion is presented as both crucial and mandatory.[122] But this is Mary as champion of orthodoxy and champion of chastity; her ascendency is violently belligerent. As such, she bears little if any resemblance to her female devotees. This powerful image of Mary is portrayed apparently at the cost of possibilities for ordinary women. These Moschus has reduced to a one-dimensional existence.

The contrasts of these cases to those of John of Ephesus are at once apparent. Even while following established ascetic patterns—as pilgrim, charity worker, recluse, or nun—his women are not stereotypes. Their ascetic modes encapsulate the variety of practices he surveys in his more detailed and numerous reports of holy men.

The dependence of John's pragmatism on the needs created by crisis is at its most obvious in these accounts. The irony in his traditional use of language about women, so contrary to what he tells us his holy women do, serves to highlight the opposition between society's values and institutions, on the one hand, and human capacity, on the other. In accord with the earliest churches, grateful for the witness women offered as missionaries and martyrs, the Monophysites in the sixth century needed women's contributions more than they needed the institutional advantages of excluding women from their structural ranks and of restricting them to a passive presence such as that which Theodoret glorifies. John's treatment of his female subjects clarifies his views on the Monophysite situation more sharply than his treatment of men, if only because the roles and activities of his male subjects are not extraordinary to their place in society or in the church.

Far from writing a simple devotional collection, John presents the ambiguous impact of people during a pivotal era. His own missionary works in Asia Minor (with compromisingly Chalcedonian sponsorship); the ex officio ordinations performed by the "Fathers" of the Jacobite church, John of Tella, John of Hephaestopolis, and Jacob Burdʿaya; the authoritative activities of his women; all of these had an impact of a kind. Motivated by faith, performed for the sake of the Christian body, their actions were all subversive to the institutions of the state church as it existed, despite being dedicated to it. In the case of the ordinations, the results were as drastic as the step itself: a "new" church was born. The case of the Monophysite missions in Asia Minor proved ultimately ambivalent, since it was a politically successful endeavor for both sides: for the Monophysites, because of the glory and renown it cast on their leaders and traditions, as shown especially in the accounts of these missions in the later chronicles; and for the Chalcedonians, since the converted areas of Asia Minor apparently functioned as Chalcedonian. The case of women, however, laid bare the contradictions of the Monophysite cause. For, just as the early church had done in its time, the Monophysites drew profitably on the strengths of those such as Euphemia or Susan but did not finally incorporate such strengths into the structural format of their own church. Although John called for extreme steps in response to the events of his time, no call is made to give women major institutionalized positions in the church.

Like John himself, the women he writes about are empowered by their personal inspiration, but they are propelled by their times into an arena greater than they had foreseen or chosen. They fit into John's scheme because they respond to the situations at hand through their relation to God and not from their relation to the ascetic "institution" or church structure. They take the crisis upon themselves as their own. John does not change the values he is advancing for these women; rather, they bring his message to fullness. It is both practical and propagandistic for John to celebrate women for deeds such as those in the *Lives*. However, John's own prejudices—evident in his use of language, and in the vivid manipulation of Satan appearing in the Virgin Mary's image—set limits on his zeal and foreshadow the results. Rules change; but the immediacy of crisis does not necessarily call for change in existing structures.

The *Lives of the Eastern Saints* are the product of John of Ephesus' admiration for his comrades. In them, he reasserts the unique potency of asceticism as a power to be channeled into the world, and thus he affirms the ascetics' place as participants in society. At the same time, sixth-century asceticism existed in relation to a society born of specific factors: the mature self-confidence of the ascetic movement and a consequent responsive fluidity of structure. John's treatment of women ascetics points to just how flexible institutions could be. The institutional partnership of asceticism and ecclesiastical organization was strong enough and stable enough to absorb even such threatening flexibility as the sanctioning of authoritative leadership for women. The sanctioning was itself a response to crisis. But the situation allowing women certain roles of impact was possible only in a period of grave unrest. It was not to become a permanent pattern. Even during the period of crisis, women's roles, although expanded, were still at the periphery of church activities. They might head communities or dispense charity, but they did not become institutionalized leaders or gain any positions in the church hierarchy.

· VII ·

JOHN OF EPHESUS:
ASCETICISM AND SOCIETY

The playing out of the ascetic's role in which John and his subjects participated was not an innovative process. They bore witness to the authority of tradition; at the same time, they molded their inheritance to fit the immediacy of their own day. But, as in the case of women, the reaction was a pragmatic one. Flexibility and responsiveness were clearly at hand, but no evidence of deeper changes in the socioreligious structures can be found in John of Ephesus' *Lives*.

John writes hagiography as if writing a commentary on his times. But the *Lives* are very much a personal product, and we cannot generalize from John's perspective. Other hagiography of the same basic format, and overlapping chronologically with John's collection, presents a different story. Cyril of Scythopolis wrote his *Lives of Palestinian Saints* contemporaneously with John of Ephesus' work.[1] More formally biographical in style, Cyril's accounts are nonetheless written with straightforward simplicity and with methodical concern for historical detail. Almost two generations later, John Moschus wrote his *Pratum spirituale*, an informal collection of Eastern ascetic vignettes primarily set in Palestine.[2] These are told in a manner more anecdotal than that which John of Ephesus employs, but Moschus shares his eye for episodic portraiture. Though Moschus wrote later, many of his stories date back to the period covered by John of Ephesus and convey a coherent sense of the sixth century.

A comparison among these works at once evokes significant differences. The vitality in John of Ephesus' urban asceticism, the distant clarity of Cyril's monasteries, and the stillness of John Moschus' desert, seem to speak of altogether different worlds. But the eastern provinces of the empire faced a religious crisis in the midst of their worldly difficulties. These three collections each present a different view of the relationship between asceticism and society and between the temporal and spiritual worlds in this same situation. Some of their differences can be attributed to their provenance and religious standings: Cyril and John Moschus represented the Palestinian monastic tradition and had the political advantage of being of the Chalcedonian confession. But the differences between these texts do raise important issues, and in doing so they offer valuable insight as to what options were available to hagiographers in the face of such upheaval. Their differences represent not so much various ascetic responses but various interpretations of what asceticism meant for the respective authors.

CONTRASTS IN HAGIOGRAPHY

Cyril of Scythopolis, like John of Ephesus, wrote with a self-conscious sense of purpose. The times in which he lived marked him too, and the task he set himself—to honor the founders of Palestinian monasticism—was not easy. Cyril saw the events of the fifth and sixth centuries as religiously dangerous. But where John saw an essential unity in time and space between the physical and divine realms, Cyril saw a gap, bridged only by contact of a limited kind.

Cyril's *Lives* are well-crafted biographies, though he includes the standard apologia that his own skills are inadequate for the task.[3] Yet despite his formality, he does not write heavily stylized hagiography. His language is clean and unadorned, carefully worked (unlike John Moschus') but unaffected.[4] He follows his subjects from birth to death, and sometimes posthumously.[5]

Cyril writes with a fastidious attention to detail. He marks and countermarks every verifiable point: where his information came from and how he got it, locations, relationships, and, above all, dates. In fact, Cyril's preoccupation with dates is startling in literature of this kind. At frequent intervals he notes the date in various combinations from the year in secular reckoning, the age of his subject at the time, which year of which emperor's reign, and the major landmark events:[6] imperial and patriarchate dealings and successions; occurrences of plague, famine, drought, invasion; rebellion politically motivated (by the Samaritans) or religiously (by the Palestinian Origenists); and foundations and dedications of monasteries. He seems to offer us exactly what John of Ephesus does not provide, a welcome sense of order. But the contrast is deceptive and may in fact work the other way. John's carelessness is belied by the coherent discipline his subjects display. Cyril's narrative efforts, too, are belied by the content: the emphasis on historical setting appears an artificial imposition by the author and not a reflection of what these saints' lives intend.

Cyril limits himself to stories of leaders. It is here that we see his audience most clearly. He cuts himself off from the less glamorous activity John of Ephesus records. Cyril's saints are removed from the experiences of ordinary people, not only by their social class at birth but also and often by blood relations or high connections with the ecclesiastical and imperial hierarchies.[7] The disciples who follow their examples and join their monasteries are also of similar background. As a whole, theirs is a superiority of place as well as of class: none are native to Palestine. As Cyril recounts events, the work of these men effectively raises Palestine to a stature befitting its identity as the Holy Land and its authority through Jerusalem's position as patriarchal seat, sufficient stature to match the monastic and ecclesiastical authority of Egypt and Alexandria, and of Syria and Antioch. Indeed, Cyril presents Jerusalem as the patriarchate most loyal to the imperial throne. Cyril is aiming for a high audience, seeking it as far away as Constantinople; he addresses a cosmopolitan and powerful elite, centered in the great cities and their networks of great families.[8] John of Ephesus seeks only the audience of the East, a poorer and provincial lot.

The social advantages of Cyril's subjects find a spiritual correspondence in their elite place as holy men. Their ascetic practices and monastic work create a holy space that mirrors Paradise. Cyril's holy men are never wanting for food or water, whether lost in the desert or enduring widespread droughts or famine.[9] They are divinely protected from every facet of sixth-century calamity, calamities threatening the holy no less than the ordinary in John of Ephesus' *Lives*. These saints need not fear danger from fire, wild beasts, robbers, pillaging troops, or plague.[10] Indeed, their anchoretic solitude can last unbroken by any temporal care or contact for many, many years.[11]

Removed by grace from the normal hardships of the world, Cyril's saints keep themselves apart from such experiences. In no case do they minister or serve unless forcefully beseeched.[12] Claiming their own sinfulness precludes them from the position of mediator, they provide intercession only with reluctance whether to emperor or to God.[13] For these holy ones, care for the needy is the business of the church in the world: institutions founded by wealthy patrons and run by the ecclesiastical hierarchy are of little concern to those of the desert.[14] Not surprisingly, Cyril emphasizes the posthumous miracles of Saints Euthymius and Sabas, miracles entailing cures, exorcisms, rescues of various sorts, and interventions where heretical doings threaten[15]—the very kinds of activity that the world sought from the holy men while alive but that they evaded by their retreat to the desert.

The good works performed by these ascetics are hence shown to be of total disinterest to them. The world of the desert and the world of the city do not meet.[16] For Cyril, the divine protection these men receive is the mark of their sanctity—Paradise regained—and their apparent lack of concern for the society beyond their monastic communities portrays their absolute devotion to God. In their sacred abode, they feel compunction if they unwittingly harm a mule,[17] but their compassion for the larger world is not in evidence. Yet Cyril does highlight just how powerful these holy men are when they do turn to the affairs of the Christian society beyond their walls.

Thus the emphasis many scholars have placed on the imperial interventions of Saints Euthymius and Sabas must be seen in the hagiographical context that Cyril establishes for us.[18] Euthymius was only persuaded with great difficulty to meet the empress Eudocia, although Simeon the Stylite himself had sent her; and he spurned her pleas for advice more than once despite her devoted efforts and building campaigns on behalf of the church.[19] Again, one of Euthymius' posthumous miracles is instructive: during the reign of Zeno, the patriarch Martyrius of Jerusalem sent an envoy to Constantinople to plead for help in the religious turbulence rife in Palestine; but the saint appeared in a vision and forbade the journey altogether.[20]

The work of Sabas was, however, of a different kind; and it is here that Cyril writes from within a set of calamitous circumstances that match the backdrop of John of Ephesus' *Lives.* In 511, Sabas was persuaded by Elias, then patriarch of Jerusalem, to meet with the emperor Anastasius regarding the severe disturbances within the church: the Acacian schism with Rome and the Monophysite struggles of the eastern patriarchates.[21] The holy man was persuaded to make this journey because Elias pressed him hard about the perils to orthodoxy. While in Constantinople, Sabas admonished Anastasius about his Monophysite leanings and also requested fiscal reforms for Palestine, again at the patriarch's behest. Although he campaigned vigorously against Severus,

who was in Constantinople at the time, and thus incurred Anastasius'
disfavor, his presence was sufficiently impressive for him to return
to Palestine with imperial largesse for distribution among the monasteries.[22] Later, Sabas himself took the initiative to approach Anastasius,
this time by organizing and sending a petition of protest, signed by the
bulk of the Palestinian ascetic community, against Severus' activities as
patriarch of Antioch and the imperial support Severus enjoyed in these
endeavors.[23]

Some years later, Sabas was again besought to play envoy for Palestine. The province had suffered severe famine and drought for several
years, narrowly avoiding a popular rebellion; shortly thereafter, the Samaritan revolt left the cities and countryside of Palestine in ruins. Sabas
was approached by Peter, now patriarch of Jerusalem, and by the other
leading Palestinian bishops and begged to go once more to Constantinople, this time to plead for leniency and tax remission on behalf of the
battered province. In 531, the saint set off for Justinian's court.[24]

Sabas' time in Justinian's care is described by Cyril as spectacular,
and indeed it would seem to have accomplished spectacular results,
both for Palestine and for the Chalcedonian church.[25] But Sabas had
shown no more interest in or inclination for alleviating Palestine's suffering before this excursion than he had before his voyage to Anastasius'
court. On both of these occasions, he acted because he was summoned
to do so. The outrage that spurred Z'ura the Stylite and Mare the Solitary to march to the imperial presence and protest against imperial policies and the compassion that found the Amidan ascetics feeding and
clothing the stricken populace of the east, although themselves in exile
under hazardous conditions, are absent in Sabas' work and in the less
histrionic actions of Euthymius. Cyril's concern to place his holy men
firmly and accurately in their historical setting shows their disassocia-
tion from it.

However, Sabas did act on his own initiative on one occasion: the
letter of protest to Anastasius about Severus of Antioch. The major issue
for Cyril's saints is heresy, and their fear about it laces all of Cyril's accounts. The *Life of Euthymius* treats us to lengthy declarations of faith
and angry responses to the charge that the Council of Chalcedon (which
took place during the height of Euthymius' monastic reign) had blessed
Nestorianism by a different name.[26]

Indeed, Cyril's writings show that defense of Chalcedon was required as much in the sixth century as it was in the fifth.[27] However,
Cyril's *Lives* dwell above all on the theological divisions that rent the Palestinian monastic community internally during the fifth and sixth cen-

turies, culminating in Cyril's own time with the crisis of Origenism.[28] The theological divisons within the desert are Cyril's overriding concern, above all else, and are the only form of crisis that move his holy men to action of their own doing: the real world is here.

For Cyril and for his subjects, the desert is the primary scene. It is where they live and where they work; their interest is not in what lies outside it. Only the battle against heresy can stir them to action in the temporal world, for heresy is an attack on the divine. The struggling eastern populace rouses no sense of urgency for these ascetics. John of Ephesus and his subjects also perceive religious crisis as the only important reality. But for them, the crisis of true faith is found in, and battled out in, the midst of society, the community of the Christian body. Although ascetics might choose solitude for part or all of their career, John does not present us with the attitude even from hermits that the human and divine are dichotomized arenas. Such a view is, however, precisely what Cyril leaves with us.

The paradoxes are apparent in Cyril's *Lives*, too, through his treatment of women. Cyril does not choose to include any female subjects among his select group of biographies, and indeed he makes no mention of the convents and women solitaries who were part of Palestine's desert community.[29] The antipathy of his subjects towards women is made plain; even a remote resemblance to women was dangerous. Euthymius and Sabas were both adamant that eunuchs and beardless youths must be kept separate from the primary monasteries and from the desert lavrae and cenobiae.[30] Sabas once punished severely a monk who had seen the eyes of a woman that the two had passed by: no more, but no less.[31]

Yet the few women mentioned in passing in Cyril's accounts are all shown to be virtuous;[32] in fact, Cyril himself as well as some of his subjects are seen to have been encouraged and prepared for their monastic careers by pious women.[33] The extremes of shunning women as the source of destruction, and yet encountering women as positive models of faith, do not balance out; they resemble the extremes between Cyril's conscientious historical sense and his subjects' lack of orientation to time, place, or society. In the case of women, in this context of stressed enmity, there is a peculiar edge to the physical intimacy with which Sabas heals women, touching and anointing their bodies.[34] Cyril's intent in recalling these incidents is to show that his saint is truly not of this world; but he succeeds, too, in severing the human from the holy. Consider the contrast, for example, in John of Ephesus' holy woman Susan, who neither saw the face of nor showed her face to a man for more than twenty-five years while yet living within and leading a mixed ascetic community. For her, the temporal and the holy are distinct but not unrelated realms.

For Cyril's saints, faith can be found in the temporal world, but the holy cannot be. The divine must be sought outside it. The ascetic's responsibility to the wider community of believers is fulfilled in the action of achieving a spiritual life, thereby offering a bridge between the imperfection of human society and the perfection of a life conforming to the will of God. Cyril's meticulous style, then, accurately reflects his subjects insofar as it matches the discipline of their lives in the desert.

The stylistic contrast between Cyril's formality and John Moschus' informality could hardly be greater. Cyril speaks to a sophisticated readership; Moschus looks to satisfy popular interests with favorite themes and diverting tales. The shared motifs and perspectives of the two collections are thus seen in sharp relief: one does not expect the two to tally so well.

However timeless the activity of his holy men, Cyril does set them in a historical framework. Moschus does not bother to do so, and the reader might often wonder when and where the stories take place. He too writes in a style befitting his content; spare and stark, his language easily conjures the uncluttered world he unfolds.[35] Here the Palestinian desert is remote in both place and time. The ascetics that Moschus brings to life are also remote. They can pass years, sometimes decades, without seeing or speaking with another soul;[36] they can lie dead for as long again, unchanged, until another anchorite or traveler accidentally stumbles across them.[37] They suffer often the demons of boredom and sexual desire and seem to return to towns or cities only when they have fallen from their vows and seek the debauchery of their fantasies.[38] In this black and white existence, miracles and prodigies are the norm, the Lord's favorite people plainly indicated, and the will of the divine equally explicit.

Moschus does include stories of worthy ascetics living in urban settings; but these tend to be bishops, or holy men on business, who remain as detached in their city as in the desert, though an occasional glimpse of social context emerges: the women who become prostitutes because they are starving,[39] and the citizens ruined by burdensome debts.[40] The ascetics themselves are untouched by the events of their time, events that penetrate the desert air only for didactic purposes. If plague strikes a village, one can seek out these holy men, whose prayers can save one's children and banish the epidemic.[41] If a marauding barbarian attacks, the prayers of these men can cause the enemies to be swallowed up by the earth or carried off to death by a giant bird; they can even cause the innocent person to be transported elsewhere.[42] Nor is food a problem: for these men, bread multiplies itself.[43] Moreover, for Moschus, holy women are solely occupied with battling Satan over the issue of fornication, a restricted sphere of activity even for women.[44]

Moschus' Chalcedonian faith is manifested by the same means as his ascetic vision. His orthodoxy is revealed in signs, dreams, and miracles. The gates of hell are opened to reveal what punishment awaits the heretic in the afterlife;[45] holy sacraments are consumed by lightning if defiled by Monophysite hands.[46] Divine apparitions prevent Monophysites from worshipping in the holy places of Jerusalem;[47] evil odors are emitted by Syrian Monophysite monks, however faultless their ascetic practice.[48] The question of faith is omnipresent but is forever played out in the intangible space between the temporal and divine worlds. Thus two stylites, one Chalcedonian and one Monophysite, bring their religious dispute to the test by exploring the miraculous qualities of their respective holy sacraments—the Monophysite morsel, not surprisingly, proving unable to survive the trial.[49]

Moschus presents in concrete terms the themes that underlie Cyril's seemingly less credulous biographies.[50] The similarity in perspective between them is more than a case of shared hagiographical motifs. The shared themes blend with the nature of the ascetic activity portrayed to reveal a common religious perception between the two works, despite their very different literary modes.

To be sure, there may be practical considerations affecting their lack of attention to the larger Christian community. Palestine did not suffer as intensely as Mesopotamia during the calamities that swept the sixth-century Byzantine East. Famine and plague do not appear to have been so long-lasting or debilitating when they occurred; natural disasters may not have been so frequent; warfare and marauding Saracens were not as persistent or as extensively destructive as such activity in Syria and Mesopotamia.[51] The Samaritan revolt inflicted severe damage, but Justinian paid a generous largesse to the province soon afterwards, in recompense.[52] Furthermore, the battle for orthodoxy was on a different footing for these two writers than for John of Ephesus. Origenism and Monophysites were real and present dangers for Cyril and Moschus, but their Chalcedonian faith nonetheless stood in a dominant position.

Yet the differences in misfortune are a matter of degree. Palestine was affected by the general malaise in the Byzantine East, and it did suffer accordingly. So Cyril's *Lives* and Moschus' anecdotes are not temporally divorced because their subjects were sheltered from overriding conditions, which, as can be glimpsed in their stories, they did in fact occasionally encounter. Their focus is other-worldly not by luxury of circumstance but by conscious intent. Theirs is a majestic vision of ascetic devotion to God, unbounded by time or place. But both works also admit that this grandeur was tarnished by human weakness: whether the seduction of the spirit by the flesh, or the erosion caused by petty disputes, or the insidious harm of ambitions worked out through the excuse of doctrinal conflict. Moving out of the temporal world into that of the spiritual life did not necessarily bring one closer to God. It did, however, alter the nature of religious crisis and of holy presence.

By contrast, the *Lives* of John of Ephesus jolt the reader into an awareness of their setting. Cyril's precision and Moschus' simplicity are consonant with their detachment from surrounding events. But if one looks for stylistic pointers, then John's writing also reveals much about his subjects, even if not as he intended. John's muddled style is not inappropriate for his content. The reality of his times is apparent throughout the *Lives*. As we have seen, the people his ascetics seek out and care for time and again are the victims of what befell the East. The immediacy of his portrait of human experience, and of holy presence within it, is heightened by the shared suffering he depicts: his ascetics may serve by divine grace, but grace does not protect them. John might have wished to present his subjects in a dignified manner—hence his pomposity in style—but his narrative style provides the best mirror for his context: there is no consistency, no clarity, and no escape.

The points where John seems to dovetail with Cyril and Moschus in hagiographical presentation are the very places that reveal their disparity of outlook. John's Thomas the Armenian forsook the luxury of his inheritance because he recognized that material goods were an ephemeral blessing. But his cry that "all is vanity" was not made with the derision of a cynic; he knew his father's wealth had been amassed by oppression of the poor.[53] John and his subjects recognized that life in the temporal world could not be dismissed as worthless or illusory; the world of human life belonged to God. A vow of devotion to God was a vow to care for what was His.

John describes the fervor with which Thomas took up his new career: "His soul became drunk on God."[54] He also tells us what that meant: "He devoted himself to making gifts on a large scale to the needy and the distressed, and to those who had creditors, and to churches and monasteries."[55] Further, Thomas kept enough of his wealth to establish a large monastic community, from which he provided spiritual leadership. When persecution struck, he carried on in exile as before. Thomas exemplifies John's choice of subject, although his career appears to begin in the well-worn formula of renouncing the temporal world for the spiritual.

Nor did John harbor illusions about his saints. He worried about Thomas' lack of care for the black ulcers on his legs,[56] just as he worried about the holy woman Euphemia's diseased feet.[57] His fear was that such negligence would result in the wearing out of the ascetic's ability to serve. He describes with clinical detail the grievous results when the monk Aaron left a gangrenous sore unattended on his body.[58] But John further relates the skill and ingenuity with which the doctors handled the case, once Aaron's condition had been discovered. His respect for the medical profession, an uncommon attitude among devout Christians,[59] was pragmatic: Aaron lived and labored another eighteen years after "the testing of this trial." But although he states the medical facts of the case, John still perceives the miraculous element of God's hand at work. Human effort in no way excludes divine agency.

In one of John's more hagiographically formulaic passages, he gives his sole report of a posthumous miracle: Paul the Anchorite, who had exorcised ferocious demons, continued to prove powerful after he died. John writes,

> even after his death miracles were everywhere wrought through his holy bones, men taking his skull and going around the districts, and, wheresoever locusts came or hail, or a scorching wind, or bubonic plague, and his right hand or head went, God would straightway make deliverance.[60]

The report is noteworthy because it stands alone in John's accounts. But in the context of the *Lives* as a whole, it makes sense. The populace of John's day required spiritual comfort as much as physical succor. Fear could gnaw no less than hunger, and it did gnaw. The relics of a holy man like Paul satisfied this need by providing the promise of care from the company of saints, not a small gift under the circumstances.

So, too, John tells of an incident occurring when the Amidan ascetic communities were in exile.[61] During the widespread famines, these monks provided what food they could for those who came in need to their place of shelter. But one day, such a crowd pressed upon them that their supplies nearly ran out. The monks did not hesitate to draw out some of their own reserve, but finally they approached the elders saying, "The food of the brotherhood has reached the point of exhaustion, and there are still many strangers lying at the door, and we have no means of supplying the need of these and of the brotherhood." The elders responded at once,

Glory to our Lord! Go, our sons, and bring forth and relieve the poor
and the strangers; and, if anything remains for ourselves, well, and if
not, we will keep fasting vigil today, and let the needs of the strangers
and the poor and the needy only be supplied; and let them not be cut
short by us.[62]

When the monks gathered for their meal at the day's end, they discovered food in abundance still remaining for themselves. "And the
whole brotherhood stood on the tables themselves together with all the
old heads of the convents, and they cried 'Kyrie eleeson' with great awe
many times, with many tears."[63] The contrast to the similar stories, on
the theme of a miraculous multiplication of food, told by Cyril and John
Moschus is stark. John's ascetics knew hunger firsthand.

What is most apparent in the *Lives of the Eastern Saints* is that the fundamental ascetic ideal—the basic understanding of devotion to God—
and the response to crisis are identical. Neither offers a means of retreat
or of refuge from the plight of the eastern provinces. As we have seen,
the conditions of exile rendered the Amidan ascetics easy prey for hunger and plague; and their religious status did not exempt them from the
massacres wrought by plundering foreign troops. Again, they could survive only so much Chalcedonian torture. In fact, these stories are notable for the standard hagiographical fare they do *not* include: the ascetic
nagged by boredom or distracted by lust. Indeed, these sins are the
product of too little activity and too much isolation. More pointedly,
John presents no miracles for answers. These ascetics may cure the sick
and exorcise demons and attend to those in need, but they cannot call
forth divine intervention. They can only serve.

Such different understandings of the task of devotion are not necessarily contradictory. John of Ephesus and Cyril of Scythopolis could
both record an incident they saw as miraculously performed by their
saints. If one tells us only of the physical, human details, and the other
only of the occurrence of the miracle itself, it is not because what happened in each case was different but simply because each writer had his
own idea of which details were important.

John Moschus portrays in clear and even tones what Cyril declares
in a more stately manner: an asceticism of impenetrable timelessness, in
which the temporal world is a place to be shunned, while one's faith is
played out between oneself and one's God. This too, for these two
hagiographers, is the nature and arena of religious crisis, warfare on behalf of the divine in a space far removed from the irrelevance of human
time and place.

But John of Ephesus tells us that there were times when the ascetics
of the early Byzantine Empire held themselves accountable for the con-

dition of the temporal world, not because a beleaguered population sought them out but because they perceived themselves as inextricably bound to the temporal world. These saints of the eastern Byzantine frontier found only one answer to the calamity of their time and to the urgency of religious crisis: for them, the holy is found not outside human society but rather manifestly within it.

While we have seen concrete hagiographical contrasts in our texts, it is difficult to assess these contrasts in terms of theological significance. Modern scholarship on the Christological controversy has shown how complex the issues were, and how difficult it is to distinguish belief from perception of belief. On the surface, these texts seem to point toward genuine contrasts among the authors, both in how the hagiographers presented the relationship between asceticism and society and in what holy men and women actually did. Although one could not prove these contrasts to be theologically based, these sources do confront us with actual differences in hagiography and asceticism, differences pointing toward distinctions of culture and belief.

HAGIOGRAPHY AND HISTORY

What, then, can we say about John of Ephesus as a hagiographer and as a historian?

John's faith and vocation were born of tradition, and so of a resolute stance against change; creativity is not a concern for John. Yet the *Lives of the Eastern Saints* are not a "literary" piece, determined by set hagiographic formulae or motifs; nor are they a collection molded into a predetermined format. John writes with a spontaneity that mirrors what he describes: an instinctive response to, and embracing of, whatever is encountered in God's world. He employs familiar language, and familiar phrases and themes, in order to place his biographies in their chosen context—that of hagiography—and in order to explain actions, beliefs, and events in a particular perspective. He is an interpreter as much as a reporter. His readers are guided through the *Lives* with signposts; they are being presented with a special view of history, a special kind of story. Language and imagery common to saints' lives orient John's audience to his purpose. But he employs these devices in a work otherwise highly personalized; they do not undermine the vitality of his collection.

Again, even John's fervor cannot obscure the soundness of his grounding in real history. John writes of lived experience. He is hasty on dates and locations and can mingle events in a confusing manner. He is insensitive to what falls outside his own interests, whether it be the fate

of a Jewish community, the livelihood of a remote village, or the consequences of altering forms of leadership for the Monophysite congregation. But he is true to his concern for what happened in people's lives
and to their lives. His portraits of provincial life in Amida no less than
his depictions of Constantinople are thus valuable to us, especially when
complemented with the impressions given by other sources, whether
contrasting or like-minded. We have here a measure of something that
stands beside the historicity of records: a rare glimpse of the living itself.

The literary conventions of hagiography are often used in such a
way as to hide the human qualities of their subjects and to disguise the
objective nature of the occurrences they record beneath layers of interpretations. Hagiography is a retelling of a biography or legend through a
different language; it looks through a different lens. So, too, did historiography in the ancient world dictate guidelines for the historian
through a preponderant emphasis on events and divine intervention,
on key leaders and celebrities, and on things produced or destroyed—
buildings, laws, policies, councils, wars—all set against an established
framework from the past. The orientation points of historiography were
the political and religious structures that determined the responses to
events or circumstances. Neither mode of description left much space
for people as private individuals, or for the ordinary fare of day-to-day
life apart from the exceptional: these were not their concerns.

John of Ephesus makes use of the hagiographer's method of describing persons blessed with the capacity to reveal holy presence in the
workings of the world; and he uses the historian's framework of time,
event, and situation laid out in a progressive scale to couch the *Lives* he
records. But his accounts are in the end the product of his wish to write
something of what he has seen. There is respect as much as reverence in
these saints' *Lives*. His approach thus differs from that of historical
chroniclers, yet his understanding of the holy and of the human causes
him to leave aside much that adorns the hagiographer's usual product,
whether formal or informal. So John's collection is an offering motivated
by faith and steeped in his Monophysite spirituality. The perceptions
that underlie it presuppose such a starting point. John begins in faith;
the *Lives* are his affirmation of what religious belief means.

In his preface to the *Lives*, John states that his reason for writing this
work was the duty imposed by Scripture: to glorify God by proclaiming
the works of His grace in the world through the triumphs of His holy
disciples. In the process of fulfilling this obligation, John is able to reveal
to us a rich segment of sixth-century Byzantine experience. He can do
this because he makes a simple equation between religion and life.

ABBREVIATIONS

For dictionaries, encyclopedias, and collections, full details may be found in the Bibliography.

AER	*American Ecclesiastical Review*
AJP	*American Journal of Philology*
AMS	*Acta Martyrum et Sanctorum*
Anal. Boll.	*Analecta Bollandiana*
Annales: e.s.c.	*Annales: économies, sociétés, et civilisations*
BEO	*Bulletin d'études orientales*
BHG	*Bibliotheca Hagiographica Graeca,* 3d ed., edited by F. Halkin; and idem, *Novum Auctarium BHG*
BHO	*Bibliotheca Hagiographica Orientalis,* edited by P. Peeters
BMGS	*Byzantine and Modern Greek Studies*
BZ	*Byzantinische Zeitschrift*
CBQ	*Catholic Biblical Quarterly*
CH	*Church History*
CP	*Classical Philology*
CR	*Classical Review*
CSCO	Corpus Scriptorum Christianorum Orientalium, Scriptores Syrii (unless otherwise noted)
CSEL	Corpus Scriptorum Ecclesiasticorum Latinorum
CSL	Corpus Scriptorum Latinorum
DHGE	*Dictionnaire d'histoire et de géographie ecclésiastiques*

DOP	*Dumbarton Oaks Papers*
DR	*Downside Review*
DTC	*Dictionnaire de Théologie Catholique*
ECR	*Eastern Churches Review*
EHR	*English Historical Review* '
GCS	Die griechischen christlichen Schriftsteller der ersten drei Jahrhunderte
GRBS	*Greek, Roman, and Byzantine Studies*
HE	*Historia Ecclesiastica*
HTR	*Harvard Theological Review*
JAC	*Jahrbuch für Antike und Christentum*
JAOS	*Journal of the American Oriental Society*
JBL	*Journal of Biblical Literature*
JEH	*Journal of Ecclesiastical History*
JME	*Journal of Medical Ethics*
JÖB	*Jahrbuch der Österreichischen Byzantinistik*
JRS	*Journal of Roman Studies*
JTS	*Journal of Theological Studies*
LCL	Loeb Classical Library
NT	*Novum Testamentum*
NTS	*New Testament Studies*
OCA	*Orientalia Christiana Analecta*
OCP	*Orientalia Christiana Periodica*
OLP	*Orientalia Lovaniensia Periodica*
PBA	*Proceedings of the British Academy*
PETSE	Papers of the Estonian Theological Society in Exile
PG	*Patrologia Graeca*, edited by J. P. Migne
PO	*Patrologia Orientalis*
POC	*Proche-Orient Chrétien*
RBK	*Reallexicon zur Byzantinischen Kunst*
RE	*Paulys Realenzyklopädie der classischen Altertumswissenschaft*
REJ	*Revue des études juives*
RHE	*Revue d'histoire ecclésiastique*
ROC	*Revue de l'orient chrétien*
SCH	Studies in Church History, edited by D. Baker, G. J. Cuming, S. Mews, et alii
SLNPNF	Select Library of Nicene and Post-Nicene Fathers

SSTS	Studies Supplementary to Sobornost
Sub. Hag.	Subsidia Hagiographica
TU	*Texte und Untersuchungen zur Geschichte der altchristlichen Literatur*
ZTK	*Zeitschrift für Theologie und Kirche*
ZK	*Zeitschrift für Kirchengeschichte*

Note on primary sources: For individual saints' lives not in major collections (e.g., John of Ephesus, *Lives*), see under *Vita* _____.

NOTES

Introduction. John's World

1. See, for example, Brock, "Introduction to Syriac Studies," esp. 11–13; Murray, *Symbols of Church and Kingdom,* 4; and Segal, *Edessa,* 16. See n. 3 below.

2. On Syriac's independent usage in the late Roman Empire, cf. Jones, *Later Roman Empire* 2: 865, 924, 968–69, 991, 994, 996. Herein, "Syriac" refers to a Syriac-speaking group or context only. "Syrian" refers to culture in the region of the Syrian Orient (languages spoken there varied: Syriac, Greek, Aramaic).

3. Wright, *Short History of Syriac Literature;* Duval, *Littérature syriaque;* Baumstark, *Geschichte der syrischen Literatur.*

4. Macuch, *Geschichte.*

5. So Duval, *Littérature syriaque,* 7–15. Edessa's claim to primacy in this respect is based on the legendary correspondence between its king Abgar the Black and Jesus, during his ministry. The legend is most fully recorded in the fifth-century *Doctrine of Addai,* ed. and trans. G. Phillips; it first became famous when the correspondence was translated into Greek by Eusebius of Caesarea, *HE* 1.13. See esp. Segal, *Edessa,* 62–81.

6. See, for example, Cameron and Cameron, "Christianity and Tradition"; Cameron, "Corippus' Poem"; Cochrane, *Christianity and Classical Culture;* M. L. W. Laistner, *Christianity and Pagan Culture in the Later Roman Empire* (Ithaca, 1951); Momigliano, *Conflict Between Paganism and Christianity;* and idem, "Popular Religious Beliefs."

7. Drijvers, *Cults and Beliefs at Edessa;* Segal, *Edessa,* 1–61.

8. Drijvers, "Facts and Problems"; Segal, *Edessa,* 30–61, esp. 30–31. The *Odes of Solomon, Acts of Judas Thomas,* and *Didascalia Apostolorum* are examples of texts from the Syrian Orient circulating in both Syriac and Greek. On the *Odes of*

Solomon, see subsequent discussion. See also A. F. J. Klijn, *The Acts of Thomas*, Supplements to *NT* 5 (Leiden, 1962); R. H. Connolly, *The Didascalia Apostolorum* (Oxford, 1929); A. Vööbus, *The Didascalia Apostolorum in Syriac*, CSCO 401/175, 402/176, 407/179, 408/180 (Louvain, 1979).

9. Drijvers, *Bardaisan of Edessa*; idem; *Cults and Beliefs at Edessa*; idem, "Facts and Problems"; Griffith, "Ephraem". Ephrem's comment on "the poison of the wisdom of the Greeks" is from the Hymns on Faith, 2.24.

10. On the Christianization of the Syrian Orient, see esp. Segal, *Edessa*; Murray, *Symbols of Church and Kingdom*, 4–24; and Drijvers, *Cults and Beliefs at Edessa*, 175–96, esp. 194–96. On the early resistance to Hellenic influence, see Brock, "Greek Words in the Syriac Gospels"; and idem, "From Antagonism to Assimilation." Both Segal and Murray provide ample testimony to the creativity and autonomous inspiration of early Syriac literature.

11. For the impact of Eastern and Western influences on the Syrian Orient, see esp. Segal, *Edessa*; Murray, *Symbols of Church and Kingdom*; Drijvers, *Cults and Beliefs at Edessa*; Vööbus, *History of Asceticism*; and Peeters, *Orient et Byzance*.

12. Peeters, *Orient et Byzance*; MacMullen, "Provincial Languages." Cf. Ebied, "Syriac Influence".

13. Vööbus, *History of the School of Nisibis*; Segal, *Edessa*, 87, 93, 95, 108, 116, 150–51, 166, 185.

14. Brock, "From Antagonism to Assimilation"; idem, "Aspects of Translation"; and idem, "Some Aspects of Greek Words."

15. Brock, "Aspects of Translation"; idem, "Greek into Syriac"; idem, "Towards a History"; P. Peeters, "Traductions et traducteurs dans l'hagiographie orientale à l'époque byzantine," *Anal. Boll.* 40 (1922): 241–98 (= *Orient et Byzance*, 165–218).

16. Murray, *Symbols of Church and Kingdom*; idem, "Theory of Symbolism"; Brock, *Luminous Eye*; Ephrem, *Harp of the Spirit*; Brock, "Syriac and Greek Hymnography."

17. Brock, "Greek into Syriac." For the place of Syrian prayer tradition in the larger context of Christian mysticism, see, above all, *Syriac Fathers on Prayer*, trans. S. P. Brock; Brock, "Prayer of the Heart"; and Widengren, "Researches in Syrian Mysticism." Ephrem Syrus, John the Solitary, and Isaac of Nineveh are prominent examples of Syriac writers still read today by various Orthodox and Roman Catholic monastic communities. See the excellent and sensitive discussion and translations by the Holy Transfiguration Monastery [D. Miller] in Isaac the Syrian, *Ascetical Homilies*.

18. The entire topic is well handled in Peeters, *Orient et Byzance*. Specific instances are treated in commentaries by Amiaud in *Vita Alexii, Légende syriaque*, Burkitt in *Euphemia and the Goth*, and in *Vita Pelagiae, Pélagie la pénitente*, ed. P. Petitmengin.

19. An example, in the case of Pelagia, is the transvestite saint motif. See Delehaye, *Legends of the Saints*, 150–55; Delcourt, *Hermaphrodite*, 84–102; and Patlagean, "Histoire de la femme déguisée."

20. For the disputes leading up to, and then resulting from, the Council of Chalcedon in 451, see, for example, Grillmeier and Bacht, *Konzil von Chalkedon;* and Sellers, *Council of Chalcedon.* On the popular involvement, see Gregory, *Vox Populi;* and Frend, "Popular Religion." These issues are further explored in subsequent discussion here.

21. Brock, "Aspects of Translation"; idem, "Some Aspects of Greek Words."

22. *Syriac Fathers on Prayer;* cf. Brock, "Christology of the Church."

23. See Lebon, *Monophysisme Sévèrien;* idem, "Christologie du monophysisme syrien"; and Chesnut, *Three Monophysite Christologies.* Although Severus probably knew Syriac, he wrote only in Greek. However, his writings survive almost solely in translation, the bulk being in Syriac. The Syriac translations of his works were undertaken in the sixth and seventh centuries, with major revisions in the eighth. See Graffin, "Jacques d'Edesse réviseur"; and Severus of Antioch, *Sixth Book of Select Letters,* ed. and trans. E. W. Brooks.

24. In fact, Syriac provided the bridge between Greek and Arabic culture during the Middle Ages: it was through Syriac that Greek learning (notably the work of Aristotle) was translated into Arabic. See Brock, "Aspects of Translation"; idem, "Greek into Syriac"; and Ebied, "Syriac Influence."

25. Bundy, "Criteria for Being *in communione.*"

26. Vööbus, *History of Asceticism* 1:86–97.

27. Ibid., 89–96 and passim. See now the insightful discussion in Brown, *Body and Society,* 83–102; and Bundy, "Marcion and the Marcionites." The possible exceptions are Bardaisan and the group known as the Quqites; Drijvers, *Bardaisan of Edessa;* idem, *Cults and Beliefs at Edessa.*

28. Murray, *Symbols of Church and Kingdom,* 4–24; Segal, *Edessa,* 67–69.

29. Brock, "Early Syrian Asceticism"; and Murray, *Symbols of Church and Kingdom;* both explore this aspect of Syrian spirituality in literature. Such an understanding of theological symbolism can be seen, for example, in the poetry of Ephrem Syrus. See, above all, Brock, *Luminous Eye;* idem, "Poet as Theologian"; and Murray, "Theory of Symbolism." Beggiani, *Early Syriac Theology,* considers Syrian spirituality and its symbolism through a variety of themes.

30. Cf. Brock, "Early Syrian Asceticism"; Vööbus, *History of Asceticism* 1: 39–45; Brown, *Body and Society,* 83–102.

31. Murray, *Symbols of Church and Kingdom,* 131–42; see, for example, *Odes of Solomon* 38.9–12 and 42.8–9. On the *Odes of Solomon,* see n. 46 below.

32. Esp. Matt. 22:1–14 and 25:1–13. Cf. Brock, "Early Syrian Asceticism," 5–6; idem, *Holy Spirit,* 51–52. For an especially sensitive reading of the meaning of this image for the Syrian Orient, see Brown, *Body and Society,* 83–102, 323–38.

33. Vööbus, *Celibacy;* idem, *History of Asceticism* 1:90–96; Murray, "Exhortation to Candidates."

34. Vööbus, *History of Asceticism* 1:68–83.

35. Ibid., 103–106; Brock, "Early Syrian Asceticism," 6; Murray, *Symbols of Church and Kingdom,* 12–17.

36. Gribomont, "Monachisme au sein de l'église"; Nedungatt, "Covenanters," 191–215, 419–44; Vööbus, *History of Asceticism* 1:97–103, 184–208; idem,

"Institution of the *Benai Qeiama*." Primary texts on the *bnay* and *bnath qyāmā* are as follows: Aphrahat, *Demonstrationes* 6, ed. and trans. D. I. Parisot; and the canons in *Syriac and Arabic Documents*, ed. and trans. A. Vööbus, esp. 34–50, 122, 125–26.

37. Murray, *Symbols of Church and Kingdom*, 239–76; Brock, *Holy Spirit*, 49–52.

38. For example, Vööbus, *History of Asceticism* 1:90.

39. For example, 1 Cor. 15:45–49.

40. Brock, "Early Syrian Asceticism"; cf. Vööbus, *History of Asceticism* 1: 152–53.

41. Vööbus, *History of Asceticism* 1:69; Bundy, "Criteria for Being *in communione.*"

42. Murray, *Symbols of Church and Kingdom*, 12–16; Vööbus, *History of Asceticism* 1; Guillaumont, "Monachisme et éthique judéo-chrétienne"; Judge, "Earliest Use of Monachos"; Kretschmar, "Beitrag zur Frage"; Beck, "Beitrag zur Terminologie."

43. Nowhere is this clearer than in Vööbus, *History of Asceticism*.

44. See esp. Vööbus, *History of Asceticism* 1. For the various religious models, see Brown, *Body and Society*, esp. 83–102, 323–38; Jonas, *Gnostic Religion*; Hoffmann, *Marcion*; Fiey, "Marcionites"; Bundy, "Marcion and the Marcionites"; Gribomont, "Monachisme au sein de l'église"; Widengren, *Mani and Manichaeism*; idem, *Mesopotamian Elements in Manichaeism*; and Bauer, *Orthodoxy and Heresy*.

45. On the autonomous origins of Syrian asceticism, see Vööbus, *History of Asceticism*; Gribomont, "Monachisme an sein de l'église"; and Jargy, "Origines du monachisme." The Syrians themselves lost sight of the origins of their asceticism under the impact of Egypt's fame and eventually claimed that the ascetic roots in Syria and Mesopotamia stemmed from disciples of Pachomius. See Brock, "Early Syrian Asceticism"; and Fiey, "Aonès, Awun, et Awgin." A clear example of the loss can be seen in Thomas of Marga, *Historia monastica*, in *Book of Governors*, ed. and trans. E. A. Wallis Budge.

46. *Odes of Solomon*, ed. and trans. J. H. Charlesworth, 2nd ed. (Missoula, 1977; Chico, 1982).

47. On the original language of the *Odes*, see the judicious comments by Murray, "Characteristics of the Earliest Syriac Christianity," 5. For a first-century dating see Charlesworth, "Odes of Solomon"; and Charlesworth and Culpepper, "Odes of Solomon and Gospel of John." The second-century position is bolstered by McNeil, "Odes of Solomon and Scriptures." Drijvers has been forcefully arguing for the third century, see his *East of Antioch*, chapters 6–10. The debates over the *Odes* have been fought long and hard, and the literature is extensive. See now the detailed annotated bibliography in Lattke, *Oden Salomos*, vol. 3.

48. Celibacy is assumed throughout, as, for example, in Odes 23 and 33. Betrothal to Christ is its explicit meaning, as, for example, in Ode 42. In Ode 38, false doctrine is described as the "Bridegroom who corrupts," with false bridal feast and celebration.

49. For example, Ode 6.1–2.

50. Ode 40.2–4.

51. For example, Ode 21.6–9. Cf. Aune, *Cultic Setting*, esp. 12–16, 166–94.

52. Ode 35.7; 37.1–4; 42.1–2.

53. B. McNeil, "*Odes of Solomon* and Suffering of Christ."

54. See "Martyr at the Sasanid Court," ed. and trans. S. P. Brock; Fiey, *Jalons pour une histoire*, 85–99.

55. *BHO*, 363–68; *BHG*, 731–40. I follow the texts in *Euphemia and the Goth*, ed. and trans. F. C. Burkitt. On the texts and their historicity, see idem, *Euphemia and the Goth*, 5–44; and Segal, *Edessa*, 83–86.

56. For the texts of the *Doctrina Addai*, see n. 5 above. On the historicity, see Segal, *Edessa*, 76–81; and Drijvers, "Facts and Problems."

57. Sharbil and Babai, *BHO*, 1049–51; Barsamya, *BHO*, 150–51. The texts are edited by P. Bedjan in *AMS* 1.95–130. On the later dating of these texts and their possible composition in Greek, see Segal, *Edessa*, 82–83, and commentary by Burkitt, in *Euphemia and the Goth*, 5–28.

58. Bundy, "Criteria for Being *in communione*."

59. Cf. Segal, *Edessa*, 82–86; and commentary by Burkitt in *Euphemia and the Goth*, 5–44.

60. Barnes, "Constantine and the Christians"; Brock, "Christians in the Sasanian Empire."

61. *Vita Antonii*, sec. 46–47. See the discussion in S. A. Harvey, "The Edessan Martyrs and Ascetic Tradition," *Symposium Syriacum 1988* (Forthcoming).

62. See n. 55 above. *The Martyrdom of Shmona and Guria* is in *Euphemia and the Goth*, ed. and trans. F. C. Burkitt, 90–110.

63. Ibid., 8.

64. Ibid., 14.

65. Ibid., 49.

66. Ibid., 37–38, 47.

67. Eusebius, *Martyrs of Palestine* 4, 5, 6, 10, 11, 13; *HE* 8.9.

68. For example, *The Martyrs of Lyons*, in *The Acts of the Christian Martyrs*, ed. H. Musurillo (Oxford, 1979), 62–85; *The Martyrdom of Perpetua and Felicitas, Acts of Christian Martyrs*, 106–31; Eusebius, *Martyrs of Palestine* 9.

69. *The Martyrdom of Habib*, in *Euphemia and the Goth*, ed. and trans. F. C. Burkitt, 112–28; and also in *Ancient Syriac Documents*, ed. and trans. W. Cureton, (trans.) 72–85.

70. Ibid., 30.

71. Eusebius, *Martyrs of Palestine*; idem, *HE* 8; *Vita Antonii*.

72. *Martyrdom of Habib*, in *Euphemia and the Goth*, 30.

73. Cf. Jacob of Sarug, *Homily on Habib the Martyr*, in *Ancient Syriac Documents*, ed. and trans. W. Cureton, 86–96.

74. *Acts of Sharbil*, in *Ancient Syriac Documents*, ed. and trans. W. Cureton, 41–62. On the date and languages, see n. 57 above.

75. Especially Aphrahat, *Demonstration* 1, "On Faith", and *Demonstration*

6, "On the Bnay Qyama," in Aphrahat, *Demonstrationes,* ed. and trans. D. I. Parisot, cols. 5–46, 239–312; and "Aphrahat the Persian Sage," trans. J. G. Gwynn, 345–52, 362–75. See also Neusner, *Aphrahat and Judaism.*

76. Aphrahat, *Demonstration* 18, "On Virginity," in Aphrahat, *Demonstrationes,* ed. and trans. D. I. Parisot, cols. 817–44; also Neusner, *Aphrahat and Judaism,* 76–83.

77. Aphrahat, *Demonstration* 6, "On the Bnay Qyama," and *Demonstration* 7, "On Penitence," in Aphrahat, *Demonstrationes,* ed. and trans. D. I. Parisot, cols. 5–46, 239–312, 313–60.

78. Ibid., *Demonstration* 6; Murray, "Exhortation to Candidates"; Black, "Tradition of Hasidaean-Essene"; Aune, *Cultic Setting.*

79. Ephrem, *Hymnen de fide,* 14.5, ed. and trans. E. Beck, in CSCO 154/73, 62.

80. Ephrem, *Carmina Nisibena,* 50.7, ed. and trans. E. Beck, in CSCO 240/102, 69.

81. Ibid., 69.3–5, 14; here trans. S. P. Brock in Ephrem, *Harp of the Spirit,* 77–79.

82. Ephrem, *Carmina Nisibena,* 50.3; here trans. S. P. Brock, *Harp of the Spirit,* 56.

83. These texts are discussed in Vööbus, *History of Asceticism* 1:152–54, and he attributes both to Ephrem. But the doubts on Ephrem's authorship are well stated in Gribomont, "Monachisme au sein de l'église." However, Theodoret of Cyrrhus, *Historia religiosa* 1–6, indicates that such ascetic practice was pursued in the Syrian Orient during Ephrem's lifetime.

84. Ephrem, "Ephrem's Letter to Publius," ed. and trans. S. P. Brock, 286.

85. See esp. Brown, *Body and Society,* 323–38; and Guillaumont, *Aux origines du monachisme chrétien,* 215–39. An example of Ephrem's view on the unity of body and soul can be seen in his Verse Homily I, in *Syrers sermones* 1, ed. and trans. E. Beck, esp. 11.260–79. In this passage, Ephrem describes the way in which the body reveals the soul's condition. A similar passage occurs in the *Vita Antonii,* sec. 67. But in the passage on Antony, the saint has achieved this state of harmony between body and soul through the discipline of his ascetic practice, by which he has "subjugated" his body to his soul's desire (sec. 14). For Ephrem, the one reveals the other because they are ultimately inseparable.

86. Theodoret, *Historia religiosa* 1–2, is our primary source, along with the hymns of Ephrem: on Jacob in the *Carmina Nisibena,* 13–14; and the cycle on Julian Saba, of disputed authorship but certainly from the same period, (Ephrem Syrus?), *Hymnen auf Abraham Kidunaya und Julianos Saba,* ed. and trans. E. Beck. The poems on Abraham Qidunaya are another important witness to earliest Syrian asceticism. See further Vööbus, *History of Asceticism* 1:141–46, and 2:42–51. On Julian, see also Palladius, *Historia Lausiaca* 42; and Sozomen, *HE* 3.14.

87. Theodoret, *Historia religiosa* 1.

88. Ibid., 2.

89. Ibid., 2.18.

90. Ibid., 1.11, 2.6.

91. Palladius, *Historia Lausiaca* 40. In the *Carmina Nisibena* 56.10, Ephrem calls himself *ʿallānā*, a word that can refer to a variety of pastoral positions; this is our only reference to an actual title for Ephrem's position. See the excellent discussion of Ephrem's career in Griffith, "Ephraem."

92. See Brown, "Saint as Exemplar"; and for how this was made possible, idem, *Body and Society.*

93. Brown, "Rise and Function." The economic monopoly that Syrian monasteries exerted over villages continued under the Arabs; the case of Simeon of the Olives (d. 734) and the Tur Abdin dramatically illustrates the issue. See "Fenqitho of the Monastery," ed. and trans. S. P. Brock, 174–79.

94. For example, Brown, "Rise and Function"; idem, "Saint as Exemplar"; idem, "Dark Age Crisis"; Frend, "Monks and the Survival"; Frazee, "Late Roman and Byzantine Legislation."

95. *Vita Antonii*, sec. 69–70. Cf. Chitty, *Desert a City*; Brown, *Body and Society*, 213–40.

96. Guillaumont, "Conception de désert" (= *Aux origines du monachisme chrétien*, 67–88).

97. On Basil's monastic aspirations, see Basil, *Lettres* 2, 223, and 142–44; Gregory of Nazianzus, *Lettres* 6; *Oration* 43.63; Sozomen, *HE* 6.34. For the intrigues involving Gregory of Nazianzus, see Basil, *Lettres* 14, and Gregory of Nazianzus, *Lettres* 2, 40, 46, 48–50, 59.

98. For example, Socrates, *HE* 7.7.13–15.

99. Theodoret, *Historia religiosa.* Cf. Jargy, "Premiers instituts monastiques"; Hendriks, "Vie quotidienne." See chapter 3 for specific discussion of how this precarious position affected Mesopotamia.

100. Simeon Stylites the Elder: *BHG*, 1678–88; *BHO*, 1121–26. The major documents on Simeon were collected and discussed in *Leben des heiligen Symeon Stylites*, ed. H. Leitzmann; see *The Lives of Simeon Stylites*, trans. R. Doran. On Simeon, see Drijvers, "Spätantike Parallelen"; and Harvey, "Sense of a Stylite."

101. On the physical details of stylitism, see *Saints stylites*, ed. and trans. H. Delehaye, and Vööbus, *History of Asceticism* 2:208–23.

102. Theodoret, *Historia religiosa* 26. Relevant to the discussion here are the treatments in Canivet, *Monachisme syrien*; and Peeters, "Un saint hellénisé par annexion: Syméon Stylite," in *Orient et Byzance*, 93–136.

103. Theodoret, *Historia religiosa* 26.12.

104. Ibid.

105. Ibid., 26.2, 7, 12. See the discussions in A.-J. Festugière, *Antioche païenne et chrétienne. Libanius, Chrysostome, et les moines de Syrie* (Paris, 1959), 354–57; and Canivet, *Monachisme syrien*, 76–77.

106. The Syriac vita survives in two recensions. The earlier (A), Vat. Syr. 117, was copied in A.D. 473: *Acta sanctorum martyrum orientalium*, ed. and trans. J. S. Assemani; there is an English translation in Doran (see n. 100 above). The later (B), Brit. Mus. Add. 14484, dates to early in the sixth century: *Vita Simeonis*

Stylitae, in *Acta Martyrum et Sanctorum,* ed. P. Bedjan (hereafter *AMS*); there is a German translation by H. Hilgenfeld in *Das Leben des heiligen Symeon Stylites,* ed. H. Lietzmann, 80–192; and an English one by F. Lent, "The Life of St. Simeon Stylites."

107. *AMS* 4.620, 519.

108. Ibid., 612.

109. For example, ibid., 571–72, 574.

110. Ibid., 572, 623.

111. Harvey, "Sense of a Stylite."

112. The Greek vita by Antonius has been edited by H. Lietzmann, *Leben des heiligen Symeon Stylites,* 19–78; there is a French translation of the primary Greek text by A.-J. Festugière, *Antioche paienne et chrétienne,* 493–506, and (for sec. 28–33) 373–75.

113. As opposed to Nöldeke and others, for example, "Yet it must always be remembered that in all Christendom, Egypt apart, it will be difficult to find such an insane and soul-destroying asceticism as was practised by the purely Semitic Syrians from about the fourth to the seventh centuries" (Nöldeke, *Sketches from Eastern History,* 10).

114. Tchalenko, *Villages antiques,* 1:227–76; Peña, Castellana, and Fernandez, *Stylites syriens;* Nasrallah, "Survie de Saint Siméon"; Vikan, "Art, Medicine and Magic."

115. *Saints Stylites,* ed. and trans. H. Delehaye; Delehaye, "Femmes stylites"; Peña, Castellana, and Fernandez, *Stylites syriens.*

116. Alexius the Man of God, *BHO,* 36–44. The primary Syriac text is in *Légende syriaque,* ed. A. Amiaud. See also Drijvers, "Legende des heiligen Alexius."

117. *Vita Alexii, Légende syriaque,* ed. A. Amiaud, 10 (trans. 6).

118. Ibid., 12 (trans. 8).

119. On Rabbula, see Blum, *Rabbula von Edessa.* There is an important Syriac vita in *AMS* 4:396–450.

120. The story of the Man of God was translated into most Christian languages of the Middle Ages; see the discussion in *Vita Alexii,* ed. A. Amiaud. Eventually the saint acquired a name, Alexius, and all of the standard traits missing in the fifth century vita (miracles, teachings, a body venerated at public feast days, a tomb transformed into an opulent shrine, and the adoration of both the pope and the emperors). An example of this later version can be found in C. J. Odenkirchen, *The Life of St. Alexius in the Old French Version of the Hildesheim Manuscript* (Brookline, 1978).

121. So, too, in the case of Daniel the Stylite and Simeon Stylites the Younger. See also the excellent discussion in *Theodoret of Cyrrhus, History,* trans. R. M. Price, ix–xxxvii.

122. Theodoret, *Historia religiosa* 26.23.

123. Vööbus, *History of Asceticism* 2:181–82; *Syriac and Arabic Documents,* ed. and trans. A. Vööbus, 24–33, and compare passim.

124. Vööbus, *History of Asceticism* 2:275.

125. On this point only I disagree with Drijvers, "Legende des heiligen Alexius."

126. The Syriac-speaking church in Persia followed a different course. See Labourt, *Christianisme dans l'empire perse;* Fiey, *Jalons pour une histoire;* and Brock, "Christology of the Church."

127. See Grillmeier and Bacht, *Konzil von Chalkedon;* Sellers, *Council of Chalcedon;* Young, *From Nicaea to Chalcedon,* chapter 5; and Grillmeier, *Christ in Christian Tradition.*

128. See Frend, *Rise of Christianity,* 770–73; and Sellers, *Council of Chalcedon.* It is certainly Leo's *Tome* that receives the most scathing opprobrium in Syriac sources. Cf. Mouterde, "Concile de Chalcédoine." Cf. Lebon, *Monophysisme Sévèrien,* esp. 1–82.

129. For the background of the problem of religious language, see Young, "God of the Greeks."

130. See Wigram, *Separation of the Monophysites;* and Frend, *Rise of the Monophysite Movement.*

131. Sellers, *Two Ancient Christologies;* idem, *Council of Chalcedon;* Grillmeier, *Christ in Christian Tradition;* Young, "Reconsideration of Alexandrian Christology"; idem, "Christological Ideas"; idem, *From Nicaea to Chalcedon,* chapter 5. Cf. Brock, "Orthodox-Oriental Orthodox Conversations."

132. Nonetheless, the profundity of shared understanding holds true to this day, although its affirmation has been disallowed by schism. See, for example, Fouyas, *Theologikai kai Istorikai Meletai* 1, esp. 140–217; Every, "Monophysite Question"; Murray, "What does a Catholic Hope." Cf. Lebon, *Monophysisme Sévèrien,* with Meyendorff, *Byzantine Theology.*

133. On the development of Monophysite theology, see Lebon, *Monophysisme Sévèrien;* idem, "Christologie du monophysisme syrien"; R. Chesnut, *Three Monophysite Christologies;* and Darling, "Patriarchate of Severus." For the development of Chalcedonian theology, see esp. Moeller, "Chalcédonisme et le néochalcédonisme"; Meyendorff, *Christ in Eastern Christian Thought;* and P. T. R. Gray, *Defense of Chalcedon.*

134. Gray, *Defense of Chalcedon,* 48–73, 154–64; Frend, *Rise of Christianity,* 828–68.

135. See Charanis, *Church and State;* and, in general, Frend, *Rise of the Monophysite Movement,* and Wigram, *Separation of the Monophysites.*

136. Evagrius, *HE* 3.44; pseudo-Dionysius, *Incerti auctoris chronicon,* 6–7 (John of Ephesus); John of Nikiu, *Chronicle* 9.9.

137. For example, John of Nikiu, *Chronicle* 90.20–26. See below, chapter 3.

138. Vasiliev, *Justin the First,* is essential for this whole period, as is Patlagean, *Pauvreté économique.* On Justinian's reign in general see, for example, Bury, *History of the Later Roman Empire* 2; Browning, *Justinian and Theodora;* and Stein, *Histoire du bas-empire* 2.

139. See esp. Honigmann, *Évêques et évêchés monophysites;* also Frend, *Rise of*

the Monophysite Movement; and Wigram, *Separation of the Monophysites.* The tumultuous atmosphere is well caught in John of Nikiu's account of the Constantinopolitan riots, *Chronicle* 89.39–68; but the background is equally volatile. For example, Evagrius, *HE* 3.30–44; "Chronique melkite," ed. and trans. A. de Halleux, chaps. 13–14; and Michael the Syrian, *Chronique* 9.8–10. Severus of Antioch, *Sixth Book of Select Letters,* vividly portrays the sense of uncertainty and danger felt even at Severus' level of leadership. See also Darling, "Patriarchate of Severus."

140. Vasiliev, *Justin the First,* 4, 224, 363. Egypt's resources were well worth keeping within imperial reach. See Johnson and West, *Byzantine Egypt,* for the wealth of the church esp. 66–72, 252–54; and Wipszycka, *Ressources et activités économiques.*

141. Hardy, *Christian Egypt; Jews and Christians in Egypt,* ed. and trans. H. I. Bell; Frend, "Popular Religion"; Gregory, *Vox Populi,* esp. 129–61, 163–201.

142. For example, Severus of Antioch, *Sixth Book of Select Letters,* 1.49–50, 53, 5.11, 5.15.

143. *Vita Severi* (Zachariah Rhetor), ed. and trans. M.-A. Kugener; *Vita Severi* (John of Beith-Aphthonia), ed. and trans. M.-A. Kugener; Severus of Antioch, *Sixth Book of Select Letters* 1.49–50. Cf. Hardy, *Christian Egypt,* 111–32.

144. Severus of Antioch, *Sixth Book of Select Letters* 5.11. That Egypt lived up to this guiding role is clear from John of Ephesus' *HE;* see *Fragmenta,* ed. E. W. Brooks, 3.7–8. Cf. Hardy, *Christian Egypt,* 120–43.

145. The consequences of the Plague have until recently rarely been acknowledged. We have three contemporary sources of information: Procopius, *Wars* 2.22–23; Evagrius, *HE* 4.29; and John of Ephesus, *HE,* in pseudo-Dionysius, *Incerti auctoris chronicon,* 79–89, 94–110, 112, 119. See chapter 3 below for discussion of these and recent scholarship.

146. Chapter 3 attempts to make clear the actual conditions of the eastern provinces at this time. The material discussed there complements, at least to some extent, the vicious denunciation of Justinian's treatment of the eastern provinces that Procopius gives in the *Anecdota.* Browning, *Justinian and Theodora,* 60–61, discusses examples of Justinian's occasional imperial munificence, especially in cases of disaster. Cf. Vasiliev, *Justin the First,* 344–88.

147. See esp. Vasiliev, *Justin the First;* and Patlagean, *Pauvreté économique,* 74–112.

148. Justinian and his contemporary historians are discussed in chapter 4. See esp. Cameron, *Procopius and the Sixth Century.*

I. *"These Holy Images": John of Ephesus and the* Lives of the Eastern Saints

1. A. Djakonov, *Ioann Efesskiy* (Petrograd, 1908), provided the most important breakthrough in postulating a biographical framework. The two best summaries, both dependent on Djakonov's work, are E. W. Brooks' Introduction

to John of Ephesus, *Lives of the Eastern Saints, PO* 17: iii–xv, and Honigmann, *Évêques et évêchés monophysites,* 207–15. See also "Jean d'Éphèse," *Dictionnaire de Spiritualité* 8, cols. 484–86 (D. Stiernon). John speaks of his childhood, training, and monastic travels in his *Lives,* while information about his missionary and ecclesiastical activities is mostly found in parts 2 and 3 of his *Ecclesiastical History* (see nn. 15 and 16 below). I will elaborate on places and events mentioned here in later sections.

2. John of Ephesus, *Lives* 4, *PO* 17:59–64.

3. Ibid., 84, 35; *PO* 18:608–9.

4. Ibid., 24, *PO* 18:516–22.

5. John of Ephesus, *HE,* in pseudo-Dionysius, *Incerti auctoris chronicon,* 77–78, 125.

6. John of Ephesus, *Lives,* 50, *PO* 19:153–58.

7. Ibid., 47, *PO* 18:681. Cf. pseudo-Dionysius, *Incerti auctoris chronicon,* 77–78 (seventy thousand converts, fifty-five churches built at public expense, forty-one from contributions by new converts).

8. John of Ephesus, *Lives,* 36, *PO* 18:624–25; and 38, *PO* 18:644. On Callinicus, see Brooks' Introduction to *Lives, PO* 17:vi.

9. This final period of John's life, after 566, is covered in his *Ecclesiastical History,* parts 2 and 3.

10. John speaks of his imprisonment under Justin II, and of other abuses, in his *HE* III (ed. Brooks), i.17, ii.4–7, 41, 44. For the conditions under which he wrote and circulated the final part of his *History,* see ibid., ii.50. For the texts, see n. 16 below.

11. His death was not in 586, as long held; for this important piece of redating see Allen, "New Date."

12. John of Ephesus, *Lives,* 35, *PO* 18:607; and *HE* in pseudo-Dionysius, *Incerti auctoris chronicon,* 39. Brooks would date this work to 537 (Introduction to *Lives, PO* 17:vi), following Ephrem's "descent to the east" of 536–537. But John's chronological reference in the *Lives* is vague enough to allow for a slightly later date, and one might take into account that the consequences of Ephrem's activity lasted far longer than that year. Perhaps John waited until his arrival at Constantinople in 540 to write this?

13. For both these works, see Brooks' references in the Introduction to John of Ephesus, *Lives, PO* 17:vi.

14. See Allen, "New Date," for the final date.

15. Fragments of part 2 were published in *Anecdota Syriaca,* ed. J. P. N. Land, 2:289–330, 385–92. Those found in pseudo-Dionysius' *Incerti auctoris chronicon* were further elaborated and annotated by Nau in "Étude sur les parties," and in John of Ephesus, "Analyse de la seconde partie." The best text for the fragments in pseudo-Dionysius is found in *Incerti auctoris chronicon,* ed. I.-B. Chabot, CSCO 104/53. More fragments were published by E. W. Brooks in John of Ephesus, *Historiae ecclesiasticae fragmenta.*

16. John of Ephesus, *Historiae ecclesiasticae pars tertia,* ed. and trans. E. W.

Brooks. See also Honigmann, "Histoire ecclésiastique de Jean d'Éphèse." An earlier version was edited by W. Cureton (Oxford, 1853) and translated by R. Payne-Smith, *The Third Part of the Ecclesiastical History of John, Bishop of Ephesus* (Oxford, 1860).

17. The sole document John includes is the *Henoticon;* he seems to have drawn only on Malalas as a Greek source, cf. Brooks' Introduction to John of Ephesus, *Lives*, PO 17:xii–xiii. Discussion of mutual influences between Greek and Syriac cultures can be found in Peeters, *Orient et Byzance*.

18. The theoretically separate literary genres of secular and ecclesiastical histories had long faced mutual infringement of their respective territories. See, for example, Cameron and Cameron, "Christianity and Tradition"; Downey, "Perspective of Early Church Historians"; and Momigliano, "Popular Religious Beliefs."

19. Even these writers, so consciously traditional, could not successfully maintain their chosen narrative boundaries. See Allen, *Evagrius Scholasticus;* Cameron, *Procopius and the Sixth Century;* and idem, *Agathias*.

20. See, for example, Allen, "'Justinianic' Plague"; Cameron, "Empress Sophia"; and idem, "Early Religious Policies."

21. Brooks' edition in *Patrologia Orientalis* was preceded by *Anecdota Syriaca*, ed. J. P. N. Land, 2:2–288, with a Latin translation by J. P. N. Land and W. J. van Douwen, *Commentarii de Beatis Orientalibus*. There are two possible exceptions to John's practice of firsthand knowledge. His account of Abraham of Kalesh, *Lives*, 4, took place before he was born. Also, some scholars think the story of the two holy fools in Amida, *Lives*, 52, is a pious fiction, but I do not; see the later discussion, pp. 91–93 and the notes thereon.

22. Introduction to John of Ephesus, *Lives*, PO 17:vi.

23. These officially began in 519, soon after the accession of Justin I, though they may not have reached Mesopotamia until 520 or 521. See chapter 3.

24. On the manuscript tradition of the *Lives* and questions on their transmission, see Brooks' Introduction to *Lives*, PO 17:iii–xv. John's *Lives* survive almost intact as a collection and are independently attested in the *Chronicles* of both pseudo-Dionysius and Michael the Syrian, each of whom gives a chapter list for the work. See the discussion by Brooks in his Introduction, *Lives*, PO 17:ix–xii.

25. On hagiography in general, see Delehaye, *Legends of the Saints;* and Aigrain, *Hagiographie*. For this particular genre, introductions to the primary collections can be found, for example, in *Dictionnaire de spiritualité* 1, cols. 1624–34; and for the early collections, Quasten, *Patrology;* and Altaner, *Patrology*. Duval, *Littérature syriaque*, 113–53, is arranged by literary categories and thus places the Syriac collections in relation to the martyr cycles and lives of the saints. The sources on which I base my generalizations are Palladius, *Historia Lausiaca* (for the texts, see nn. 31 and 32 below); Theodoret of Cyrrhus, *Historia religiosa* (for the texts, see nn. 31 and 32 below); John Moschus, *Pratum spirituale*, trans. M.-J.

Rouët de Journel; John of Ephesus, *Lives of the Eastern Saints;* and Thomas of Marga, *Historia monastica, Book of Governors,* ed. and trans. E. A. Wallis Budge.

26. For the contrast between the monastic interests of these collections, and the different (often society-oriented) interests in standard vitae, cf. Patlagean, "À Byzance"; Brown, "Rise and Function"; and Hackel, *Byzantine Saint,* esp. 117–68.

27. Especially in John of Ephesus, *Lives,* 3, 5, 14, 17, 18, 19, 20, 27, 29, 32.

28. Ibid., 20, *PO* 17:278–83.

29. Ibid., 58, *PO* 19:206–27.

30. Ibid., 24, *PO* 18:521.

31. Palladius, *Lausiac History of Palladius,* ed. and trans. C. Butler; the work also has been translated and annotated in *Palladius: The Lausiac History,* trans. R. T. Meyer. For Theodoret of Cyrrhus, *Théodoret de Cyr, Histoire,* ed. and trans. P. Canivet and A. Leroy-Molinghen; there is now an English translation with notes in *Theodoret of Cyrrhus, History,* trans. R. M. Price; see also the general discussion in Canivet, *Monachisme syrien.*

32. For sixth-century Syriac manuscripts that contain selections from Palladius, *Historia Lausiaca,* see Wright, *Catalogue of the Syriac Manuscripts* 3. The Old Syriac texts have now been edited by R. Draguet, *Formes syriaques.* The seventh-century Syriac translation by Anan-Isho in fact was a collection of earlier Syriac renditions of Palladius, Jerome, and other stories and *apophthegmata;* see Anan-Isho, *Book of Paradise,* ed. and trans. E. A. Wallis Budge. On the Syriac versions of Theodoret's *Historia religiosa*—mainly select chapters—cf. *Théodoret de Cyr, Histoire,* ed. and trans. P. Canivet and A. Leroy-Molinghen, 1:60–63.

33. See Hunt, "Palladius of Helenopolis"; and Draguet, "Histoire lausiaque."

34. Cf. Turner, "Lausiac History of Palladius," esp. 345–51.

35. See Draguet, "Histoire lausiaque"; A. Guillaumont, *Les "Kephalaia Gnostica" d'Evagre le Pontique et l'histoire de l'origénisme chez les grecs et chez les syriens,* Patristica Sorbonensia 5 (Paris, 1962); and Vööbus, *History of Asceticism* 2:308–10.

36. In general, cf. Frend, *Rise of the Monophysite Movement.*

37. John Rufus, *Plérophories, témoignages et révélations,* written about 512, well illustrates the venom of Monophysite anti-Chalcedonian sentiments. Ironically, one thirteenth-century manuscript, Paris Syr. 234, contains extracts both from Theodoret's *Historia religiosa* and from John of Ephesus' *Lives!*

38. Cf. Thomas of Marga, *Historia monastica, Book of Governors* 1, ed. and trans. E. A. Wallis Budge.

39. Notably John of Tella, Severus of Antioch, and Jacob Burdʿaya. See chapter 5 below.

40. On standard hagiographical formulae see, for example, Delehaye, *Legends of the Saints;* idem, *Cinq leçons;* and Festugière, "Lieu communs."

41. For example, John of Ephesus, *Lives,* 2, *PO* 17:20 (Zʿura); 23, *PO* 17:303 (Simeon the Solitary).

42. Ibid., 4, *PO* 17:81–82 (Maro).

43. Ibid., 1, *PO* 17:10 (Habib).

44. See, for example, John Moschus, *Pratum spirituale* 15, 20, 21, 99; Procopius, *Wars* 1.7.5–11. In general, see the discussions on motifs in Delehaye, *Legends of the Saints;* Festugière, "Lieux communs"; and idem, *Moines d'orient* 1.

45. *Lives*, 6, *PO* 17:112–16 (Paul the Anchorite); 27, *PO* 18:549–50, 555–57 (Susan).

46. *Vita Antonii*, chaps. 8–10; *Vita Simeonis Stylitae, AMS* 4:523, 529, 535–38; *Vita Danielis Stylitae*, chap. 14 (where Daniel recalls the model of Antony), 15, 18.

47. See chapter 6.

48. *Lives*, 12, *PO* 17:171–86. For the understanding of hagiography in terms of the *imitatio Christi*, see Drijvers, "Byzantine Saint"; and esp. Patlagean, "À Byzance."

49. *Lives*, 52, *PO* 19:164–79 (The Two Antiochenes); 53, *PO* 19:179–85 (Priscus). See the discussion of these pp. 91–93.

50. de Gaiffier, "Intactam sponsam relinquens."

51. Especially in *Lives*, 8 (Addai), 12 (Mary), 16 (Simeon the Mountaineer), 17 (the poor stranger), and 29 (Malkha).

52. Especially in *Lives*, 5 (Simeon and Sergius), 23 (Simeon the Solitary), and 33 (Hala).

53. For example, *Lives*, 3 (John the Nazarite), 14 (Abbi), and 29 (Malkha).

54. For example, *Lives*, 29 (Malkha), 45 (Isaac), and 55 (Sosiana).

55. These and other characteristic traits are discussed at length in Vööbus, *History of Asceticism.*

56. *Lives*, 1, *PO* 17:12; 4, *PO* 17:69–71.

57. For example, ibid. 2, *PO* 17:20; 4, *PO* 17:60–65.

58. Ibid., 1, *PO* 17:14–15; 3, *PO* 17:42–43; 15, *PO* 17:220–24.

59. For example, Brown, "Rise and Function."

60. For an analysis of a specific case where John employs a motif literally that occurs thematically (and so literarily) elsewhere in hagiography, see Harvey, "Physicians and Ascetics." In this instance, the motif involves how a hagiographer writes about disease and illness when they occur in a saint, as opposed to such an occurrence in a layperson. Another clear example is John's striking treatment of women; see chap. 6.

61. *Lives*, Preface, *PO* 17:2.

62. The collection probably was written while John was living in his monastery outside Constantinople. John became leader of the Monophysites there in 566. The *Lives* appear to have been written between 566 and 568. See Brooks' comments in his Introduction to *Lives, PO* 17:vii.

63. We are still lacking sufficient work on bilingualism in the ancient world, though much ground has been broken in Peeters, *Orient et Byzance;* Brock, "Some Aspects of Greek Words"; idem, "Greek Words in the Syriac Gospels"; and idem, "Review of M. Black, *An Aramaic Approach to the Gospels and Acts," JTS* 20 (1969): 276–78.

64. See chap. 4.

65. Cf. Allen, *Evagrius Scholasticus*, 51, on John and other church historians of late antiquity who direct their writings only to those who are like-minded.

66. Cf. John of Ephesus, *Lives*, 1, *PO* 17:15–16; 5, *PO* 17:89–90; 16, *PO* 17:246; 24, *PO* 18:521; 58, *PO* 19:206–27. John alludes to the scholarly training of Mare, bishop of Amida, in *Lives*, 13, *PO* 17:190; we know more precisely that Mare was learned in Greek as well as Syriac from pseudo-Zachariah Rhetor, *HE* 7.5. For an example of what kind of library a Syriac monastery might have, see Wallis Budge's comments in Thomas of Marga, *Historia monastica, Book of Governors* 1.lix–lxiv. John of Ephesus mentions that teaching was an occupation ascetics sometimes undertook: *Lives* 5, *PO* 17:89; 16, *PO* 17:246. But the monks of Beth Abhe in the seventh century were so opposed to running a school in their monastery that the majority of them mutinied and left when such a proposition was put to them, claiming that they could not fulfill their religious vows with the distractions and noise of a school around them. See Thomas of Marga, *Historia monastica, Book of Governors* 2.7–10.

67. Vööbus, *History of the School of Nisibis;* and see the surveys in the literary histories by Wright, *Short History of Syriac Literature;* Duval, *Littérature syriaque;* and Baumstark, *Geschichte der syrischen Literatur.*

68. *Lives,* 1, *PO* 17:15–16; 5, *PO* 17:89–90; 16, *PO* 17:246. But see Segal, "Mesopotamian Communities."

69. Cf. Brock, "Aspects of Translation"; and idem, "Greek into Syriac."

70. For example, *Vita Danielis Stylitae* 3, 10, 14, 17, 19, 28; Theodoret of Cyrrhus, *Historia religiosa* 5, 6, 8, 14.

71. Cf. John of Ephesus, *Lives,* 21, *PO* 17:283–98; and cf. Peeters, *Orient et Byzance.*

72. John of Ephesus, *Lives* 21, *PO* 17: 283–98; and Cyril of Scythopolis, *Vita Euthymii,* 37 (text in *Kyrillos von Skythopolis,* ed. E. Schwartz).

73. *Vita Sabae* (Cyril of Scythopolis), 20 and 32, where Armenian monks are allowed to use their own language for only part of the worship services, and only as a gesture to prove how accommodating Saint Sabas and the Patriarch of Jerusalem (in this case, Elias) could be.

74. Cameron, "Agathias on the Sassanians."

75. For the text see pseudo-Zachariah Rhetor, *Historia ecclesiastica,* ed. and trans. E. W. Brooks; and in English translation, *Syriac Chronicle,* ed. and trans. F. J. Hamilton and E. W. Brooks. See the discussion in Allen, "Zachariah Scholasticus."

76. John of Ephesus, *Lives,* 13, *PO* 17:190.

77. Cf. Brown, *World of Late Antiquity.*

78. For a contrast beyond the scope of this study, Brown, "Eastern and Western Christendom," provides an excellent comparison of the *Lives* of John of Ephesus with those of his Latin contemporary, Gregory of Tours. The insights offered can be compared with those put forth from a different perspective by Nelson, "Symbols in Context."

*II. "Let Your Light So Shine Before Men":
The Ascetic Vision*

1. Cf. Brown, "Rise and Function."
2. John of Ephesus, *Lives*, 1, PO 17:5–18.
3. Ibid., 9.
4. Ibid., 15.
5. Ibid., 12.
6. John states that Habib "travelled in all the districts of Syria," ibid., 11.
7. "Life of Z'ura" is John's second chapter, ibid., 18–35; however, Z'ura's discipleship is also stressed in the "Life of Habib," for example, ibid., 10, 17. See also Michael the Syrian, *Chronique* 9.23.
8. *Lives*, 2, PO 17:20. For the ramifications of the master-disciple relationship, see Brown, "Saint as Exemplar"; and Flusin, *Miracle et histoire*, 188–91.
9. *Lives*, 12, PO 17:181.
10. *Lives*, 11, PO 17:158–66.
11. Ibid., 164.
12. Theodoret, *Historia religiosa* 26.2, 12; and the Syriac *Vita Simeonis Stylitae*, AMS 4:571–77.
13. *Lives*, 8, PO 17:124–35.
14. Ibid., 129.
15. Ibid., 130.
16. Cf. *Vita Antonii*, chap. 14. See Douglas, *Purity and Danger*, 94.
17. *Lives*, 7, PO 17:118–24.
18. Ibid., 120.
19. Ibid., 123. A similar incident is recounted in the "Life of Habib," *Lives*, 1, PO 17:12; but the story seems to fit more appropriately here, in the "Life of Abraham."
20. *Lives*, 31, PO 18:576–85.
21. Ibid., 577.
22. *Lives*, 30, PO 18:575–76.
23. For example, Brown, "Rise and Function"; and Patlagean, "À Byzance."
24. *Lives*, 15, PO 17:220–28.
25. Ibid., 223–24.
26. Ibid., 224.
27. Ibid., 22, PO 17:299–300.
28. Ibid., 299.
29. Compare the panic Theodoret depicts in villages that did not have a holy man or woman to look after them. One village went so far as to kidnap a neighboring town's recluse, who was shortly thereafter kidnapped back. See Theodoret, *Historia religiosa* 19.
30. *Lives*, 19, PO 17:278–83.
31. Ibid., 18, PO 17:260–65. Cf. *Syriac and Arabic Documents*, ed. and trans. A. Vööbus, 33 (canon 26).

32. Ibid., 7, *PO* 17:118–24.

33. Cf. Brown, "Saint as Exemplar," on the dissemination of a central value system.

34. *Lives*, 38, *PO* 18:641–45.

35. Ibid., 3, *PO* 17:40; see also 17:36–55.

36. Ibid., 35, *PO* 18:612; see also 18:607–23.

37. Theodoret, *Historia religiosa* 26.26.

38. *Lives*, 4, *PO* 17:56–84. Maro also appears during the Monophysite persecutions in *Lives*, 5, *PO* 17:98–101.

39. Ibid., 4, *PO* 17:83–84.

40. Ibid., 60.

41. See the discussion of this incident in chap. 1, pp. 28–29. Compare the first miracle worked by Theodore of Sykeon, for which the suppliant had to explain to Theodore how to do it; *Life of Theodore of Sykeon*, in *Three Byzantine Saints*, chap. 18, 99–100.

42. *Lives*, 4, *PO* 17.64.

43. Ibid., 64–65.

44. Ibid., 65–67.

45. Ibid., 70.

46. Ibid.

47. Cf. Douglas, *Purity and Danger*, esp. 99–113.

48. *Lives*, 5, *PO* 17:84–111.

49. Ibid., 90–91.

50. Ibid., 93. This incident is discussed in both Nöldeke, *Sketches from Eastern History*, chap. 7; and Segal, "Jews of North Mesopotamia," 60–61.

51. On the position of the Jews, see Segal, "Jews of North Mesopotamia"; Jones, *Later Roman Empire* 2:944–50; and A. Sharf, *Byzantine Jewry from Justinian to the Fourth Crusade* (London, 1971), esp. 19–41. Sharf comments on the anomalous legal status of the Jewish religion, which was explicitly permitted as a deliberate Christian policy: "Judaism had to be preserved as a living testimony to the Christian interpretation of the scriptures, to the victory of Christianity. Jews were thus sharply distinguished from both pagans and heretics—who had no rights and no civil status" (Sharf, *Byzantine Jewry*, 20). Cf. Procopius, *Anecdota* 28.16–18, on Justinian's persecution of the Jews.

52. *AMS* 4:636–38. Cf. for example, Nau, "Deux épisodes"; and Severus of Antioch, *Sixth Book of Select Letters* 1.15.

53. *Lives*, 5, *PO* 17:95–103; discussed in chap. 3, pp. 72–73.

54. For example, Palladius, *Historia Lausiaca* 3.

55. For example, Theodoret, *Historia religiosa* 1, 2.

56. *Lives*, 29, *PO* 18:563.

57. Ibid., 30, *PO* 18:575–76.

58. See, for example, Chitty, *Desert a City*; and Hunt, "Palladius of Helenopolis."

59. Peeters, *Orient et Byzance*, chap. 5, supposes that Theodoret may have

written the *Historia religiosa* partly to regain favor with Syrian ascetics, and partly as a reaction against Egyptian monasticism and thus against Cyril of Alexandria. Canivet, *Monachisme syrien*, disagrees altogether and does not believe that a political motive lies behind the work.

    60. *Lives*, 32, *PO* 18:586–92. There are two other instances of misbehaving monks: two monks deceived by a vision from Satan, who immediately seek confession and penance when they realize what has happened; and a monk who joined the Amidan monasteries without following canonical procedure but who repented and received absolution before death. See *Lives*, 15, *PO* 17:220–28; 18, *PO* 17:260–65. Both instances are more fully discussed here later.

    61. Palladius, *Historia Lausiaca* 25, 53, 58.

    62. *Lives*, 9, *PO* 17:135, see also 17:135–37.

III. Amida: The Measure of Madness

    1. See the articles "Amid," *DHGE* 2:1237–49 (Karalevsky); *RBK* 1:133–37 (Restle); and *RE* 1:1833 (Baumgartner). For an archaeological overview of the city, see Van Berchem and Strzygowski, *Amida*. On the military and trading importance of the city, see Dilleman, *Haute mésopotamie*; and especially, N. Pigulevskaja, *Villes de l'état iranien*. Segal, "Mesopotamian Communities," 109–39, is most helpful for setting Amida in a cultural and political context.

    2. Van Bercham and Strzygowski, *Amida*, 163; Vööbus, *History of Asceticism* 1:228–29, 2:37–39. Vööbus considers the background of Persian-Byzantine hostilities, as well as the constant invasions in this area, crucial to the development of asceticism in north Mesopotamia.

    3. Sozomen, *HE* 3.14; John of Ephesus, *Lives*, 58, *PO* 19:208; Vööbus, *History of Asceticism* 2:231–32. Van Bercham and Strzygowski, *Amida*, 163–65, cites the attestations of Amida's early importance as a Christian center. Evidence for the origins of asceticism at Amida is sparse and obscure, as for Mesopotamia in general; cf. Vööbus, *History of Asceticism* 2.

    4. John of Ephesus, *Lives*, 58, *PO* 19:207–9.

    5. Ibid., 209.

    6. This account follows John of Ephesus, *Lives*, 58, *PO* 19:209–12.

    7. Ibid., 212.

    8. Ibid.

    9. For example, John of Ephesus, *Lives*, 17, *PO* 17:249–50; 19–20, *PO* 17:266–83; 24, *PO* 18:521; and 35, *PO* 18:607–23. See also Vööbus, *History of Asceticism* 2:233; and Van Berchem and Strzygowski, *Amida*, 165.

    10. Pseudo-Zachariah Rhetor, *HE* 8.2; "Joshua the Stylite," *Chronicle* XXXIII–XLIX; *Chronicon Edessenum*, ed. and trans. I. Guidi, LXXVI–LXXIX; Jacob of Edessa, *Chronicon*, ed. and trans. E. W. Brooks, 314–15; *Chronicon anonymum 846*, ed. and trans. E. W. Brooks, 218–19; pseudo-Dionysius, *Incerti auctoris chronicon*, 3–4 (John of Ephesus); Michael the Syrian, *Chronique* 9.7. See, for example, Se-

verus of Antioch, *Sixth Book of Select Letters* 5.12, on the meaning of the signs appearing in the skies.

11. Hostilities between Byzantium and Persia had been increasing for some time, and an outright breach of peace was inevitable: cf. "Joshua the Stylite," *Chronicle* VII–XX; pseudo-Zachariah Rhetor, *HE* 7.3; Procopius, *Wars* 1.2–7; Michael the Syrian, *Chronique* 9.7, for ancient accounts of the background to the Persian Wars. Pigulevskaja, *Villes de l'état iranien*, 216–17, provides helpful insight on the Persians' motives, taking into account Kawad's problems of domestic social unrest owing to religious disputes, severe famine at home (as in Mesopotamia), and various financial and political considerations. "Joshua the Stylite," *Chronicle* XX, seems to acknowledge such contributing factors within Persia itself, though in so doing he expresses much hostility to the Persians. Bury, *History of the Later Roman Empire* 2:10–15, gives a summary of the events of this war. Dillemann, *Haute mésopotamie*, 313–15, discusses some specific textual problems about the siege of 502–503.

12. "Joshua the Stylite," *Chronicle* L, LVIII; pseudo-Zachariah Rhetor, *HE* 7.3–4; Procopius, *Wars* 1.7; pseudo-Dionysius, *Incerti auctoris chronicon*, 5 (John of Ephesus); Michael the Syrian, *Chronique* 9.8; *Chronicon anonymum 1234* LI, ed. and trans. J.-B. Chabot, CSCO 81/36 and 109/56.

13. This capture of the city did not lose its importance as a historical landmark in Syrian tradition; in addition to the sources mentioned, see also *Chronicon Edessenum* LXXX; Jacob of Edessa, *Chronicon*, 315; *Chronicon anonymum 819*, ed. A. Barsaum, 7; *Chronicon anonymum 846*, 219; *Narrationes variae*, ed. and trans. E. W. Brooks, XVII and XVIII.

14. Pseudo-Zachariah Rhetor, *HE* 7.4; Procopius, *Wars* 1.7.23; Michael the Syrian, *Chronique* 9.7; *Chronicon anonymum 1234* LI.

15. "Joshua the Stylite," *Chronicle* LIII; pseudo-Dionysius, *Incerti auctoris chronicon*, 5 (John of Ephesus).

16. John of Ephesus, *Lives*, 58, *PO* 19:217–19.

17. Frend, *Rise of the Monophysite Movement*, 185, includes other incidents to support this speculation, but for Amida, at any rate, it seems unlikely. The Monophysite position in Byzantium was hardly so bleak at this time; in Persia, by contrast, the outbreak of war with the Romans in 502 sparked off bitter Monophysite persecution, and the refugees flocking into Roman territory made their presence felt. See Charanis, *Church and State*, 29–30; and Segal, "Mesopotamian Communities," 113.

18. "Joshua the Stylite," *Chronicle* LIII (trans. Wright, 42).

19. Ibid., LVI, LXVI–LXIX, LXXI–LXXXI (on the Amidan women, see LXXVI–LXXVII); pseudo-Zachariah, *HE* 6.4; Procopius, *Wars* 1.9; Michael the Syrian, *Chronique* 9.8; *Narrationes variae* XVIII.

20. Procopius, *Wars* 1.7.33–35.

21. A helpful summary of these wars under Justin I and Justinian is found in Bury, *History of the Later Roman Empire* 2:75–123. See also Downey, "Persian Campaign." Being garrisoned, even by one's own protectors, proved an agoniz-

ing experience for the townspeople involved; see for example, "Joshua the Sty-lite," *Chronicle* LIV, LXX, LXXVII, LXXXII, XCVI. For the Persian invasions of Mesopotamia, see also pseudo-Dionysius, *Incerti auctoris chronicon*, 69, 90 (John of Ephesus); and Jacob of Edessa, *Chronicon*, 320. Syrian bitterness towards Persia left its influence; see Cameron, "Agathias on the Sassanians," 69–70, 113–14.

22. Cf. Vasiliev, *Justin the First*, 313–17; and Stein, *Histoire du bas-empire* 2:97–98, 105, 267–68, and 293. Although Vasiliev, and Brooks, in John of Ephesus, *Lives*, PO 17:19, n. 2, date the raids as starting in 515 (cf. Stein, *Histoire*, 2:105), the problem was obviously already present in 502; see n. 24 below. Cf. also Procopius, *Anecdota* 18.22–23, 30; 23.6–10.

23. For example, John of Ephesus, *Lives*, 2, PO 17:19–20; 4, PO 17:78–83; 16, PO 17:245.

24. Procopius, *Wars* 1.7.8, states that during the Amidan siege of 502–503 the Hephthalitae were overrunning the Mesopotamian countryside. Khosroes also used Hunnic mercenaries, cf. Procopius, *Wars* 2.26.

25. For example, pseudo-Zachariah Rhetor, *HE* 8.5, 9.14; *Chronicon Edessenum* CIII (both on the invasion of 531/2).

26. John of Nikiu, *Chronicle* 90.1.

27. Monophysite sources distinctly mark Justin's accession as the beginning of their woes; cf. pseudo-Zachariah Rhetor, *HE* 8; pseudo-Dionysius, *Incerti auctoris chronicon*, 15–16 (John of Ephesus); John of Nikiu, *Chronicle* 90; Jacob of Edessa, *Chronicon*, 317; *Chronicon anonymum 846*, 222; Michael the Syrian, *Chronique* 9.12; and *Chronicon anonymum 1234*, 53. Compare, for example, Evagrius, *HE* 4.1, where Justin's accession passes without remarks on religious policy; Evagrius, *HE* 4.9, comments on these matters instead when recounting the crowning of Justinian. For the background to and significance of Justin's change in government policy regarding the Chalcedonian faith, see esp. Charanis, *Church and State*; Vasiliev, *Justin the First*; and Wigram, *Separation of the Monophysites*, 64–65.

28. On the persecutions of the Monophysites, see in general Vasiliev, *Justin the First*; Frend, *Rise of the Monophysite Movement*; Wigram, *Separation of the Monophysites*; and Honigmann, *Évêques et évêchés monophysites*.

29. Vasiliev, *Justin the First*, 235–36. See pseudo-Dionysius, *Incerti auctoris chronicon*, 19, 21–24, 26; and Michael the Syrian, *Chronique* 9.14.

30. This assumption of duties probably occurred in 521; Vasiliev, *Justin the First*, 230; Honigmann, *Évêques et évêchés monophysites*, 101.

31. Evagrius, a Chalcedonian, claims that Paul resigned voluntarily; *HE* 4.4. On Euphrasius' accession and subsequent death, see Vasiliev, *Justin the First*, 239–40; and pseudo-Zachariah Rhetor, *HE* 8.1. But Honigmann, *Évêques et évêchés monophysites*, 148, claims that the oriental monks were first driven out by Euphrasius, which contradicts the account in Michael the Syrian, *Chronique* 9.14, based on part 2 of John of Ephesus' *HE*, wherein Paul "the Jew" is blamed.

32. Pseudo-Dionysius, *Incerti auctoris chronicon*, 70 (John of Ephesus); Michael the Syrian, *Chronique* 9.26 (Chabot, II, 220–21).

33. The best biography of Ephrem is in Lebon, "Éphrem d'Amid." See also

Vasiliev, *Justin the First*, 122–24. Both pseudo-Zachariah Rhetor, *HE* 7.4; and John of Nikiu, *Chronicle* 90.23, praise Ephrem as a civil administrator.

34. For the implications of this, see esp. Cameron, "Images of Authority," 28–31; Boojamra, "Christian *Philanthropia*"; Wigram, *Separation of the Monophysites*, 100; and Segal, "Mesopotamian Communities," 114–15.

35. For a shady incident, see pseudo-Zachariah Rhetor, *HE* 9.15, 9.19; and Michael the Syrian, *Chronique* 9.23.

36. See esp. Gray, *The Defense of Chalcedon*, 141–54. Cf. also Lebon, "Éphrem d'Amid," 203–14; Moeller, "Chalcédonisme et le néo-chalcédonisme," 680–85; and Sellers, *Council of Chalcedon*, 313–15, 320–23, 332–43.

37. For example, John Moschus, *Pratum spirituale* 36, 37; *Vita Sabae* (Cyril of Scythopolis), 85; Evagrius, *HE* 4.25.

38. Cf. pseudo-Zachariah Rhetor, *HE* 10.5; and Michael the Syrian, *Chronique* 9.24. Evagrius, *HE* 4.6, considers Ephrem's deeds on behalf of Antioch before his consecration as a manifestation of divine providence. See Downey, "Ephraemius," for other episodes of Ephrem's civil activity while patriarch.

39. Monophysite sources unanimously condemn Ephrem, and their indignation at his use of the army was harshly expressed. See, for example, pseudo-Zachariah Rhetor, *HE* 10.1; pseudo-Dionysius, *Incerti auctoris chronicon*, 38–44 (John of Ephesus); Michael the Syrian, *Chronique* 9.13–23. Michael is particularly scathing about the army in *Chronique* 9.24 (Chabot II, 206); he claims that Ephrem gave the appearance of being a learned sage but was in reality a pagan! *Chronique* 9.16 (Chabot II, 181). Honigmann, *Évêques et évêchés monophysites*, 148–49, assesses Ephrem's activities as patriarch.

40. Michael the Syrian, *Chronique* 9.26 (Chabot II, 223).

41. The primary account is found in pseudo-Dionysius, *Incerti auctoris chronicon*, 32–44; Michael the Syrian, *Chronique* 9.13–23, 26, draws almost all his material from this same source, which is clearly John of Ephesus' *HE*, pt. II. See also Jacob of Edessa, *Chronicon*, 319–20; and *Chronicon anonymum 846*, 225–27.

42. Michael the Syrian, *Chronique* 9.26 (Chabot II, 223–4). Pseudo-Dionysius, *Incerti auctoris chronicon*, 37 (John of Ephesus), also accuses Abraham of adhering to the Chalcedonian faith not willingly but obsequiously.

43. John of Ephesus, *Lives*, 18, *PO* 17:261, mentions a local plague slightly earlier than the bubonic outbreak of 542. *Lives*, 53, *PO* 19:185; pseudo-Dionysius, *Incerti auctoris chronicon*, 79–88, 112 (John of Ephesus); pseudo-Zachariah Rhetor, *HE* 10.9–14; Jacob of Edessa, *Chronicon*, 320–21; and Michael the Syrian, *Chronique* 9.32, deal with the Great Plague and continual famine in Mesopotamia and Amida. See Biraben and LeGoff, "Peste dans le haute moyen age"; and esp. Allen, "'Justinianic' Plague." Allen observes that famine was a chronic sixth-century problem, both creating conditions ripe for the outbreak of plague and becoming also a result of its occurrence.

44. The major accounts of the plague of madness are found in pseudo-Dionysius, *Incerti auctoris chronicon*, 15–16; Michael the Syrian, *Chronique* 9.32; and *Chronicon anonymum 1234*, LXII. The version found in pseudo-Dionysius is

clearly the original for all other accounts and is included in the collection of fragments attributed to John of Ephesus, *HE*, pt. 2, in John of Ephesus, "Analyse de
la seconde partie," ed. F. Nau, 468–69. There is no reason not to attribute this
passage to John; but even if the writer of pseudo-Dionysius had drawn on other
material at this point, the account would probably still have come from a contemporary given the nature of sources used by this historian. (I am indebted to
L. Michael Whitby for this observation.)

45. *Spurious Life of James* (Jacob Burdᶜaya), *PO* 19: 259–62; *Narrationes variae* XVII.

46. Besides the calamities mentioned, comets were seen in the Byzantine
East in the years 500, 538, 543/4, 556, 565, and 599; earthquakes occurred in the
same area in 499, 503, 515, 525, 526, 528, 529, 530, 533, 536, 538/9, 539, 541, 542,
543, 546, 551, 554, 557, 558, 558/9, 561, 567, 568, 580/1, 583, 584/5, 588, and 601.
See Grumel, *Chronologie*, 457–81, on natural disasters. See Patlagean, *Pauvreté
économique*, 74–92; and Vasiliev, *Justin the First*, 344–53, 360–62, 382–83, on the
cumulative economic effect of the natural calamities.

47. For a discussion of such "psychic epidemics"—including dance fren-
zies, witch hunts, and revival movements—see, above all, Rosen, *Madness in Society*, 118, 192–225. Cf. also J. J. Lhermitte, *True and False Possession*, trans. P. J.
Hepburne-Scott (New York, 1963; orig. French, 1956); Zax and Cowen, *Abnormal
Psychology*, 25–58; and cf. Trethowan, "Exorcism," on physical and mental
symptoms in cases of severe hysteria.

Also relevant are the comparable situations seen in Cohn, *Pursuit of the Millenium*; for the obvious parallels in Europe during the fourteenth century, see
Ziegler, *Black Death*. Professor A. A. M. Bryer has pointed out to me that Amida
would again suffer a similar constellation of tragedy in the fourteenth to mid-
fifteenth centuries but without again evidencing such a major social breakdown;
see Sanjian, *Colophons of Armenian Manuscripts*. In this instance, the influence of
Islamic fatalism—through which plague was seen as a martyrdom and a mercy
for the faithful Muslim—may have contained public reaction, as it did in general
during the Black Death in the Muslim domain; see Dols, *Black Death*, 236–54
and, for a sensitive comparison with Western reactions, 281–302.

48. Rosen, *Madness in Society*, 21–136; J. S. Neaman, *Suggestion of the Devil:
The Origins of Madness* (New York, 1975). Animal-like behavior, general disorien-
tation, and excessive violence are among the primary symptoms. Rosen, 192–
225, also discusses the occurrence of animal-like behavior during certain psychic
epidemics, especially in revival movements. Cf. John of Ephesus, *Lives*, 1, *PO*
17:14–15; and pseudo-Zachariah Rhetor, *HE* 7.14, for madness displayed through
similar symptoms. For a sense of how this pattern of madness fits with the
changes in late antique understandings of insanity, see Festugière, "Épidémies
«hippocratiques»."

49. See nn. 43 and 46 above on natural disasters in the Syrian Orient; and, for
example, "Joshua the Stylite," *Chronicle*; Procopius, *Wars* 1–2; pseudo-Dionysius,
Incerti auctoris chronicon, 3–118; pseudo-Zachariah Rhetor, HE 7–12; John of

Nikiu, *Chronicle* 90.23–32; Michael the Syrian, *Chronique* 9; *Chronicon anonymum 1234*, LIII.

50. I have discussed Amida's plague of madness with psychiatrist Sir William Trethowan and with psychologist Dr. James B. Ashbrook and have gratefully drawn upon their professional expertise in the present discussion. Both see no reason to doubt the genuine occurrence of this outbreak, especially in the cumulative circumstances of the time.

The events of the sixth century may offer some solutions as to why Amida, present-day Diyar Bekir, exhibits almost no archaeological remains from pre-Islamic times apart from its walls and the cathedral shell. See Van Berchem and Strzygowski, *Amida.* Destruction of property, such as the Persian Wars wrought, could hardly have been repaired substantially in light of subsequent events and circumstances.

51. Consider the regular mention in later Syriac chronicles of the events of the Persian conquest of Amida in 503, and the plague of madness in 560. These sources are listed in the notes above, but the point is especially made by the two late fragments *Narrationes variae* XVII and XVIII.

52. For example, Brown, "Rise and Function"; Vööbus, *History of Asceticism* 2; Brock, "Early Syrian Asceticism."

53. Patlagean, "À Byzance"; Brown, "Eastern and Western Christendom."

54. Theodoret, *Historia religiosa* 26. Cf., for example, John of Ephesus, *Lives*, 4, *PO* 17:56–84. Cf. Vööbus, *History of Asceticism* 2:325; and Brock, "Early Syrian Asceticism," 14.

55. See John of Ephesus, *Lives*, 52, *PO* 19:164–79, and 53, *PO* 19:179–85.

56. Procopius, *Wars* 1.9.18. "Joshua the Stylite" tells how the Edessenes, preparing for a Persian siege against them, pulled down all the monasteries and inns in the area just outside the city walls—presumably to avoid such atrocities, but perhaps also to avoid giving the besiegers a base for men and equipment close to the walls; "Joshua the Stylite," *Chronicle* 59.

57. John of Ephesus, *Lives*, 4, *PO* 17:78–83.

58. Procopius, *Wars* 1.7.5–11.

59. John of Ephesus, *Lives*, 2, *PO* 17:19–20. The paralysis in midair of an attacking enemy is a common literary *topos;* compare, for example, John Moschus, *Pratum spirituale* 15, 70, 75.

60. John of Ephesus, *Lives*, 16, *PO* 17:245.

61. John of Ephesus, *Lives*, 6, *PO* 17:111–18. The appearance of the demons first in the guise of panicked villagers fleeing from the raiders is interesting for its similarity to the incident sparking off Amida's plague of madness.

62. It is worth noting that in the first half of the fifth century, a monk named Dada from the region of Amida was sent by the people of the city to Constantinople; his purpose was to plead for tax relief, as Amida had suffered harshly from war and famine. Dada seems to have been a prolific writer, but nothing by him survives for us. See Wright, *Short History of Syriac Literature*, 54–55; Duval, *Littérature syriaque*, 339.

63. John of Ephesus, *Lives*, 35, PO 18:608. For the account of the Amidan monasteries, see *Lives*, PO 18:607–23; and 58, PO 19:207–27; pseudo-Dionysius, *Incerti auctoris chronicon*, 39–44; and Michael the Syrian, *Chronique* 9.17–19. I have drawn from these sources for the present summary; the brief translations are from John's thirty-fifth "Life."

64. John of Ephesus, *Lives*, 35, PO 18:608.

65. Under Paul "the Jew," the expulsion was perhaps as late as 521; Mesopotamia was the last place in which the persecutions were undertaken. There may well have been concern among civil and ecclesiastical officials about entering Mesopotamia, an area more fully committed to the Monophysite faith than elsewhere in the East, apart from Egypt, where the economic factor of the empire's need for grain mattered more than imperial religious policies. See Vasiliev, *Justin the First*, 229; and Wigram, *Separation of the Monophysites*, 95.

66. The village of Ḥzyn in Ṭysfʾ; the location is unknown.

67. See also pseudo-Zachariah Rhetor, *HE* 8.5; and Michael the Syrian, *Chronique* 9.15.

68. John of Ephesus, *Lives*, 35, PO 13:620.

69. This was part of the campaign involved in Ephrem's "descent to the east." Cf. John of Ephesus, *Lives*, 58, PO 19:224; pseudo-Zachariah Rhetor, *HE* 1.1; pseudo-Dionysius, *Incerti auctoris chronicon*, 38–44; Michael the Syrian, *Chronique* 9.14. Abraham bar Kaili was also commanding soldiers during this expulsion.

70. John of Ephesus, *Lives*, 35, PO 18:620; but pseudo-Dionysius, *Incerti auctoris chronicon*, 40, says there were "a thousand men or more," whereas John, *Lives*, 14, PO 17:214, states that the number during the first persecution was 750.

71. John of Ephesus, *Lives*, 35, PO 18:621.

72. Ibid., 622–23. Cf. the related situation in Armenia, similar in impact and also encouraged by Ephrem: idem, *Lives*, 21, PO 17:293–94.

73. For example, Wigram, *Separation of the Monophysites*, 67–68; Frend, *Rise of the Monophysite Movement*, 79, 141–44; idem, "Popular Religion"; Brown, "Rise and Function"; and idem, "Dark Age Crisis."

74. For example, Frend, *Rise of the Monophysite Movement*, 260–61. The decision to ordain Monophysite bishops—a step eventually leading to the creation of a separate Monophysite ecclesiastical hierarchy—was made largely because popular fears over communion at Chalcedonian hands had become so urgent and widespread. It was not a move engineered by ambitious or contentious Monophysite leaders.

75. Cf. Wigram, *Separation of the Monophysites*, 68.

76. Pseudo-Zachariah Rhetor, *HE* 8.5 (*Syriac Chronicle*, trans. F. J. Hamilton and E. W. Brooks, 211–12). Cf. Michael the Syrian, *Chronique* 9.14.

77. John of Ephesus, *Lives*, 35, PO 18:607–23.

78. Ibid., 618.

79. Ibid., 58, PO 19:221–17.

80. Ibid., 225–26.

81. Ibid., 20, *PO* 17:278–83.

82. Ibid., 24, *PO* 18:521.

83. For example, ibid. 14 and 18, *PO* 17:213–20, 260–65; 29, *PO* 18:562–74.

84. Ibid., 14, *PO* 17:213–20 (Abbi); 17, *PO* 17:248–59 (the poor stranger); 19, *PO* 17:266–80 (Zacharias). Cf. also 20, *PO* 17:281–83; 28, *PO* 18:559–62; 51, *PO* 19:159–60.

85. Ibid., 18, *PO* 17:260–65.

86. Ibid., 260. On the ruling against leaving a monastery without release, see *Syriac and Arabic Documents*, ed. and trans. A. Vööbus, 33 (canon 26).

87. John of Ephesus, *Lives*, 33, *PO* 18:592–601; 3, *PO* 17:42–44; 34, *PO* 18:601–6.

88. Ibid., 33, *PO* 18:599.

89. Ibid., 35, *PO* 18:614–17.

90. Pseudo-Dionysius, *Incerti auctoris chronicon*, 39–40 (John of Ephesus). See also Michael the Syrian, *Chronique* 9.19. Cf. the parallel situation in John of Ephesus, *Lives*, 21, *PO* 17:293–97.

91. Pseudo-Dionysius, *Incerti auctoris chronicon*, 40–44 (John of Ephesus); Michael the Syrian, *Chronique* 9.19.

92. John of Ephesus, *Lives*, 23, *PO* 17:300–304.

93. Ibid., 304.

94. Ibid., 5, *PO* 17:98 (my trans.).

95. Ibid., 96–99.

96. Ibid., 96–101.

97. Ibid., 101–3 (my trans.).

98. Ibid., 103–11.

99. Ibid., 12, *PO* 17:176–78. Cf. pseudo-Dionysius, *Incerti auctoris chronicon*, 43–44 (John of Ephesus), for another account of secret aid by villagers when the Amidans were driven out of the monastery of the Poplars by Ephrem's troops, during the second persecution.

100. John of Ephesus, *Lives*, 12, *PO* 17:171–86. On the significance of Euphemia's work, see chap. 6.

101. John of Ephesus, *Lives*, 12, *PO* 17:184 (my trans.).

IV. Purpose and Places

1. John of Ephesus, *Lives*, 48, *PO* 18:685; pseudo-Zachariah Rhetor, *HE* 8.5. It is probably to the Egyptian desert as a gathering place that this famous passage of pseudo-Zachariah refers.

2. Egypt's reputation for ascetic excellence was a serious factor for the Monophysite monks who came from elsewhere in the East, including Mesopotamia. For the nature of Egypt's spiritual authority in this realm, see Rousseau, "Spiritual Authority"; idem, "Blood-relationships."

3. John of Ephesus, *Lives*, 27, *PO* 18:554. For an impression, from the Egyp-

tian viewpoint, of how Egypt itself was affected by the persecutions, see esp. Hardy, *Christian Egypt*; see also Evelyn-White, *Monasteries of the Wâdi 'N Natrûn*, 219–40.

4. John of Ephesus, *Lives*, 27, *PO* 18:541–58. Arzanene was visited by Simeon the Persian Debater while on his missionary travels, *Lives*, 10, *PO* 17:145; and its clergy were ordained during the persecutions by John of Tella, *Lives*, 24, *PO* 18:519.

5. In the "Life of Susan," ibid., *PO* 18:547–48, John says the spot was about two miles from Mendis; and elsewhere, about twelve miles distant from the monastery of Mar Menas, *PO* 17:209. Mendis itself, he claims, was twenty-four miles above Alexandria, *Lives*, 13, *PO* 17:190 (see also Brooks' footnote). Mar Menas was a celebrated monastery and its reputation was no doubt attractive to the newcomers; proximity may have seemed desirable. Cf. Hardy, *Christian Egypt*, 125–26 ("The shrine of St. Menas had become the Lourdes of the ancient world"); and see "Karm Abu Mena," *RBK*, 1116–58 (M. Krause).

6. John of Ephesus, *Lives*, 27, *PO* 18:548.

7. Ibid., 550 (my trans.).

8. Ibid., 554–56. Susan's activities and John's reactions to them are discussed in chap. 6.

9. Cf. Severus of Antioch, "Sévère d'Antioche en Égypte," ed. and trans. W. E. Crum.

10. *Lives*, 48, *PO* 18:684–90.

11. Ibid., 685. Here John carelessly gives the impression that Severus was received by the patriarch Theodosius, who was not consecrated to the see until 535 (and then somewhat violently: see pseudo-Zachariah Rhetor, *HE* 9.14; Michael the Syrian, *Chronique* 9.12). Theodosius was banished in 536 to Thrace and then to Constantinople, where he remained, guiding the Monophysites until his death in 566.

12. John of Ephesus, *Lives*, 48, *PO* 18:685.

13. See esp. *Vita Severi* (John of Beith-Aphthonia); and for the sense of how this aura grew with Severus' legend, see *Vita Severi* (Athanasius Scriptor), *Conflict of Severus*, ed. and trans. E. J. Goodspeed and W. E. Crum.

14. John is referring here (*Lives*, 48, *PO* 18:685) in particular to the doctrinal dispute between Severus and Julian of Halicarnassus. See esp. pseudo-Zachariah Rhetor, *HE* 9.9–13; and Michael the Syrian, *Chronique* 9.27, 30. The argument centered on Julian's belief that the body of Christ was incorruptible; an excellent summary is in Casey, "Julian of Halicarnassus." Cf. Hardy, *Christian Egypt*, 128–32.

15. For example, Severus of Antioch, *Sixth Book of Select Letters* 1.49, 2.3.

16. Pseudo-Zachariah Rhetor, *HE* 9.13. In the letters pseudo-Zachariah Rhetor cites here, Severus describes himself contending against the Chalcedonians from Egypt, "I [am] a man who changes about from one place to another and have no convenient time for other things that are required" (*HE* 9.11 [*Syriac Chronicle*, ed. and trans. F. J. Hamilton and E. W. Brooks, 235]). See also Severus of Antioch, *Sixth Book of Select Letters* 1.53.

17. *Lives*, 21, *PO* 17:283–98. See also 54, *PO* 19:186; 55, *PO* 19:192; 56, *PO* 19:197–99.

18. John of Ephesus, *HE, Fragmenta* 3.7–8.

19. *Lives*, 13, *PO* 17:187–213.

20. On Amida's bishops at this time, see Honigmann, *Évêques et évêchés monophysites*, 100–101; also, "Joshua the Stylite," *Chronicle* LXXXIII; and pseudo-Zachariah Rhetor, *HE* 8.5. For Abraham bar Kaili, apparently consecrated by Paul "the Jew" of Antioch, see chap. 3.

21. John of Ephesus, *Lives*, 13, *PO* 17:188.

22. Ibid., 188–89.

23. Ibid., 189–90. Cf. the description of Mare's adventures in pseudo-Zachariah Rhetor, *HE* 8.5.

24. John of Ephesus, *Lives*, 13, *PO* 17:190.

25. John's account of the lives of Mary and Euphemia reflects the same intent, *Lives*, 12, *PO* 17:166–86. See the discussion of their story in chap. 6.

26. *Lives*, 13, *PO* 17:192.

27. John of Ephesus, ibid., 25, *PO* 18:528, says of this campaign: "severe fighting and much slaughter took place in Alexandria, as is common in that great city." See also, for example, ibid., 37, *PO* 18:629–30; Procopius, *Anecdota* 26.35–44; John of Nikiu, *Chronicle* 90.81–89, 92.5–7; Michael the Syrian, *Chronique* 9.21, 25.

28. See the *Life of John the Almsgiver*, in *Three Byzantine Saints*, trans. E. A. Dawes and N. Baynes, 195–270; Monks, "Church of Alexandria"; Hardy, *Christian Egypt*, 139–41, 154–61.

29. Michael the Syrian, *Chronique* 9.25. Cf. John of Ephesus' more general description of the persecutions throughout the East, in very similar language; *Lives*, 24, *PO* 18:524–25.

30. *Lives*, 48, *PO* 18:687. See also, for example, Michael the Syrian, *Chronique* 9.27. Cf. Severus of Antioch, "Sévère d'Antioche en Égypte," ed. and trans. W. E. Crum.

31. See Evagrius, *HE* 4.9, for the pro-Chalcedonian view of Alexandria and Constantinople as the two main centers of religious dissent.

32. A point that particularly rankled Procopius: see the *Anecdota*. On Theodora, see Browning, *Justinian and Theodora*; Bury, *History of the Later Roman Empire* 2:27–35; and Diehl, *Théodora*.

33. Procopius, *Anecdota* 10.14–15.

34. Ibid. (*Opera*, ed. and trans. H. B. Dewing, 7:125).

35. Evagrius, *HE* 4.10. Cf. Allen, *Evagrius Scholasticus*, chap. 8, on Evagrius' treatment of Justin I and Justinian. Allen here points out that Evagrius adds credibility to Procopius' *Anecdota*, which thus cannot be dismissed as personal ranting.

36. Evagrius, *HE*, 4.10.

37. On Theodora's good deeds toward the Monophysites, see, for example, Severus of Antioch, *Sixth Book of Select Letters* 1.63; John of Ephesus, *Lives*; idem, *HE, Fragmenta* 3.2–5; pseudo-Zachariah Rhetor, *HE* 9.14; John of Nikiu, *Chron-*

icle 90.87–88; Jacob of Edessa, *Chronicon,* 321; *Chronicon anonymum 819,* 10; *Chronicon anonymum 1234,* LIV–LV; Michael the Syrian, *Chronique* 9.15, 20, 21.

38. *Chronicon anonymum 1234,* LV; Michael the Syrian, *Chronique* 9.20. This tradition still appeals to the Syrian Orthodox; it is retold in the play "Theodora," written in Arabic (1956) by Mor Faulos Behram, Metropolitan of Baghdad, and translated into Syriac (1977) by Mor Iuhannon Philoxenos Dolobani, the late Metropolitan of Mardin.

39. Browning, *Justinian and Theodora,* 40.

40. For example, Procopius, *Anecdota* 17.27; Evagrius, *HE* 4.10–11. It is notable, for example, that the pro-Chalcedonian *Melkite Chronicle* of the seventh century—in its reports on ecclesiastical and theological events involving imperial circles—does not once mention the energetic empress. See "Chronique melkite," ed. and trans. A. de Halleux, 13–18. This may be a simple case of male chauvinism, of course; pseudo-Zachariah Rhetor often omits mention of Theodora in places where her activity was decisive, for example, *HE* 8.5, 9.15 (cf. 9.19).

41. Pseudo-Zachariah Rhetor, *HE* 8.5, 9.1; John of Nikiu, *Chronicle* 90.49–59; Michael the Syrian, *Chronique* 9.34. It is interesting that John of Nikiu seems to transfer the respective characteristics of the imperial couple from one to the other. At *Chronicle* 93.1–3, he lists those figures who had most greatly adorned Rome: Romulus, Numa, Caesar, Augustus, "and subsequently came the empress Theodora, the consort of the emperor Justinian"!

42. The same respect is shown in his *Ecclesiastical History* for the emperor Justin II. See Cameron, "Early Byzantine *Kaiserkritik.*"

43. For Theodora's correspondence with the Persian queen, *Lives,* 10, *PO* 17:157 (cf. Procopius, *Anecdota* 2.32–37); the hospitals she founded, *Lives,* 51, *PO* 19:161–62; and her prostitution, *Lives,* 13, *PO* 17:189. John's statement that Theodora "came from the brothel" (*porne* is his word) substantiates the leering charges of Procopius with none of the latter's scorn; see Procopius, *Anecdota* 9.1–30.

44. For example, *Lives,* 57, *PO* 19:200–206.

45. *Lives,* 37, *PO* 18:680. See also John's *HE, Fragmenta* 3.6, where John says the emperor was anxious to fulfill the will of his wife even after her death. Michael the Syrian, *Chronique* 9.29, speaks of Justinian's grief at Theodora's death, with the implication that this led him to treat the patriarchs Anthimus and Theodosius with leniency.

46. *Lives,* 47, *PO* 18:681; pseudo-Dionysius, *Incerti auctoris chronicon* 77–78, 125 (John of Ephesus); and Michael the Syrian, *Chronique* 9.25, 33. John also converted the Manicheans in Constantinople at Justinian's request; pseudo-Dionysius, *Incerti auctoris chronicon,* 75–76 (John of Ephesus); and Michael the Syrian, *Chronique* 9.25.

47. Michael the Syrian, *Chronique* 9.25. It may be that the new converts could not appreciate the theological arguments waged over the Council of Chalcedon; but the missions to Nubia (not led by John of Ephesus) produced a self-consciously Monophysite following. See Frend, *Rise of the Monophysite Movement,* 297–303; Hardy, *Christian Egypt,* 141–43.

48. A good example is in John's *HE, Fragmenta* 3.4, where John went so far as to offend the emperor but does not appear to have suffered for his frankness (here he seems to have acted, at least in part, through intermediaries).

49. Cf. Cameron, "Early Religious Policies."

50. Gray, *Defense of Chalcedon*, esp. 154–64; Wigram, *Separation of the Monophysites*, chap. 8. Justinian seems to have shown high respect for certain of his theological opponents; for example, John of Ephesus, *HE, Fragmenta* 3.8. His aphthartodocetic views were similar to those of Julian of Halicarnassus; see n. 14 above.

51. Pseudo-Zachariah Rhetor, *HE* 8.5. For Severus' cynicism, John of Ephesus, *HE, Fragmenta* 3.3. Darling, "Patriarchate of Severus," sees this attitude of Severus increasing over time, beginning as early as his years in Antioch.

52. See the documents in Brock, "Orthodox-Oriental Orthodox Conversations"; and "Conversations with the Syrian Orthodox," ed. and trans. S. P. Brock. Cf. pseudo-Zachariah Rhetor, *HE* 9.15; and Michael the Syrian, *Chronique* 9.22.

53. Brock, "Orthodox-Oriental Orthodox Conversations," 226.

54. Ibid., 225; pseudo-Zachariah Rhetor, *HE* 9.15.

55. Pseudo-Zachariah Rhetor, *HE* 9.16; see also Evagrius, *HE* 4.11.

56. John of Ephesus, *HE, Fragmenta* 3.3; idem, *Lives,* 48, *PO* 18:687; and Severus of Antioch, *Sixth Book of Select Letters* 4:7.

57. John of Ephesus, *HE, Fragmenta* 3.3, 8; pseudo-Zachariah Rhetor, *HE* 9.19; Evagrius, *HE* 4.11; "Chronique melkite," 17–18; *Chronicon anonymum 846,* 223; Michael the Syrian, *Chronique* 9.22.

58. John of Ephesus, *HE, Fragmenta* 3.4; Michael the Syrian, *Chronique* 9.30.

59. For example, John of Ephesus, *HE, Fragmenta* 3.1; pseudo-Zachariah Rhetor, *HE* 12.6; Evagrius, *HE* 4.36; "Chronique melkite," 19–23; Michael the Syrian, *Chronique* 9.30. But the complexity of the picture is best gained in the overviews given by Frend, *Rise of the Monophysite Movement;* and Wigram, *Separation of the Monophysites.*

60. Best encapsulated in his *HE, Fragmenta* 3.2–8. The gradual wear does not seem to have crushed John's own spirit until matters internal to the Monophysites broke down under Justin II and Tiberius; see his *HE,* pt. III.

61. The significance of Constantine's example did not escape his contemporaries as can be seen in the works of Eusebius of Caesarea and, more generally, Lietzmann, *History of the Early Church,* vols. 3 and 4.

62. Here, too, the populace was highly influenced by ascetics, in this case by the "Sleepless" monks. The Trishagion riots were a case in point. Evagrius, *HE* 3.44; pseudo-Dionysius, *Incerti auctoris chronicon,* 6–7 (John of Ephesus); John of Nikiu, *Chronicle* 9.9.

63. For a general sense of how Constantinople "worked," see Jones, *Later Roman Empire* 2:687–709; for its changing circumstances in the sixth century, see Cameron, "Corippus' Poem"; and idem, "Theotokos."

64. John of Ephesus, *Lives,* 2, *PO* 17:18–35. See chap. 2, for a description of Z'ura's career in Mesopotamia.

65. Frend, *Rise of the Monophysite Movement*, 270, 272. John gives no indication of the date.

66. For mention of Zʿura, see Severus of Antioch, *Sixth Book of Select Letters* 3.2; "Chronique melkite," 18; Michael the Syrian, *Chronique* 9.23; Bar Hebraeus, *Chronicon ecclesiasticum* 1:206–12. Further references are noted by Frend, *Rise of the Monophysite Movement*, 272; the stylite apparently baptized Theodora, a considerable honor for both parties. Michael's account, as usual, primarily follows John's; so, too, does that of Bar Hebraeus.

67. *Lives*, 2, PO 17:22.

68. Cf. Severus of Antioch, *Sixth Book of Select Letters* 11.1, where the patriarch begs a would-be solitary not to follow his own selfish desire for withdrawal but instead to face the religious crisis with action because the urgency of the times is so great.

69. *Vita Danielis Stylitae*, chaps. 72–85.

70. *Lives*, 2, PO 17:24–25.

71. Inaccuracy of this kind is characteristic of John's historical method; he tended to make his points by whatever means of emphasis seemed necessary. Procopius mentions two, or possibly three, severe illnesses contracted by Justinian: *Buildings* 1.6.5–8, 1.7.6–16; idem, *Wars* 2.23.20, which records the emperor's bout of bubonic plague. The first of these (*Buildings* 1.6.5–8) in particular bears a resemblance to John's account involving Zʿura, since Procopius claims that Justinian was healed by the intervention of Saints Cosmas and Damian after doctors proved unable to treat his near-fatal illness, and that this became the occasion for a shrine dedicated to the saints by the emperor.

This passage and its circumstances, rather than the vague story of an "eastern monk" and a gruesome apparition in Procopius, *Anecdota* 12.23–26, as Brooks suggests (*PO* 17:24 n.), seem an appropriate basis for John's story of Zʿura—unless the passage refers to the emperor's case of plague, which would have it happen at too late a date (Zʿura was banished from Constantinople in 536, and the plague did not arrive until 542). But this seems unlikely since Procopius would surely have mentioned it if the illness had been plague. If Zʿura had been involved, the emperor clearly could not have paid him tribute; the choice of Saints Cosmas and Damian would have been particularly appropriate, since their very popular cult had reached the Greco-Roman world through the Syrian Orient (in fact, the saints may originally have been Arab tribesmen). See Peeters, *Orient et Byzance*, 65–68. The church dedicated to Saints Cosmas and Damian may be the building now known as the Atik Mustafa Pasa Camii; see B. Aran, "The Nunnery of the Anagyres and the Mustafa Pasha Mosque: Notes," *JÖB* 26 (1977): 247–53; and Mathews, *Byzantine Churches of Istanbul*, 16. For an alternative, cf. Janin, *Constantinople byzantine*, 123.

72. *Lives*, 2, PO 17:25–26.

73. Ibid., 26–31; also Michael the Syrian, *Chronique* 9.23; and Bar Hebraeus, *Chronicon ecclesiasticum* 1:206–12, where the two later chroniclers are primarily

dependent on John's account. See pseudo-Zachariah Rhetor, *HE* 9.15, 19, for another version of Agapetus' visit and death in Constantinople that, while not mentioning Zʿura by name, substantiates John's story with regard to the pope's death. Agapetus in fact did die of fever, as pseudo-Zachariah Rhetor indicates.

74. *Lives*, 2, PO 17:34–35.

75. Ibid. Theodosius was exiled from Alexandria in 536, in accordance with the general banishment order decreed at that time against Severus and the other Monophysite leaders. The "Chronique melkite," chap. 18, includes Zʿura's name in the list of those who were banned.

76. *Lives*, 37, PO 18:624–41.

77. Ibid., 631. John might not have felt so embarrassed if Mare had directed his anger in this fashion toward anyone else; but his own position of favor in the imperial court made his reaction to the encounter necessarily awkward. It was not the passion but the disrespect that alarmed him. On this very incident Nöldeke remarked, "All this was in execrable taste; yet it is a real pleasure to see that there still were some people capable of confronting the servile 'Byzantinism' of the day in a way that was manly and independent" (Nöldeke, *Sketches from Eastern History*, 230–31).

78. *Lives*, 37, PO 18:632–33.

79. Ibid., 639.

80. Ibid., 640.

81. Ibid., 9, PO 17:136–37.

82. A summarizing chronological account of Theodora's patronage and its recipients is in Duchesne, "Protégés de Théodora."

83. *Lives*, 13, PO 17:187–213.

84. Ibid., 207.

85. Ibid., 212.

86. Ibid., 47, PO 18:677.

87. In this chapter of the *Lives* (47, PO 18:676–84), John gives a tantalizingly confused picture of the Monophysite residences in Constantinople, mentioning in particular the palace of Hormisdas and a martyrion dedicated to Saint Sergius. The picture is hampered by both insufficient corroborative documentation and incomplete archaeological remains; John himself describes severe damage by fire to the Monophysite quarters. An effort to clarify John's presentation in this instance is made by Mango, "Church of Saints Sergius and Bacchus"; and idem, "Church of Sts. Sergius and Bacchus Once Again." On the Palace of Hormisdas, see Guilland, *Études de topographie* 1:294–305. On the Church of Saints Sergius and Bacchus, see Van Millengen, *Byzantine Churches*, 62–83. Neither Van Millengen nor Guilland uses John of Ephesus, despite his detailed (if confused) descriptions. Cf. Janin, *Constantinople byzantine*, 358–59.

88. John of Ephesus, *Lives*, 47, PO 18:677.

89. Ibid., 679.

90. Ibid., 680.

91. Ibid., 48, *PO* 18:684–90. The patriarchs John includes are Severus of Antioch, Theodosius of Alexandria, Anthimus of Constantinople, Sergius of Antioch, and Paul ("the Black") of Antioch.

92. See the accounts of these events in Frend, *Rise of the Monophysite Movement*, 270–73; idem, *Rise of Christianity*, 842–43.

93. Their leadership was of paramount import to the movement, and the act of their communion (which must have been around 535/6) with one another remained a critical landmark in Monophysite tradition. Following their ritual of communion, they maintained contact, sending numerous encyclicals to one another while in exile, and these were circulated with considerable impact within the church body. See, for example, pseudo-Zachariah Rhetor, *HE* 9.14–26; John of Ephesus, *HE, Fragmenta* 3.5–6; Evagrius, *HE* 4.11; "Chronique melkite," 17; Jacob of Edessa, *Chronicon*. 319–21; *Chronicon anonymum 846*, 223, 228; and Michael the Syrian, *Chronique* 9.21. Severus was patriarch in Antioch from 512–518, when he was deposed; he died in Egypt in 538. Theodosius held the seat in Alexandria from 535–537 and remained in exile in Constantinople until his death in 566. Anthimus served as patriarch only from 535–536, when he resigned under imperial pressure; he survived in exile, hidden by Theodora, perhaps another seven or eight years.

94. See Frend, *Rise of the Monophysite Movement*; Wigram, *Separation of the Monophysites*; and Hardy, *Christian Egypt*.

95. For Severus' problems, while exiled, in maintaining the internal discipline of the Monophysites, see, for example, Severus of Antioch, *Sixth Book of Select Letters* 1.49, 53, 57, 2.3.

96. *Lives*, 44, *PO* 18:661–68.

97. Ibid., 664.

98. Ibid., 664–65.

99. Ibid., 661.

100. Ibid., 33–34, *PO* 18:592–606; 38–41, *PO* 18:641–58; 46, *PO* 18:671–76.

101. Ibid., 57, *PO* 19:200–206.

102. Ibid., 200. This was the chamberlain Mishael, who served in the court of Anastasius; see Severus of Antioch, *Sixth Book of Select Letters* 1.19 and 9.1, and further references in Brooks' footnote, *Lives*, 57, *PO* 19:200, n. 1. In *Sixth Book of Select Letters*, 9.1, Severus, who was patriarch in Antioch at the time, urged Mishael not to abandon his career in the court to become a solitary because the urgency of the Monophysite cause made a presence, such as his, in the palace all the more necessary. He offers high praise for the asceticism Mishael practiced while following a lay career, and he urges the chamberlain to accept his situation as one that bestows the crown of martyrdom.

103. *Lives*, 57, *PO* 19:201.

104. Ibid., 205.

105. For example, John of Ephesus, *HE, Fragmenta* 3.5–6; and Michael the Syrian, *Chronique* 9.23.

106. For example, pseudo-Dionysius, *Incerti auctoris chronicon*, 75–76, 125

(John of Ephesus); Procopius, *Anecdota* 11.14–31, 28.16–18; and Michael the Syrian, *Chronique* 9.25, 32.

107. *Lives*, 33, PO 18:592–601.

108. Ibid., 600–601.

109. Frend, *Rise of the Monophysite Movement*, 322–23; and especially Wigram, *Separation of the Monophysites*, chap. 12. The conduct of the Monophysite community in Constantinople was not, of course, the direct cause of the renewed persecutions in the 570s. But their activity may have been seen to contribute to Justin II's failure to secure a religious solution by theological dialogue; certainly, the nature of their presence in the capital must have been exasperating for those who sought a pro-Chalcedonian answer.

110. On holy fools, see Rydén, "Holy Fool"; and I. Špidlik and F. Vandenbroucke, "Fous pour le Christ," *Dictionnaire de Spiritualité* 5, cols. 752–70. The practice of holy foolery came to prominence in the Byzantine realm with the career of the Syrian ascetic Simeon Salos in the sixth century; but its inspiration derived from the Pauline teachings, 1 Cor. 4:10–13, once again a literalizing of symbols. The earliest appearance of a holy fool in Greek literature is in Palladius, *Historia Lausiaca* 39, where a nun feigning madness is revealed by divine vision as the holiest of ascetics. An elaborate Syriac version of the same story is in the "Life of Onesima," in John the Stylite, *Select Narrations of Holy Women*, ed. and trans. A. Smith Lewis. For an excellent analysis of the meaning of this form of ascesis, see Syrkin, "On the Behavior."

111. *Lives*, 52, PO 19:164–79. For another couple leading similar lives, see the *Life of John the Almsgiver* by Leontius of Neapolis, chap. 24 in *Three Byzantine Saints*, trans. E. A. Dawes and N. Baynes, 232–34. De Gaiffier, "Intactam sponsam relinquens," catalogs the variations on this theme; John's couple are treated at pp. 171–72. I am grateful to Professor Lennart Rydén for these references and others, and for discussing this chapter of John's *Lives* with me.

112. *Lives*, 52, PO 19:178.

113. Professor Lennart Rydén believes that this chapter is a novelette and is highly unlikely to have any basis in fact; de Gaiffier, "Intactam sponsam relinquens," takes this position and views John's account as a literary device. The general scepticism found in editor Brooks' own notes to the text indicates a similar perspective. Brooks is bothered in particular by the erratic chronology of the story. This I do not find to be a serious concern because it is a chronic problem in John's writings. Against Professor Rydén's view (and others), I must emphasize the chapter's uniqueness in the *Lives* if it is fictional and further point to the fool in *Lives*, 53, which undoubtedly reflects a genuine encounter and admittedly lacks the romantic tone of *Lives*, 52. Nöldeke, *Sketches from Eastern History*, 234–35, believes that the basic story of the Amidan couple was true, but that it simply underwent elaboration in being told twice over. I do not believe that John, for all his carelessness, would insert a full-blown fictional account into his collection. Thus, if this story should turn out to be a pious fiction, then probably it was a later interpolation.

114. *Lives*, 52, *PO* 19:172.
115. Ibid., 169.
116. See chap. 3.
117. *Lives*, 53, *PO* 19:179–85.
118. Ibid., 183.

V. *Spirituality and Accountability: Consequences of the Ascetic Vow*

1. On the Monophysite missions see, above all, Hendriks, "Activité apostolique," where considerable attention is given to the situation discussed here—
the remarkable role of the Monophysite ascetic in the matter of missions. Hendriks notes the singular fire and rigor of these monks; it is on this very point that
John of Ephesus enlightens us. In general, see also Frend, *Rise of the Monophysite
Movement*, chaps. 8–9; and Wigram, *Separation of the Monophysites*, 138–40. The
role of the persecutions cannot be overemphasized, especially in that it placed
these Christians in new places among new people, with impressive stories to
tell, although John reminds us that persecution was not the motivating force.
The parallel situation for the Nestorians accounts for both the similarities and
differences between the two groups in this regard. For a sense of how Nestorian
tradition preserves this heritage of persecution and mission, see Mar Aprem,
Nestorian Missions.
2. *Lives*, 16, *PO* 17:229–47.
3. Ibid., 229.
4. Ibid., 233–34.
5. Ibid., 235–36.
6. Ibid., 241. On the Sons and Daughters of the Covenant (*bnay* and *bnath
qyāmā*), see p. 6 above.
7. *Lives*, 16, *PO* 17:241–42.
8. Ibid., 245.
9. Ibid., 247.
10. There is one indirect reference to invasions by the Huns, ibid., 245, discussed earlier here in chap. 3, but no other connection is made to the events
dominating the eastern provinces at that time.
11. Vööbus, *History of Asceticism* 1:307–25, 2:342–60.
12. *Syriac and Arabic Documents*, ed. and trans. A. Vööbus, 121–22 (on the
date, 115).
13. *Lives*, 10, *PO* 17:137–58. Additional material on Simeon of Beth Arsham
is in pseudo-Zachariah Rhetor, *HE* 8.3; Michael the Syrian, *Chronique* 9.8–9; and
Bar Hebraeus, *Chronicon ecclesiasticum* 1:190, 2:86. On Simeon's writings, see Duval, *Littérature syriaque*, 136–40, 342, 358–59. The shorter version of his famous
letter on the persecution of the Christians in Najran is preserved from John of
Ephesus' *HE* in pseudo-Dionysius, *Incerti auctoris chronicon*, 54–57; for discus-

sion of the letter, its versions, and problems, see I. Shahid, *The Martyrs of Najran*, Sub. Hag. 49 (Bruxelles, 1971).

14. On the origins and history of Persian Christianity, see Labourt, *Christianisme dans l'empire perse;* Fiey, *Jalons pour une histoire;* Brock, "Christians in the Sasanian Empire"; and Vööbus, *History of the School of Nisibis.* For the continuing survival of Marcionism, see Fiey, "Marcionites." In accordance with Syrian tradition, John includes Bardaisan in the same category as Mani and Marcion. This is an unjust affiliation, as Bardaisan seems to have been "orthodox" and not of the same ascetically dualistic orientation as the other two. Cf. Bardaisan, *"Book of the Laws,"* ed. and trans. H. J. W. Drijvers; and Drijvers, *Bardaisan of Edessa.*

15. *Lives*, 10, *PO* 17:144.

16. Ibid., 10, *PO* 17:138. Cf. for example, idem, *HE, Fragmenta* 3.2–4, 8.

17. *Lives*, 10, *PO* 17:140–41.

18. Ibid., 138.

19. Ibid., 142–43, 152–53, 157. In the incident with Anastasius, the Nestorians persuaded the Persian king that the "orthodox" (Monophysite) believers were traitors to the Persian throne, "since their faith also and their rites agree with those of the Romans." When Anastasius demanded that the persecutions be stopped, he also secured a royal decree that the Christian peoples of Persia should "not harm one another by reason of occasions of enmity" (ibid., 142–43).

20. Ibid., 152.

21. See, for example, *Lives*, 39, *PO* 18:645–47; 40, *PO* 18:647–51; 43, *PO* 18:658–60; 51, *PO* 19:159–64.

22. Ibid., 47, *PO* 18:681.

23. Pseudo-Dionysius, *Incerti auctoris chronicon*, 75–78, 125 (John of Ephesus); Michael the Syrian, *Chronique* 9.25, 33. Paganism was a problem that vexed the church like a festering sore. As Justinian's measures and John of Ephesus' enterprises showed, its continued presence was not viewed as a sign of lingering death but rather as a malignant cancer. It was not so many years earlier that pseudo-Zachariah Rhetor had written his *Life of Severus of Antioch*—less a biography than a treatise against persisting pagan worship and a refutation of the charges that the great patriarch had once been involved in such practices himself; see *Vita Severi* (Zachariah Rhetor). In fact, Severus had been a pagan as a youth and converted to Christianity while a law student in Beyrouth; for this evidence, see Garitte, "Textes hagiographique," esp. 335–46.

24. *Lives*, 40, *PO* 18:650; 43, *PO* 18:658.

25. Ibid., 43, *PO* 18:659–60.

26. Ibid., 46, *PO* 18:671–76.

27. Ibid., 24, *PO* 18:513–26. Apart from the *Lives*, our major source is the contemporary (written c. 542) *Vita Iohannis Episcopi Tellae*, ed. and trans. E. W. Brooks; see also, for example, Severus of Antioch, *Sixth Book of Select Letters* 5.14; pseudo-Zachariah Rhetor, *HE* 8.4–5, 10.1; and *Chronicon anonymum 846*, 223. Honigmann, *Évêques et évêchés monophysites*, 51–52, summarizes John of Tella's life and activities. John left us a number of ecclesiastical and monastic canons;

see the references in Honigmann on p. 52, and the discussion and texts in *Syriac and Arabic Documents*, ed. and trans. A. Vööbus, 55–61.

28. This was a very early inclination—while a young child, according to Elias. See the *Vita Iohannis Episcopi Tellae*, 40–42.

29. Cf. pseudo-Zachariah Rhetor, *HE* 8.5.

30. Ibid., 515–56.

31. See esp. Frend, "Severus of Antioch"; idem, "Monophysites and the Transition"; and Vööbus, "Origin of the Monophysite Church." More generally, cf. Frend, *Rise of the Monophysite Movement*; and Wigram, *Separation of the Monophysites*. Compare the altogether different perspective of the Nestorians in Brock, "Christians in the Sasanian Empire," esp. 8–9.

32. The scene is vividly described in Severus' *Sixth Book of Select Letters* 1, "On ordinations." He frequently quotes from the letters of the Cappadocian Fathers, and, indeed, the overlap between their situations is fascinating—especially for the way in which Severus chose to interpret the rather unsavory manipulation of ecclesiastical structure and law that Basil employed, and which Gregory of Nazianzus painfully suffered. See Basil, *Lettres*, ed. and trans. Y. Courtonne; and Gregory of Nazianzus, *Lettres*, ed. and trans. P. Gallay. Severus was, in part, converted by the writings of the Cappadocians while a student. See *Vita Severi* (Zachariah Rhetor); and *Vita Severi* (John of Beith-Aphthonia).

33. The controversy over Chalcedon had never been a dispute between theologians alone; from its beginnings it had stirred popular passions. See Frend, "Popular Religion"; and Gregory, *Vox Populi*.

34. John of Ephesus, *Lives*, 24, *PO* 18:517.

35. Frend, "Severus of Antioch," 273; idem, *Rise of the Monophysite Movement*, 260–61. In both places, the author has misconstrued the year of John of Ephesus' ordination, 840 of the Greeks (= 529/30), for the number of ordinations performed by John of Tella in one year; *Lives*, 24, *PO* 18:521.

36. Ibid., 518.

37. Ibid.

38. Ibid., 519.

39. Ibid., 521–22. John of Ephesus would have been in his early twenties at the time.

40. Severus of Antioch, *Sixth Book of Select Letters* 5.14. For John of Tella in Marde, see also John of Ephesus, *Lives*, 15, *PO* 17:228.

41. Severus of Antioch, *Sixth Book of Select Letters* 1, "On ordinations." The question of canonicity, particularly with regard to ordinations, was always provocatively argued when proceedings of diverse interests were conducted in the church. Severus, *Sixth Book of Select Letters* 1.2, points out that church discipline on ordinations was often remiss in times of persecution. He cites the (less than flattering) case of Basil's orchestrated consecration to Caesarea in 370; Gregory of Nazianzus, *Lettres*, 40–45, presents the other side of that incident. Monophysite tradition, however, was something to be reckoned with: in his *Vita Severi*, John of Beith-Aphthonia remarks that Peter the Iberian's consecration in 452 was per-

formed under adverse circumstances and would have been uncanonical but for the intervention of the Holy Spirit, who filled in for the requisite but missing third bishop. As John of Tella was primarily ordaining deacons and priests, the situation was not as awkward as that of Jacob Burd'aya and his comrade Theodore of Arabia, as discussed later here. For discussion of the concern with purity and the exclusive closing inward for persecuted or marginal groups, see Douglas, *Purity and Danger.*

42. *Lives,* 24, *PO* 18:520.

43. Ibid., 522–24.

44. Ibid., 522.

45. Ibid., 25, *PO* 18:526–40. For John of Hephaestopolis, see further Honigmann, *Évêques et évêchés monophysites,* 165–67.

46. *Lives,* 25, *PO* 18:526–27. Cf. the discussion of Hendriks, "Activité apostolique."

47. *Lives,* 25, *PO* 18:529.

48. Ibid.

49. Ibid., 530–31.

50. Ibid., 534.

51. Ibid., 536.

52. Ibid., 538.

53. Ibid., 540.

54. *Lives,* 49, *PO* 18:692.

55. Ibid., 50, *PO* 19:153. Important background here is laid by Trimingham, *Christianity Among the Arabs.*

56. *Lives,* 50, *PO* 19:153–54. In fact, another bishop, Cyrus, had already been performing some ordinations in Persia, much after the manner of the two Johns; but he was inaccessible to the Monophysites in Roman territory because of the wars in progress between Byzantium and the Sasanians. See pseudo-Zachariah Rhetor, *HE* 10.13; Michael the Syrian, *Chronique* 9.29.

57. *Lives,* 49, *PO* 18:690–97.

58. Ibid., 691–92.

59. Ibid., 50, *PO* 19:154. See Honigmann, *Évêques et évêchés monophysites,* 158–63.

60. *Lives,* 49, *PO* 18:696.

61. Ibid., 697; idem, 50, *PO* 19:155–56.

62. Ibid., 49, *PO* 18:696–97; 50, *PO* 19:156–58. Cf. *Chronicon anonymum 819,* 10.

63. The question is treated in detail in Bundy, "Jacob Baradaeus." Principal sources for Jacob are the following: John of Ephesus, *Lives,* 49, *PO* 18:690–97; and 50, *PO* 19:153–58; idem, *HE,* pt. III; the letters to and from Jacob, in *Documenta ad origines monophysitarum illustrandas,* ed. and trans. J.-B Chabot, *Letters* 7, 23, 29, 31, 32, 33, 35, 36; pseudo-Zachariah Rhetor, *HE* 10.12; Michael the Syrian, *Chronique* 9.29–31; and Bar Hebraeus, *Chronicon ecclesiasticum* 1.213–18, 233–44. There is also the spurious *Vita Iacobi Baradaei,* falsely attributed to John of

Ephesus, edited and translated by E. W. Brooks; the attribution to John was supported by the plagiarism of certain passages from John's *Lives*, but it also indicates how venerable a historian John was held to be in later tradition, and the marked influence of his particular biographical rendering of Jacob's life even where legend had grown extensively. To this spurious *Vita*, 268–73, editor Brooks appends a short text that concerns the transfer in 622 of Jacob's relics from the Egyptian monastery at Casium where he died, to his former home, the monastery of Fsiltha at Tella.

64. See esp., *Sévère ibn-al-Moqaffa, évêque d'Aschmounain, Réfutation de Saʿid ibn-Batriq* (*Eutychius*), (*Le Livre des Conciles*), ed. and trans. P. Chébli, *PO* 3 (Paris, 1909), 208ff.; Chronicle of Seert, *Histoire nestorienne*, ed. and trans. A. Scher, 140–42; and *Le Livre de la Lampe des ténèbres par Abû l-Barakât Ibn Kabour*, ed. and trans. L. Villecourt, E. Tisserant, and G. Wiet, *PO* 20 (Paris, 1929), 733.

65. Jacob's demise is perhaps best summarized in Wigram, *Separation of the Monophysites*.

66. Honigmann, *Évêques et évêchés monophysites*, is indispensable for understanding the structural evolution that took place in the Monophysite movement during the sixth century.

VI. *Some Implications: The Case of Women*

1. The critical analysis is Fiorenza, *In Memory of Her.*

2. Luke 8:1–3, 10:38–42.

3. Fiorenza, *In Memory of Her;* idem, "Word, Spirit, and Power: Women in Early Christian Communities," in McLaughlin and Ruether, *Women of Spirit,* 29–70; C. Parvey, "The Theology and Leadership of Women in the New Testament," in Ruether, *Religion and Sexism,* 117–49.

4. 1 Cor. 14:33–35; 1 Tim. 2:11–14; Titus 2:3–5; Eph. 5:22–24.

5. Gal. 3:27–28.

6. Chadwick, *Early Church,* 58–59.

7. "The Acts of Paul," in *New Testament Apocrypha* 2: 322–90 (trans. 352–90), esp. 330–33, and 353–64 (trans. "The Acts of Thecla").

8. Cf., for example, A. Harnack, *The Mission and Expansion of Christianity in the First Three Centuries,* trans. J. Moffat (New York, 1908), book 4, chap. 2. The role of mothers and wives as "missionaries" for the faith continued. Examples are legion; but, for instance, in the fourth century Augustine of Hippo was profoundly influenced by his pious mother Monica overshadowing his religiously unconvinced father. The two brothers Basil of Caesarea and Gregory of Nyssa had the example of their devout mother Emmelia and, even more, their great sister Macrina.

9. For the inception and development of ministry and hierarchy for the ecclesiastical body, see, for example, Kirk, *Apostolic Ministry;* Fliche and Martin, *Histoire de l'église* 1:259–78, 373–86, 2:387–402. What happened to women in

the midst of this process is delineated in Fiorenza, *In Memory of Her*; idem, "Word, Spirit, and Power" (see n. 3 above); Parvey, (see n. 3 above); and Danielou, "Ministère des femmes."

10. Clark, *Ascetic Piety and Women's Faith*. The developing situation for the Western church is well sketched in the two volumes *Religion and Sexism* and *Women of Spirit* (see n. 3 above). For the development in the eastern provinces of the empire, cf. Patlagean, "Histoire de la femme déguisée"; idem, *Pauvreté économique*, esp. 113–55; Grosdidier de Matons, "Femme dans l'empire byzantine"; Beauchamp, "Situation juridique"; and Buckler, "Women in Byzantine Law."

11. J. C. Engelsman, *The Feminine Dimension of the Divine* (Philadelphia, 1979), sets out the basic issues of this subject.

12. See Lucian, *De dea Syria*, and Apuleius, *Metamorphoses* 8.23–31, for ancient views on her cult. For her place in ancient Near Eastern religion and in the Greco-Roman world, see Segal, *Edessa*, 45–61; Drijvers, *Cults and Beliefs at Edessa*, esp. 76–121; Strong and Garstang, *Syrian Goddess*; and Nock, *Conversion*.

13. Segal, *Edessa*; Murray, *Symbols of Church and Kingdom*.

14. P. Bird, "Images of Women in the Old Testament," in Ruether, *Religion and Sexism*, 41–88; J. Hauptmann, "Images of Women in the Talmud," in Ruether, *Religion and Sexism*, 184–212. But the confines of women's lives were rigidly monitored, and no less in the early Christian era than before. See Neusner, *History of the Mishnaic Law*.

15. Trible, *God and the Rhetoric*.

16. Von Rad, *Wisdom in Israel*, esp. 144–76. For a survey of scholarship and discussion of Christianity's inheritance of the Wisdom tradition, see J. D. G. Dunn, *Christology in the Making: An Inquiry into the Origins of the Doctrine of the Incarnation* (London, 1980), 163–212, 324–38. Von Rad does not address the issue of whether Wisdom's female persona is significant in itself. Engelsman, *Feminine Dimension of the Divine*, attempts to treat the issue, but here (as also for Demeter and the Virgin Mary) she mishandles the sources. On the Shekinah, see Goldberg, *Untersuchungen über die Vorstellung*.

17. The psychological attraction of a Mother Goddess figure is shown especially in the Greco-Roman world by the adoption of the Isis cult, but similarly of Cybele, the Syrian Goddess, and indeed Diana of the Ephesians. Greek and Roman counterparts did not inspire the same response as these oriental mystery cults. See Pomeroy, *Goddesses, Whores, Wives, and Slaves*; and Nock, *Conversion*. The Great Mother of Greek mythology, probably at her strongest in Minoan Crete, was considerably scaled down in power and diffused as a cult once the pantheon of Zeus and Hera emerged. Lucian commented that one would have to combine Hera, Athena, Aphrodite, Artemis, Nemesis, Rhea, Selena, and the Fates in order to encompass the power of the Syrian Goddess; Lucian, *De dea Syria*, 32.

18. See Murray, *Symbols of Church and Kingdom*, 312–20.

19. See especially Odes 8, 19, 28, 35, and 36; and Murray, *Symbols of Church and Kingdom*, 312–20, for discussion of this kind of imagery. For recent assess-

ments of Ode 19, see Lagrand, "How was the Virgin Mary"; and Drijvers, "19th Ode of Solomon." It is not until a considerably later date that Western tradition attempts to explore these possibilities. See McLaughlin, "'Christ my Mother.'"

20. Esp. Ode 19:6–10, in *Odes of Solomon*, ed. and trans. J. H. Charlesworth, 81–84.

21. Graef, *Mary* 1:34–35. Graef's suggestion that Ode 19 confuses Mary with the goddess Isis misses the mark: people knew the differences between them.

22. See Brock, "Mary in Syriac Tradition"; idem, "Mary and the Eucharist"; Murray, "Mary, the Second Eve"; and Graef, *Mary* 1:57–62, 119–29. Compare Graef, *Mary;* and idem, "Theme of the Second Eve," for parallel developments in later Greek and Western traditions.

23. The origin of the *Protevangelion* remains in dispute. For the principal theories, see *New Testament Apocrypha,* 1:370–88; Strycker, *Forme la plus an cienne;* and Smid, *Protevangelium Jacobi.* Strycker argues for an Egyptian author, Smid for a Syrian one. Every, "*Protevangelion of James,*" suggests an origin in Ephesus.

24. The Syriac version of the *Protevangelion* is in *Apocrypha Syriaca*, ed. A. Smith-Lewis, Studia Sinaitica 11 (London, 1902). For the Syriac Life of the Virgin, see *History of the Blessed Virgin*, ed. and trans. E. A. Wallis Budge.

25. Cf. also Brown et al., *Mary in the New Testament*, 241–82, 293–94, for Mary's place in Greco-Latin works of the second century.

26. Above all, see Brock, *Holy Spirit,* esp. 79–88, 129–33; and Beggiani, *Early Syriac Theology*, esp. 101–13.

27. Brock, *Holy Spirit*, 130–32.

28. For examples from the Syrian Orthodox, Church of the East, and Maronite liturgies, see Brock, *Holy Spirit*, 79–88, 129–33; and Beggiani, *Early Syriac Theology*, 101–14.

29. For example, Pomeroy, *Goddesses, Whores, Wives, and Slaves;* and Nock, *Conversion.*

30. See Murray, *Symbols of Church and Kingdom*, 312–20. For a vivid example of the transformation of *meltha,* see the Gospel of John in the Peshitta. Brock, "Aspects of Translation," 87, sees both instances as a logical consequence of translation technique. Cf. also Brock, "Towards a History," 10.

31. Murray, "Mary, the Second Eve," esp. 373.

32. As Murray himself points out, ibid.; but also, for example, this reverence can be seen in the *Odes of Solomon.*

33. Segal, *Edessa,* 38–39.

34. As discussed in the Introduction here. See esp. Bundy, "Marcion and the Marcionites"; Brown, *Body and Society,* 83–102; Bauer, *Orthodoxy and Heresy;* and Vööbus, *History of Asceticism* 1, for the impact of Marcionism on the Syrian Orient.

35. For example, Tertullian, *Adversus Marcionem* 1.29. Cf. Frend, *Rise of Christianity,* 215–16.

36. Marcion himself came from Asia Minor—Tertullian, *Adversus Marcionem* 1.1, says from the Pontus—but he made his career in Rome. The particular fertility of the Syrian Orient for his teachings, however, finds an important parallel in the "Phrygian heresy" of Montanism. Both groups granted women positions of high responsibility and sacerdotal import; both Phrygia and the Syrian Orient had worshiped goddesses of magnificent character. A natural extension, in both cases, from religious thought to societal consequences may have unconsciously been at work. Certainly these two heresies were the source of particular bitterness for the mainstream church, and their similar settings are striking. Eusebius, *HE* 5.14–19, describes the Montanists as spreading "like venomous reptiles." It is interesting to speculate here on the consequences of following a historical tradition written by and about men: contemporary sources tell us that some members of the Montanist sect chose to call themselves Priscillianists after their female foundress Prisca (Priscilla). For the scandalized reaction to heresies that granted authoritative roles to women, see, for example, Tertullian, *De praescriptione haereticorum* 41.

37. See the earlier discussion in the Introduction here. Cf. Brown, *Body and Society*, 259–84.

38. In general, see Vööbus, *History of Asceticism*. We have little evidence for women stylites beyond the mere records of their existence: Vööbus, *History of Asceticism* 2:273–74; Delehaye, "Femmes stylites." Fiey, "Cénobitisme féminin ancien," deals mainly with Iraq and reads the lack of evidence more pessimistically.

39. See esp. Vööbus, *History of Asceticism;* and *Syriac and Arabic Documents,* ed. and trans. A. Vööbus. Vööbus, *History of Asceticism* 2:257, rightly judges the negative motivation behind the authority granted deaconesses to distribute communion: it was the mark of the unworthiness of the nuns that they were not to receive it at the hands of a priest. Cf. also Danielou, "Ministère des femmes."

40. Theodoret, *Historia religiosa* 29, 30.

41. For a similar presentation, see J.-M. Fiey, "Une hymne nestorienne sur les saintes femmes," *Anal. Boll.* 84 (1966): 77–110.

42. Febronia, *BHO*, 302–3; *BHG*, 208–9.

43. Our oldest manuscript dates back to the sixth century. The Syriac text is in *Vita Febroniae,* and an English translation is in *Holy Women of the Syrian Orient,* trans. S. P. Brock and S. A. Harvey, 150–76. Febronia's cult remains popular to this day; cf. Gülcan, "Renewal of Monastic Life."

44. Cf. the similar interchange in the martyrdom of Maḥya. I. Shahid, *The Martyrs of Najran,* Sub. Hag. 49 (Bruxelles, 1971), xix–xxii; translated in *Holy Women of the Syrian Orient,* trans. S. P. Brock and S. A. Harvey, 109–111.

45. Pelagia, *BHO*, 919; *BHG*, 1478–79. The Syriac text is in *Vita Pelagiae,* and an English translation is in *Holy Women of the Syrian Orient,* trans. S. P. Brock and S. A. Harvey, 40–62. It is unlikely that the Pelagia and Bishop Nonnus of our text can be identified with the courtesan mentioned by John Chrysostom, or

with the Bishop Nonnus of Theophanes, for reasons of lack of evidence in the former case and inaccurate chronology in the latter. See now the monograph, *Pélagie la pénitente*, ed. P. Petitmengin; and for a deeply sensitive treatment of her story and theme, Ward, *Harlots of the Desert*.

46. See Delehaye, *Legends of the Saints*, 150–55; Delcourt, "Female Saints in Masculine Clothing," in *Hermaphrodite*, 84–102; and Patlagean, "Histoire de la femme déguisée."

47. "The Acts of Thecla," *New Testament Apocrypha*, 2:330–33, 353–64.

48. Consider, for example, Matrona of Constantinople (c. 425–524), *BHG*, 1221–23; the sixth-century Anastasia, *BHG*, 79–80, who seems to have been a correspondent of Severus of Antioch. When the Piacenza Pilgrim visited the Holy Land around 570, he not only visited Pelagia's tomb but also reported a recent exploit like Anastasia's; Piacenza Pilgrim, *Travels*, 34, ed. P. Geyer; also in Wilkinson, *Jerusalem Pilgrims*, 78–89.

49. See the discussion in Patlagean, "Histoire de la femme déguisée."

50. Fiey, "Une hymne nestorienne" (see n. 41 above).

51. For example, *Lives*, 1, *PO* 17:12; 4, *PO* 17:69–71. Compare the parallel case when John himself nearly died as a baby; *Lives*, 4, *PO* 17:61–64.

52. John claims the preponderance of females in need of exorcism without hesitation. See esp. *Lives*, 4, *PO* 17:65; and cf., for example, the cases in 1, *PO* 17:12, 14–15; 15, *PO* 17:223–28.

53. Ibid., 44, *PO* 18:666–68.

54. Ibid., 4, *PO* 17:63. Cf. Simeon the Stylite, who had the same rule; Theodoret, *Historia religiosa* 26.21.

55. Lives, 47, *PO* 18:676–84.

56. See chap. 4 for detailed discussion.

57. *Lives*, 47, *PO* 18:683–84.

58. *Lives*, 15, *PO* 17:220–28.

59. The account of Jacob as unwilling exorcist is discussed in chap. 2.

60. *Lives*, 15, *PO* 17:225.

61. Ibid., 226–27.

62. Ibid., 228.

63. Ibid., 226.

64. Ibid., 56, *PO* 19:198–99.

65. Ibid., 31, *PO* 18:578–85. Elijah and Theodore are discussed in chap. 2.

66. *Lives*, 31, *PO* 18:582–85.

67. Ibid., 21, *PO* 17:290–93, 297–98.

68. Cf. McLaughlin and Ruether, *Women of Spirit*.

69. *Lives*, 12, *PO* 17:166–67; 27, *PO* 18:542.

70. Ibid., 27, *PO* 18:541.

71. Ibid., 28, *PO* 18:559.

72. Examples abound, perhaps most graphically in the *Gospel of Thomas*, Logion 114. Cf. *Vita Macrinae*, in Gregory of Nyssa, *Opera*, ed. W. Jaeger, 8.1.371; Palladius, *Historia Lausiaca* 9; Theodoret, *Historia religiosa* 29; and, in the sayings

of Sarah, *Apophthegmata patrum*, PG 65.419–22 [and the additional Saying 9, in *Sayings of the Desert Fathers*, trans. B. Ward (London, 1975), 192].

73. *Lives*, 12, PO 17:166–71. John does not title her "the Pilgrim," but the label serves here to distinguish her from Mary the Anchorite, discussed later. The passages quoted from John's text are my own translations.

74. Ibid., 169.

75. Ibid., 169–70.

76. Ibid. For miracles worked by presence rather than by will, cf. Theodoret, *Historia religiosa* 24.7.

77. See chap. 2; and *Lives*, 4, PO 17:56–84.

78. *Lives*, 12, PO 17:171–86. The passages quoted are my own translations.

79. *Lives*, 12, PO 17:171.

80. Ibid., 174–75.

81. Ibid., 175–76. Euphemia was not the only one of John's ascetics who refused to take the sins of others upon herself. See also *Lives*, 4, PO 17:67; and 44, PO 18:665.

82. *Lives*, 12, PO 17:179–80.

83. Ibid., 181.

84. Ibid., 181. Compare the similar juxtaposition of Thomas and Stephen, *Lives*, 13, PO 17:187–213, discussed earlier in chap. 4.

85. See chap. 4; *Lives*, 27, PO 18:541–58.

86. Cf. Clark, "Piety, Propaganda and Politics"; and idem, "Ascetic Renunciation and Feminine Advancement."

87. *Lives*, 27, PO 18:552–53.

88. Ibid., 557.

89. Ibid., 28, PO 18:559–62.

90. Ibid., 560.

91. Ibid., 562.

92. See chap. 3.

93. *Lives*, 28, PO 18:559.

94. For example, Patlagean, "Sur la limitation"; and esp. idem, *Pauvreté économique*, 113–55.

95. *Lives*, 44, PO 18:660–68.

96. Ibid., 54, PO 19:185–91.

97. Ibid., 54–56, PO 19:185–99; John of Nikiu, *Chronicle* 90.13.

98. Palladius, *Historia Lausiaca*. Cf. the studies collected in Clark, *Ascetic Piety and Women's Faith*.

99. Severus of Antioch, *Sixth Book of Select Letters*, 10.7.

100. There is a lacuna of a leaf or two in the manuscript at the beginning of John's chapter about her; PO 19:186, and 186, n. 3. He may have included mention of her change in circumstance in the missing portion. But it also may not have been of concern to him, considering the situation in which he knew her— as an ascetic, within an ascetic community.

101. The suffering of members of the nobility who took up asceticism is a

recurring theme in hagiographical literature. Cf., for example, the case of Arsenius in the Egyptian desert of Scete, *Apophthegmata patrum*, PG 65.88–107. See also Clark, "Authority and Humility."

102. *Lives*, 54, PO 19:187.

103. Ibid., 188. Cf. Melania's vast knowledge of patristics, Palladius, *Historia Lausiaca* 55.

104. Some of these are treated by John in *Lives*, 55–56, PO 19:191–99.

105. Ibid., 54, PO 19:189.

106. Ibid., 190.

107. Ibid., 191.

108. Cf. Melania, who exploited her temporal position for the sake of the ascetics she so loved. Palladius, *Historia Lausiaca* 46, 54. See also Clark, "Ascetic Renunciation and Feminine Advancement"; idem, "Authority and Humility."

109. *Lives*, 55, PO 19:191–96.

110. Ibid., 192.

111. Ibid., 193–95.

112. See the discussion in chap. 1.

113. Palladius, *Historia Lausiaca* 28–30, 33–35, 37, 49, 69–70.

114. Ibid., 5, 31, 60, 63–64, 69.

115. Ibid., 9, 41, 46, 54–57, 61, 67.

116. Ibid., 59. Amma Talis governed a convent of sixty women: "[These women] loved her so much that no lock was placed in the hall of the monastery, as in others, but they were held in check by their love for her. The old woman [Amma Talis] had such a high degree of self-control that when I had entered and taken a seat, she came and sat with me, and placed her hands on my shoulders in a burst of frankness" (*Palladius*, trans. R. T. Meyer, 140).

117. Again, Palladius states that the responsibility for sin is women's when in fact he also indicates that the fault is not theirs at all. Of Taor he says, "She was so graceful in appearance that even a well-controlled person might be led astray by her beauty were not chastity her defense and did not her decorum turn sinful eyes to fear and shame" (*Historia Lausiaca* 59; *Palladius*, trans. R. T. Meyer, 140). And on another excellent holy woman, "All the clergy confirmed that when she was a young maiden of about 20, she was exceedingly pretty and really to be avoided because of her beauty, lest one be suspected of having been with her" (*Historia Lausiaca* 63; *Palladius*, trans. R. T. Meyer, 144).

118. Theodoret, *Historia religiosa* 29, 30.

119. Ibid., 29.

120. John Moschus, *Pratum spirituale* 76, 88, 135–36, 152, 188, 207, 217. Chap. 128 speaks of women's weakness in the face of demons, and of their inability to lead others.

121. Ibid., 3, 14, 19, 31, 39, 45, 60, 75, 78, 179, 189, 204–6.

122. Ibid., 45–48, 50, 75. For discussion of the Marian witness of John Moschus, see Chadwick, "John Moschus"; and Vasey, "John Moschus, Monk

Marian Witness." John Moschus, *Pratum spirituale* 20, speaks also of the potency of Saint Thecla as intercessor.

VII. *John of Ephesus: Asceticism and Society*

1. Cyril of Scythopolis, *Vitae*, in *Kyrillos von Skythopolis*, ed. E. Schwartz. See also Festugière, *Moines d'Orient* 3:1–3, *Les moines de Palestine*. Cyril's biographies record the lives of Saints Euthymius, Sabas, John the Hesychast, Cyriacus, Theodosius, Theognius, and Abraamius. On Cyril as a hagiographer, see, above all, Flusin, *Miracle et histoire*.

2. John Moschus, *Pratum spirituale*, PG 87.3.2851–3112.

3. *Vita Euthymii* 6; *Vita Sabae*, Prologue.

4. Festugière, *Moines d'Orient* 3.1:10, praises him for "une candeur charmante"; Cyril does, of course, use familiar hagiographical themes—for example, friendship with lions, divine protection, and temptation by Satan in the wilderness—that might be called "thematic stylization." But the presence of these incidents in no way undermines the historical integrity of his biographical narrative.

5. *Vita Euthymii* 41–60; *Vita Sabae* 77–90.

6. Cf., for example, *Vita Euthymii* 36, 40, 43; *Vita Sabae* Prologue, 6, 10, 15, 19, 27, 68, 77; *Vita Iohannis Hesychasti* 5, 11; *Vita Kyriaki* 8, 10. For example, Festugière, *Moines d'Orient* 3.1:42–44; *Dictionnaire de Spiritualité* 2.2, cols. 2687–90 (I. Hauscherr). On Cyril's use of dates, see, above all, *Kyrillos von Skythopolis*, ed. E. Schwartz, 340–55.

7. For example, *Vita Euthymii* 2, 16; *Vita Sabae* 1, 2, 9, 25; *Vita Iohannis Hesychasti* 1, 3; *Vita Abraami*. Cf. Flusin, *Miracle et histoire*, 89–90; and cf., for example, the parallel situations of the Cappodocian Fathers, especially Basil's network of contacts; and the situation in fifth-century Egypt. On Basil, see in particular *Saint Basile, Lettres*; and the discussions in Kopecek, "Social Class"; Ramsey, "Life in the Days of St. Basil the Great," in *Pauline and Other Studies*, 369–406; idem, "Noble Anatolian Family"; and Ruether, *Gregory of Nazianzus*. On the Egyptian situation, consider the connections laid out especially by Palladius, *Historia Lausiaca*; cf. Rousseau, "Blood-relationships." The *Vita Antonii*, and Theodoret in his *Historia religiosa*, both struggle to justify the presence of uneducated, lower-class ascetic leaders.

8. For the political context, see F. T. Noonan, "Political Thought in Greek Palestinian Hagiography (ca. 526–ca. 630)" (Ph.D. diss., University of Chicago, 1975).

9. *Vita Euthymii* 17, 25, 38, 44; *Vita Sabae* 11, 17, 58, 64, 66, 67; *Vita Iohannis Hesychasti* 12; *Vita Kyriaki* 8, 9, 17; Flusin, *Miracle et histoire*, 126, 181–82.

10. *Vita Euthymii* 13; *Vita Sabae* 5, 14, 23, 34, 49; *Vita Iohannis Hesychasti* 13, 18; *Vita Kyriaki* 10, 16.

11. *Vita Sabae* 25; *Vita Kyriaki* 18, 19.

12. For example, *Vita Euthymii* 25; *Vita Sabae* 67; *Vita Abraami*.

13. For example, *Vita Euthymii* 10, 12, 19, 23; *Vita Sabae* 39, 45; *Vita Kyriaki* 9, 10; *Vita Abraami*.

14. *Vita Euthymii* 30, 35; *Vita Sabae* 31, 72, 73; *Vita Iohannis Hesychasti* 5; *Vita Theodosii* 3; *Vita Abraami*. This setup is closely aligned with Basil's welfare and social service program as instituted in Caesarea. Cf. Basil, *Lettres* 94, 142–54; and Gregory of Nazianzus, *Oration* 43.63. This became the model for Byzantine *philanthropia*; see Constantelos, *Byzantine Philanthropy and Social Welfare*; Boojamra, "Christian *Philanthropia*"; and Downey, "*Philanthropia*."

15. *Vita Euthymii* 41, 43, 44, 48–60; *Vita Sabae* 78–84.

16. *Vita Euthymii* 17, 25; *Vita Sabae* 58, 64, 65, 67; Flusin, *Miracle et histoire*, 123–25.

17. For example, *Vita Sabae* 44.

18. For example, the treatment in Frend, *Rise of the Monophysite Movement*.

19. *Vita Euthymii* 30, 35. There is a familiar motif here of spurning a woman's audience, however virtuous or pious she may be; the summary model is that of Arsenius, in the *Apophthegmata patrum*, PG 65.95–98. See also Festugière, *Moines d'Orient* 1, *Culture ou Sainteté*, 47–48.

20. *Vita Euthymii* 43.

21. *Vita Sabae* 50–54.

22. Ibid., 55.

23. Ibid., 56–57. Cf. Evagrius, *HE* 3.31, 33.

24. *Vita Sabae* 64, 66–67, 70. Cf. Procopius, *Anecdota* 11.24–26.

25. *Vita Sabae* 71–75. Sabas treats Theodora rather more kindly than Euthymius treated Eudocia, even while holding her Monophysitism in utter disdain.

26. *Vita Euthymii* 2, 20, 26–27.

27. *Vita Euthymii* 30; *Vita Sabae* 38, 52, 55, 74; *Vita Iohannis Hesychasti* 27.

28. *Vita Euthymii* 27, 30, 43, 45; *Vita Sabae* 30, 33, 35–36, 38, 50, 56–57, 60, 72, 74, 83–90; *Vita Kyriaki* 11–15; *Vita Theodosii* 1; *Vita Theognii*. Cyril's condemnation of Leontius of Byzantium is scathing. The contrast to the opinion of modern scholars is noteworthy. Cf. Gray, *Defense of Chalcedon,* 90–103; Wigram, *Separation of the Monophysites,* 120; Moeller, "Chalcédonisme et le néo-chalcédonisme"; Sellers, *Council of Chalcedon.*

29. Cyril does mention an anchoress in the desert: *Vita Kyriaki* 18–19. There may not have been convents within the specific geographical area Cyril writes about outside Jerusalem, but the convents in and around the Holy City were certainly renowned. Consider those founded by Jerome and Paula, and Rufinus and Melania. There were also desert communities of women south of Cyril's region, in lower Palestine. Cf., for example, C. J. Kraemer, Jr., ed., *Excavations at Nessana* 3, *Non-Literary Papyri* (Princeton, 1958), P. Nessana 25 (?), 29, 31, 62, 79; and the Piacenza Pilgrim, *Travels* 12, 16, 22, 34; which mention communities throughout the Holy Land. I am indebted to Peter Donovan for these references.

30. *Vita Euthymii* 16, 31; *Vita Sabae* 7, 29, 69; *Vita Kyriaki* 4. Compare the similar attitude in Egypt, Chitty, *Desert a City,* 66–67.

31. *Vita Sabae*, 47. Women were not allowed to enter the monasteries even when in need: *Vita Euthymii* 54.

32. *Vita Euthymii* 1, 3, 23, 30, 35, 52, 54; *Vita Sabae* 53, 62–63, 68, 70–71, 80; *Vita Kyriaki* 18–19; *Vita Iohannis Hesychasti* 23–24.

33. *Vita Euthymii* 1, 3; *Vita Sabae* 75; *Vita Iohannis Hesychasti* 20, 23–24; *Vita Theodosii* 1; *Vita Theognii*.

34. *Vita Sabae* 62–63. Cf. Flusin, *Miracle et histoire*, 180–81.

35. Cf. Baynes, "The *Pratum Spirituale*," in *Byzantine Studies*, 261–70; Chadwick, "John Moschus"; and "Jean Moschus," *Dictionnaire de Spiritualité* 8, cols. 632–40 (E. Mani).

36. John Moschus, *Pratum spirituale* 179.

37. Ibid., 84, 87, 89, 120–21, 170, 179. Cf. Cyril, *Vita Sabae* 24; *Vita Kyriaki* 18–19.

38. John Moschus, *Pratum spirituale* 14, 19, 39, 45, 97, 135.

39. Ibid., 136, 186, 207.

40. Ibid., 186, 193, 201, 207.

41. Ibid., 131–32.

42. Ibid., 20–21, 99. Cf. Cyril, *Vita Sabae* 14; *Vita Kyriaki* 16; *Vita Iohannis Hesychasti* 13.

43. John Moschus, *Pratum spirituale* 38; cf. Cyril, *Vita Euthymii* 17.

44. See chap. 6.

45. John Moschus, *Pratum spirituale* 26.

46. Ibid., 30.

47. Ibid., 48–49.

48. Ibid., 106.

49. Ibid., 29, cf. 36.

50. Another shared motif is the relationship between holy men and wild beasts, particularly lions. For example, Cyril, *Vita Euthymii* 13; *Vita Sabae* 23, 33–34, 49; *Vita Iohannis Hesychasti* 13; *Vita Kyriaki* 49–50; and John Moschus, *Pratum spirituale* 2, 18, 58. For a measure of realism beyond the motif, compare these with the nuns' lion in the Piacenza Pilgrim, *Travels* 34. In general, see Festugière, "Lieux communs"; and idem, *Moines d'Orient* 1:53–57. Cf., for example, Theodoret, *Historia religiosa* 6.

51. Archaeological evidence appears to indicate that the sixth century witnessed an expansionist period in Palestine, despite the plague and other factors. For example, H. D. Colt, ed., *Excavations at Nessana* 1 (London, 1962), and C. J. Kraemer Jr., ed., *Excavations at Nessana* 3, *Non-Literary Papyri* (Princeton, 1958); and Cameron, "Late Antiquity." But cf. Patlagean, *Pauvreté économique*, 74–92, on Palestine's share of catastrophes, particularly of famine. Six earthquakes only are recorded for Palestine in the sixth century, of which two, in 502 and 531, were serious. Cf. Kallner-Amiran, "Revised Earthquake-Catalogue," 1–2. For a particular case in point see Downey, *Gaza in the Early Sixth Century*.

52. Cyril, *Vita Sabae* 72–74; Cf. Procopius, *Anecdota* 11.24–29. See Avi-Yonah, *Jews of Palestine*, 241–43.

53. John of Ephesus, *Lives*, 21, *PO* 17:287–88.

54. Ibid., 289.

55. Ibid.

56. Ibid., 291–92.

57. Ibid., 12, *PO* 17:180–81.

58. Ibid., 38, *PO* 18:643–45. On this episode see Harvey, "Physicians and Ascetics." What makes this episode so striking is the contrast to how other hagiographers portray illness and healing. Cf., for example, Adnès and Canivet, "Guérisons miraculeuses." Furthermore, John is prepared to call on "secular" doctors. Cf. Constantelos, "Physician-priests."

59. Cf. Hopkins, "Contraception in the Roman Empire"; Patlagean, "Sur la limitation"; and Sigerist, *Civilization and Disease* (New York, 1944), esp. 69–71.

60. *Lives*, 6, *PO* 17:118.

61. Ibid., 25, *PO* 18:614–18.

62. Ibid., 615.

63. Ibid., 616.

BIBLIOGRAPHY

Primary Sources

For individual saints' lives not in major collections (e.g., John of Ephesus, *Lives*) see under *Vita* _____.

Acta Martyrum et Sanctorum. 7 vols. Edited by P. Bedjan. Paris, 1890–97; Hildesheim, 1968.

Acta sanctorum martyrum orientalium. Edited by J. S. Assemani. Pars 2. Rome, 1748.

Anan-Isho. *The Book of Paradise: Being the Histories and Sayings of the Monks and Ascetics of the Egyptian Desert. The Syrian Texts, According to the Recension of Anan-Isho of Beth Abhe.* 2 vols. Edited and translated by E. A. Wallis Budge. London, 1904.

Ancient Syriac Documents. Edited and translated by W. Cureton. London, 1864; Amsterdam, 1967.

Anecdota Syriaca. Vol. 2. Edited by J. P. N. Land. Leiden, 1868.

Aphrahat. *Aphraatis sapientis persae demonstrationes.* Edited and translated by D. I. Parisot. *Patrologia Syriaca*, Vol. 1, Edited by R. Graffin. Paris, 1894. *Demonstrations* 1, 5–6, 8, 10, 17, 21–22 are translated in *Aphrahat the Persian Sage* by J. Gwynn, SLNPNF 13, 345–412. Oxford, 1898. *Demonstrations* 11–13, 15–19, 21, and part of 23 are translated in *Aphrahat and Judaism* by J. Neusner. Leiden, 1971.

The Apocryphal New Testament. Translated by M. R. James. Oxford, 1972.

Apophthegmata patrum. PG 65, cols. 71–440.

Apuleius, *Metamorphoses.* Translated by J. Lindsay. *Apuleius: The Golden Ass.* Bloomington, 1962.

Bardaisan. *"The Book of the Laws of the Countries" or: "Dialogue on Fate."* Edited and translated by H. J. W. Drijvers. Assen, 1965.

Bar Hebraeus. *Gregorii Bar Hebraei chronicon ecclesiasticum*. 3 vols. Edited and translated by J. B. Abbeloos and T. J. Lamy. Louvain, 1872–77.

———. *The Chronography of Bar Hebraeus, Being the first part of his Political History of the World*. 2 vols. Edited and translated by E. A. Wallis Budge. Oxford, 1932.

Basil of Caesarea. *Saint Basile, Lettres*. 3 vols. Edited and translated by Y. Courtonne. Paris, 1966.

Chronicon anonymum. Edited and translated by I. Guidi, CSCO 1/1, 2/2. Paris, 1903.

Chronicon anonymum ad annum Christi 819 pertinens. Edited by A. Barsaum, CSCO 81/36; and translated by J.-B. Chabot, CSCO 109/56. Paris, 1920–37.

Chronicon anonymum ad annum Domini 846 pertinens. Edited and translated by E. W. Brooks and J.-B. Chabot, CSCO 3/3, 4/4. Paris, 1904.

Chronicon anonymum ad annum Christi 1234 pertinens. Edited and translated by J.-B. Chabot, CSCO 81/36, 82/37, and CSCO 109/56. Paris, 1916–20; Louvain, 1937. And by A. Abouna and J.-M. Fiey, CSCO 354/154. Louvain, 1974.

Chronicon Edessenum. Edited and translated by I. Guidi, CSCO 1/1, 2/2. Paris, 1903.

"La chronique melkite abrégée du ms. sinaï syr. 10." Edited and translated by A. de Halleux. *Le Muséon* 91 (1978): 5–44.

Chronicle of Seert. *Histoire nestorienne (Chronique de Seert)*. Edited and translated by A. Scher. *PO* 7:95–203. Paris, 1911.

"The Conversations with the Syrian Orthodox Under Justinian (532)." Edited and translated by S. P. Brock. *OCP* 47 (1981): 87–121.

Cyril of Scythopolis. *Vitae*. In *Kyrillos von Skythopolis*. Edited by E. Schwartz. *TU* 49.2. Leipzig, 1939. Also in *Les moines de Palestine, Les moines d'Orient* 3.1–3. Translated by A.-J. Festugière. Paris, 1962–63.

Doctrine of Addai. Edited and translated by G. Phillips. London, 1876. Also in *The Teaching of Addai*. Retranslated by G. Howard. Missoula, 1981.

Documenta ad origines monophysitarum illustrandas. Edited and translated by J.-B. Chabot, CSCO 17/17, 103/52. Paris and Louvain, 1908–33.

Ephrem Syrus. *Des heiligen Ephraem des syrers carmina Nisibena* 1–2. Edited and translated by E. Beck, CSCO 218/92, 219/93, 240/102, 241/103. Louvain, 1961–63.

———. *Des heiligen Ephraem des syrers hymnen de fide*. Edited and translated by E. Beck, CSCO 154/73, 155/74. Louvain, 1955.

———. *Des heiligen Ephraem des syrers sermones* 1. Edited and translated by E. Beck, CSCO 305/130, 306/131. Louvain, 1970.

———. *Ephraim the Syrian, Hymns and Homilies*. Translated by J. Gwynn, SLNPNF 13, 165–344. Oxford, 1898.

———. "Ephrem's Letter to Publius." Edited and translated by S. P. Brock. *Le Muséon* 89 (1976): 261–305.

———. *The Harp of the Spirit: 18 Poems of St. Ephrem*. 2d ed. Translated by S. P. Brock, SSTS 4. London, 1983.

[Ephrem Syrus?] *Des heiligen Ephraem des syrers hymnen auf Abraham Kidunaya und Julianos Saba.* Edited and translated by E. Beck, CSCO 322/140, 323/141. Louvain, 1972.

Epiphanius of Salamis. *Adversus Haereses (Panarion).* Edited by K. Holl, GCS 25, 31, 37. Leipzig, 1915–33.

Euphemia and the Goth with the Acts of Martyrdom of the Confessors of Edessa, Shmona, Guria and Habib. Edited and translated by F. C. Burkitt. London and Oxford, 1913.

Eusebius of Caesarea. *Historia ecclesiastica.* Edited by E. Schwartz, GCS 9. Leipzig, 1903.

———. *The Ecclesiastical History and the Martyrs of Palestine.* Translated by H. J. Lawlor and J. E. L. Oulton. London, 1954.

Evagrius Scholasticus. *Historia ecclesiastica.* Edited by J. Bidez and L. Parmentier. London, 1898; New York, 1979. Translated by A.-J. Festugière. *Byzantion* 45 (1975): 187–471.

"The Fenqitho of the Monastery of Mar Gabriel in Tur Abdin." Edited and translated by S. P. Brock. *Östkirchliche Studien* 28 (1979): 168–82.

Gregory of Nazianzus. *Saint Grégoire de Nazianze, Lettres.* 2 vols. Edited and translated by P. Gallay. Paris, 1967.

———. *Opera Omnia.* PG 35–38.

Gregory of Nyssa. *Opera.* 8 vols. Edited by W. Jaeger. Leiden, 1959.

The History of the Blessed Virgin, and the History of the Likeness of Christ Which the Jews of Tiberias Made to Mock At. Edited and translated by E. A. Wallis Budge. Vols. 4 and 5, Luzac's Semitic Text and Translation Series. London, 1899.

Holy Women of the Syrian Orient. Translated by S. P. Brock and S. A. Harvey. Berkeley and Los Angeles, 1987.

"Une hymne nestorienne sur les saintes femmes." Edited and translated by J.-M. Fiey. *Anal. Boll.* 84 (1966): 77–110.

Isaac the Syrian. *The Ascetical Homilies of Saint Isaac the Syrian.* Translated by Holy Transfiguration Monastery [D. Miller]. Boston, 1984.

Jacob of Edessa. *Chronicon.* Edited and translated by E. W. Brooks, CSCO 5/5, 6/6. Paris, 1905–1907.

Jews and Christians in Egypt: The Jewish Troubles in Alexandria and the Athanasian Controversy. Edited and translated by H. I. Bell. London, 1924; Westport, 1976. (Documents).

John of Ephesus. *Ioannis Ephesini historiae ecclesiasticae fragmenta quae e prima et secunda parte supersunt.* Edited by E. W. Brooks, CSCO 104/53, 402–20. Louvain, 1965.

———. "Analyse de la seconde partie inédite de *l'Histoire Ecclesiastique* de Jean d'Asie, patriarche jacobite de Constantinople (†585)." Edited by F. Nau. *ROC* 2 (1897): 455–93.

———. *Ioannis Ephesini historiae ecclesiasticae pars tertia.* Edited and translated by E. W. Brooks, CSCO 105/54, 106/55. Paris, 1935–36.

———. *Lives of the Eastern Saints.* Edited and translated by E. W. Brooks. *PO*

17–19. Paris, 1923–25. Also in *Commentarii de beatis orientalibus*. Translated by J. P. N. Land and W. J. van Douwen. Amsterdam, 1889.

John Moschus. *Ioannis Moschi pratum spirituale*. PG 87.3, cols. 2851–3112. Also in *Jean Moschus, Le pré spirituel*. Translated by M.-J. Rouët de Journel. Sources Chrétiennes. Paris, 1946.

John of Nikiu. *Chronicle*. Edited and translated by R. H. Charles. London, 1916; 1981.

John Rufus. *Plérophories, témoignages et révélations contre le concile de Chalcédoine*. Edited and translated by F. Nau. *PO* 8:5–208. Paris, 1912.

John the Stylite of Beth-Mar-Qanun. *Select Narrations of Holy Women*. Edited and translated by A. Smith Lewis. *Studia Sinaitica* 9–10. London, 1900.

"Joshua the Stylite." *Chronicle*. Edited and translated by W. Wright. Cambridge, 1882.

Lucian. *Opera*. 8 vols., LCL. Edited and translated by A. H. Harmon. London/ Cambridge (Mass.), 1969.

———. *Lucian, The Syrian Goddess (De dea syria)*. Translated by H. W. Attridge and R. A. Oden. Missoula, 1976.

"A Martyr at the Sasanid Court under Vahran II: Candida." Edited and translated by S. P. Brock. *Anal. Boll.* 96 (1978): 167–81. (= Brock, S. P. *Syriac Perspectives*, chap. 9.)

Michael the Syrian. *Chronique de Michel le syrien*. 3 vols. Edited and translated by J.-B. Chabot. Paris, 1899–1905.

The Nag Hammadi Library in English. 2d ed., ed. J. M. Robinson. San Francisco, 1988.

Narrationes variae. Edited and translated by E. W. Brooks, CSCO 5/5:259–63 and 6/6:331–35. Paris, 1905–1907.

Nessana Papyri. In *Excavations at Nessana*. Vol. 3, *Non-Literary Papyri*. Edited and translated by C. J. Kraemer, Jr. Princeton, 1958.

New Testament Apocrypha. 2 vols. Edited by E. Hennecke and W. Schneemelcher, translated by R. M. Wilson. London, 1973.

Odes of Solomon. 2d ed. Edited and translated by J. H. Charlesworth. Missoula, 1977; Chico, 1982.

Palladius. *Historia Lausiaca*. In *The Lausiac History of Palladius*. 2 vols. Edited and translated by C. Butler. Cambridge, 1898–1904. Also in *Palladius: The Lausiac History*. Translated by R. T. Meyer. Ancient Christian Writers 34. London, 1965. For the Syriac versions, *Les formes syriaques de la matière de l'histoire lausiaque*. 2 vols. Edited and translated by R. Draguet, CSCO 389/169, 398/ 173. Louvain, 1978.

Patrologiae cursus completus, Series Graeca. Edited by J. P. Migne. Paris, 1867–1934.

Patrologia Orientalis. Edited by R. Graffin, F. Nau, and F. Graffin. Paris, 1907–.

Piacenza Pilgrim. *Travels*. Edited by P. Geyer, CSEL 39, 159–91. Vienna, 1898. (= CSL 175, 127–53.) Also in *Jerusalem Pilgrims Before the Crusades*, 79–89. Translated by J. Wilkinson. Jerusalem, 1977.

Procopius. Opera. 7 vols., LCL. Edited and translated by H. B. Dewing. London, 1961. (*Wars*, vols. 1–5; *Anecdota*, vol. 6; *Buildings*, vol. 7.)

Pseudo-Dionysius of Tell-Mahre. *Incerti auctoris chronicon anonymum pseudo-Dionysianum vulgo dictum.* Edited and translated by J.-B. Chabot, CSCO 91/43, 121/66, and 104/53. Louvain, 1927–49; 1933.

Les saints stylites. Edited and translated by H. Delehaye, Sub. Hag. 14. Bruxelles, 1923.

Severus of Antioch. *Les homiliae cathedrales de Sévère d'Antioche, Homélie 77.* Edited and translated by M.-A. Kugener and E. Triffaux, *PO* 16:761–863. Paris, 1922.

———. "Sévère d'Antioche en Égypte." Edited and translated by W. E. Crum. *ROC* 3 (1922–23): 92–104. [Coptic fragments]

———. *The Sixth Book of Select Letters of Severus, Patriarch of Antioch by Athanasius of Nisibis.* 4 vols. Edited and translated by E. W. Brooks. Oxford, 1902; 1969.

Simeon the Stylite. "The Letters of Simeon the Stylite." Edited and translated by C. C. Torrey. *JAOS* 20 (1899): 253–76.

Socrates. *Historia ecclesiastica.* Edited by J. Bidez and G. C. Hansen, GCS 50. Berlin, 1960.

Sozomen. *Historia ecclesiastica.* Edited by J. Bidez and G. C. Hansen, GCS 50. Berlin, 1960.

Syriac and Arabic Documents Regarding Legislation Relative to Syrian Asceticism. Edited and translated by A. Vööbus, PETSE 11. Stockholm, 1960.

The Syriac Fathers on Prayer and the Spiritual Life. Translated by S. P. Brock, Cistercian Studies 101. Kalamazoo, 1987.

Tertullian. *Adversus Marcionem.* Edited by A. Kroymann, CSEL 47. Vienna, 1906.

———. *De cultu feminarum.* Edited by A. Kroymann, CSEL 70, 59–88. Vienna, 1942.

———. *De praescriptione haereticorum.* Edited by A. Kroymann, CSEL 70, 1–58. Vienna, 1942.

Theodoret of Cyrrhus. *Historia religiosa.* In *Théodoret de Cyr, Historie des moines de syrie.* Edited and translated by P. Canivet and A. Leroy-Molinghen. Sources Chrétiennes 234, 257. Paris, 1977–79. Also in *Theodoret of Cyrrhus, A History of the Monks of Syria.* Translated by R. M. Price, Cistercian Studies 88. Kalamazoo, 1985.

Thomas of Marga. *Historia monastica.* In *The Book of Governors: The Historia Monastica of Thomas Bishop of Marga A.D. 840.* 2 vols. Edited and translated by E. A. Wallis Budge. London, 1893.

Three Byzantine Saints. Translated by E. A. Dawes and N. Baynes. Oxford, 1948; London, 1977.

Vita Abraami (Cyril of Scythopolis). Edited by E. Schwartz, *TU* 49.2, 244–47. Also in *Les moines d'Orient* 3.3, 73–79. Translated by A.-J. Festugière. Paris, 1962–63.

Vita Alexii. In *La légende syriaque de Saint Alexis l'homme de Dieu.* Edited and translated by A. Amiaud. Paris, 1889.

Vita Antonii. PG 26, cols. 837–976. Also in *The Life of Antony.* Translated by R. T. Meyer. Ancient Christian Writers 10. London, 1950. And in *Athanasius: The Life of Antony and the Letter to Marcellinus.* Translated by R. C. Gregg. New York, 1980. For the Syriac version, *La Vie primitive de S. Antoine.* Edited and translated by R. Draguet, CSCO 417/183, 418/184. Louvain, 1980.

Vita Danielis Stylitae. In *Les Saints Stylites,* edited by H. Delehaye, 1–94. Also in *Three Byzantine Saints,* translated by E. Dawes and N. Baynes, 1–71.

Vita Euthymii (Cyril of Scythopolis). Edited by E. Schwartz, *TU* 49.2, 3–85. Also in *Les moines d'Orient* 3.1. Translated by A.-J. Festugière. Paris, 1962.

Vita Febroniae (Thomaïs). *AMS* 5:573–615. Also in *Holy Women of the Syrian Orient,* translated by S. P. Brock and S. A. Harvey, 150–76.

Vita Iacobi Baradaei. In "A Spurious Life of James." Edited and translated by E. W. Brooks, *PO* 19:228–68. Paris, 1925.

Vita Iohannis Eleemosynarii (Leontius of Neapolis). In *Leontios' von Neapolis leben des heiligen Johannes des Barmherzigen erzbishofs von Alexandrien.* Edited by H. Gelzer. Freiburg/Leipzig, 1893. Also in *Three Byzantine Saints,* translated by E. Dawes and N. Baynes, 207–62.

Vita Iohannis Episcopi Tellae (Elias). Edited and translated by E. W. Brooks, CSCO 7/7: 29–95 and 8/8: 21–60. Paris, 1907.

Vita Iohannis Hesychasti (Cyril of Scythopolis). Edited by E. Schwartz, *TU* 49.2, 201–22. Also in *Les moines d'Orient,* 3.3, 13–34. Translated by A.-J. Festugière. Paris, 1962–63.

Vita Isaiae Monachi (Zachariah Rhetor). Edited and translated by E. W. Brooks, CSCO 7/7: 1–16 and 8/8: 1–10. Paris, 1907.

Vita Kyriaki (Cyril of Scythopolis). Edited by E. Schwartz, *TU* 49.2, 222–35. Also in *Les moines d'Orient,* 3.3, 39–52. Translated by A.-J. Festugière. Paris, 1907.

Vita Macrinae (Gregory of Nyssa). Edited by V. W. Callahan. In Greg. Ny., *Opera,* edited by W. Jaeger, 8.1, 347–414.

Vita Pelagiae (Jacob the Deacon). *AMS* 6:616–49. For the versions, *Pélagie la pénitente: Metamorphoses d'une legende.* Vol. 1, *Les textes et leur histoire.* Edited by P. Petitmengin. Études Augustiniennes. Paris, 1981. Also in *Holy Women of the Syrian Orient,* translated by S. P. Brock and S. A. Harvey, 40–62.

Vita Petri Iberi (John Rufus). In *Petrus der Iberer.* Edited and translated by R. Raabe. Leipzig, 1895.

Vita Sabae (Cyril of Scythopolis). Edited by E. Schwartz, *TU* 49.2, 85–200. Also in *Les moines d'Orient,* 3.2. Translated by A.-J. Festugière. Paris, 1962.

Vita Severi (Athanasius Scriptor). In "Athanasius Scriptor of Antioch, *The Conflict of Severus.*" Edited and translated by E. J. Goodspeed and W. E. Crum, *PO* 4 (1908): 575–726.

Vita Severi (John of Beith-Aphthonia). In "*Vie de Sévère* par Jean de Beith-Aphthonia." Edited and translated by M.-A. Kugener, *PO* 2:204–64. Paris, 1907.

Vita Severi (Zachariah Rhetor). In "*Vie de Sévère, Patriarche d'Antioche 512–518* par Zacharie le scholastique." Edited and translated by M.-A. Kugener, *PO* 2:7–115. Paris, 1907.

Vita Simeonis Stylitae. In *Das leben des heiligen Symeon Stylites,* Edited by H. Lietz-

mann, *TU* 32.4. Liepzig, 1908. The Syriac *Vita* is in *AMS* 4:507–644. Also in
"The Life of St. Simeon Stylites." Translated by F. Lent. *JAOS* 35 (1915–17):
103–98. Also in *The Lives of Simeon Stylites*. Translated by R. Doran. Cistercian Studies 112. Kalamazoo, 1989.

Vita Simeonis Stylitae Iunioris. In *La vie ancienne de S. Syméon Stylite le jeune (521–*
592). 2 vols. Edited and translated by P. Van den Ven, Sub. Hag. 32. Bruxelles, 1962–70.

Vita Theodosii (Cyril of Scythopolis). Edited by E. Schwartz, *TU* 49.2, 235–41. Also
in *Les moines d'Orient*, 3.3, 57–62. Translated by A.-J. Festugière. Paris, 1907.

Vita Theognii (Cyril of Scythopolis). Edited by E. Schwartz, *TU* 49.2, 241–43. Also
in *Les moines d'Orient*, 3.3, 65–67. Translated by A.-J. Festugière. Paris, 1907.

Vitae virorum apud Monophysitas celeberrimorum. Edited and translated by E. W.
Brooks, CSCO 7/7, 8/8. Paris, 1907.

Women in the Early Church. Translated by E. A. Clark. Wilmington, 1983.

Zachariah Rhetor. *Historia ecclesiastica Zachariae Rhetori vulgo adscripta*. Edited and
translated by E. W. Brooks, CSCO 83/38, 84/39, 87/41, 88/42. Louvain and
Paris, 1919–24. Also in *The Syriac Chronicle Known as that of Zachariah of*
Mitylene. Translated by F. J. Hamilton and E. W. Brooks. London, 1899; New
York, 1979.

Secondary Sources

Adnès, A., and Canivet, P. "Guérisons miraculeuses et exorcismes dans l''Histoire Philothée' de Théodoret de Cyr." *Revue de l'Histoire des Religions* 171
(1967): 53–82, 149–79.

Aigrain, R. *L'hagiographie: Ses sources, ses méthodes, son histoire*. Paris, 1953.

Allen, P. *Evagrius Scholasticus the Church Historian*. Louvain, 1981.

———. "The 'Justinianic' Plague." *Byzantion* 49 (1979): 5–20.

———. "A New Date for the Last Recorded Events in John of Ephesus' *Historia*
Ecclesiastica." *OLP* 10 (1979): 251–54.

———. "Zachariah Scholasticus and the *Historia Ecclesiastica* of Evagrius Scholasticus." *JTS* 31 (1980): 471–88.

Altaner, B. *Patrology*. Freiburg, 1960.

Ashtor, E. "An Essay on the Diet of the Various Classes in the Medieval Levant."
In *Biology of Man in History*, edited by R. Forster and O. Ranum, 125–62.
(=*Annales: e.s.c.* 23 [1968]: 1017–53.)

Atiya, A. S. *A History of Eastern Christianity*. London, 1968.

Aune, D. E. *The Cultic Setting of Realized Eschatology in Early Christianity*. Leiden,
1972.

Avi-Yonah, M. *The Jews of Palestine: A Political History from the Bar Kokhba War to*
the Arab Conquest. Oxford, 1976.

Baker, A. "Early Syrian Asceticism." *DR* 88 (1970): 393–409.

———. "Syriac and the Origins of Monasticism." *DR* 86 (1968): 342–53.

Barnes, T. D. "Angel of Light or Mystic Initiate? The Problem of the *Life of An-*
tony." *JTS* 37 (1986): 353–68.

———. "Constantine and the Christians of Persia." *JRS* 75 (1985): 126–36.

Bauer, W. *Orthodoxy and Heresy in Earliest Christianity*. Edited and translated by R. A. Kraft and G. Krodel. Philadelphia, 1971.

Baumstark, A. *Geschichte der syrischen Literatur, mit Ausschluss der christlich—Palästinensischen Texte*. Bonn, 1922; Berlin, 1968.

Baynes, N. H. *Byzantine Studies and Other Essays*. London, 1955.

Beauchamp, J. "La situation juridique de la femme à Byzance." *Cahiers de civilization médiévale Xe–XIIe siècles* 20 (1977): 145–76.

Beck, E. "Ein Beitrag zur Terminologie des ältesten syrischen Mönchtums." *Studia Anselmiana* 38 (1956): 254–67.

Beggiani, S. J. *Early Syriac Theology, with Special Reference to the Maronite Tradition*. Lanham, 1983.

Biraben, J.-N., and LeGoff, J. "La peste dans le haute moyen age." *Annales: e.s.c.* 24 (1969): 1484–1510. (="The Plague in the Early Middle Ages." In *Biology of Man in History*, edited by R. Forster and O. Ranum, 48–80.)

Black, M. "The Tradition of Hasidaean-Essene Asceticism: Its Origins and Influences." In *Aspects du Judéo-Christianisme*, edited by M. Simon, 19–33. Paris, 1965.

Blum, G. G. *Rabbula von Edessa*. CSCO 300/Sub. 34. Louvain, 1969.

Boojamra, J. L. "Christian *Philanthropia*: A Study of Justinian's Welfare Policy and the Church." *Byzantina* 7 (1975): 345–73.

Breydy, M. "Les laics et les *bnay qyomo* dans l'ancienne tradition de l'église syrienne." *Kanon Jahrbuch f.d. Recht der Östkirchen* 3 (1977): 51–75.

Brock, S. P. "Aspects of Translation Technique in Antiquity." *GRBS* 20 (1979): 69–87. (= *Syriac Perspectives*, chap. 3.)

———. "Baptismal Themes in the Writings of Jacob of Serugh." *Symposium Syriacum 1976*, OCA 205 (1978): 325–47.

———. "Christians in the Sasanian Empire: A Case of Divided Loyalties." In *Religion and National Identity*, SCH 18 (1982), 1–19. (= *Syriac Perspectives*, chap. 6.)

———. "The Christology of the Church of the East in the Synods of the Fifth to Early Seventh Centuries: Preliminary Considerations and Materials." In *Aksum-Thyateira: A Festschrift for Archbishop Methodios of Thyateira and Great Britain*, edited by G. D. Dragas, 125–42. Athens, 1985.

———. "Early Syrian Asceticism." *Numen* 20 (1973): 1–19. (= *Syriac Perspectives*, chap. 1.)

———. "From Antagonism to Assimilation: Syriac Attitudes to Greek Learning." In *East of Byzantium: Syria and Armenia in the Formative Period*, edited by N. Garsoïan, T. Mathews, and R. Thomson, 17–34. Washington, 1982. (= *Syriac Perspectives*, chap. 5.)

———. "Genesis 22 in Syriac Tradition." In *Mélanges Dominique Barthélemy: Études Bibliques offertes à l'occasion de son 60e anniversaire*, edited by P. Casetti. *Orbis Biblicus et Orientalis* 38:1–30. Freiburg and Göttingen, 1981.

———. "Greek into Syriac and Syriac into Greek." *Journal of the Syriac Academy* (Baghdad) 3 (1977): 1–17. (= *Syriac Perspectives*, chap. 2.)

——. "Greek Words in the Syriac Gospels." *Le Muséon* 80 (1967): 389–426.

——. *The Holy Spirit in the Syrian Baptismal Tradition.* Edited by J. Vellian, Syrian Churches Series 9. Poona, 1979.

——. "An Introduction to Syriac Studies." In *Horizons in Semitic Studies: Articles for the Student,* edited by J. H. Eaton, 1–33. Birmingham, 1980.

——. *The Luminous Eye: The Spiritual World Vision of St. Ephrem.* Rome, 1985.

——. "Mary and the Eucharist: An Oriental Perspective." *Sobornost* 1.2 (1979): 50–59.

—— "Mary in Syriac Tradition." The Ecumenical Society for the Blessed Virgin Mary, Oxford, 1978.

——. "The Orthodox-Oriental Orthodox Conversations of 532." *Apostolo Varnava* 41 (1980): 219–28. (= *Syriac Perspectives,* chap. 11.)

——. "The Poet as Theologian." *Sobornost* 7.4 (1978): 243–50.

——. "The Prayer of the Heart in Syriac Tradition." *Sobornost/ECR* 4.2 (1982): 131–42.

——. "Some Aspects of Greek Words in Syriac." *Abhand. Ak. Wiss. Göttingen* 96 (1975): 80–108. (= *Syriac Perspectives,* chap. 4.)

——. "Syriac and Greek Hymnography: Problems of Origin." In *Studia Patristica* 16.2, edited by E. A. Livingstone, 77–81. Berlin, 1985.

——. *Syriac Perspectives on Late Antiquity.* London, 1984.

——. "Towards a History of Syriac Translation Technique." *Symposium Syriacum 1980, OCA* 221 (1983): 1–14.

Brown, P. *The Body and Society: Men, Women and Sexual Renunciation in Early Christianity.* New York, 1988.

——. "A Dark Age Crisis: Aspects of the Iconoclastic Controversy." *EHR* 88 (1973): 1–34. (= *Society and the Holy,* 251–301.)

——. "Eastern and Western Christendom in Late Antiquity: A Parting of the Ways." In *The Orthodox Churches and the West,* SCH 13 (1976), 1–24. (= *Society and the Holy,* 166–95.)

——. *Religion and Society in the Age of St. Augustine.* London, 1972.

——. "The Rise and Function of the Holy Man in Late Antiquity." In *Society and the Holy,* 103–52. [Revised from *JRS* 61 (1971): 80–101.]

——. "The Saint as Exemplar in Late Antiquity." *Representations* 1.2 (1983): 1–25.

——. *Society and the Holy in Late Antiquity.* Berkeley and Los Angeles, 1982.

——. "Town, Village and Holy Man: The Case of Syria." In *Society and the Holy,* 153–65. (Also in *Assimilation et résistance à la culture gréco-romaine dans le monde ancien,* edited by D. M. Pippidi, 213–20. Bucharest, 1976.)

——. *The World of Late Antiquity.* London, 1971.

Brown, R. E.; Donfried, K. P.; Fitzmyer, J. A.; and Reuman, J., eds. *Mary in the New Testament.* London, 1978.

Browning, R. *Justinian and Theodora.* Rev. ed. New York, 1987.

Buck, D. F. "The Structure of the Lausiac History." *Byzantion* 46 (1976): 292–307.

Buckler, G. "Women in Byzantine Law About 1100 A.D." *Byzantion* 11 (1936): 391–416.

Bundy, D. D. "Criteria for Being *in communione* in the Early Syrian Church." *Augustinianum* 25 (1985): 597–608.

———. "Jacob Baradaeus. The State of Research, a Review of the Sources, and a New Approach." *Le Muséon* 91 (1978): 45–86.

———. "Marcion and the Marcionites in Early Syriac Apologetics." *Le Muséon* 101 (1988): 21–32.

Burkitt, F. C. *Early Eastern Christianity*. London, 1904.

Bury, J. B. *History of the Later Roman Empire from the Death of Theodosius I to the Death of Justinian*. 2 vols. New York, 1958.

Cameron, Averil. *Agathias*. Oxford, 1970.

———. "Agathias on the Sassanians." *DOP* 23–24 (1969–70): 69–183.

———. *Continuity and Change in Sixth Century Byzantium*. London, 1981.

———. "Corrippus' Poem on Justin II: A Terminus of Antique Art?" *Annali della Scuola Normale Superiore di Pisa* 5 (1975): 129–65.

———. "The Theotokos in Sixth-Century Constantinople." *JTS* 29 (1978): 79–108.

———. "Early Byzantine *Kaiserkritik*: Two Case Histories." *BMGS* 3 (1977): 1–17.

———. "The Early Religious Policies of Justin II." In *The Orthodox Churches and the West*, SCH 13 (1976), 51–67.

———. "The Empress Sophia." *Byzantion* 45 (1975): 5–21.

———. "Images of Authority: Elites and Icons in Late Sixth Century Byzantium." *Past and Present* 84 (1979): 3–35.

———. "Late Antiquity: the Total View." *Past and Present* 88 (1980): 129–35.

———. "A Nativity Poem of the Sixth Century A.D." *CP* 74 (1979): 222–32.

———. *Procopius and the Sixth Century*. Berkeley, 1985.

———. "The Sceptic and the Shroud." Inaugural Lecture, presented at King's College, University of London, London, 1980.

———. "The 'Scepticism' of Procopius." *Historia* 15 (1966): 466–82.

Cameron, A., and Cameron, A. "Christianity and Tradition in the Historiography of the Late Empire." *Classical Quarterly* 14 (1964): 316–28.

Canart, P. "Le nouveau-né qui dénonce son père. Les avatars d'un conte populaire dans la littérature hagiographique." *Anal. Boll.* 84 (1966): 309–33.

Canivet, P. *Le monachisme syrien selon Théodoret de Cyr*. Théologie Historique 42. Paris, 1977.

Casey, R. P. "Julian of Halicarnassus." *HTR* 19 (1926): 206–13.

Ceran, W. "Stagnation or Fluctuation in Early Byzantine Society?" *Byzantinoslavica* 31 (1970): 192–203.

Chadwick, H. *The Early Church*. London, 1967.

———. "John Moschus and his Friend Sophronius the Sophist." *JTS* 25 (1974): 41–74.

Charanis, P. *Church and State in the Later Roman Empire: The Religious Policy of Anastasius the First, 491–518*. Madison, 1939; Thessaloniki, 1974.

Charlesworth, J. H. "The Odes of Solomon—Not Gnostic." *CBQ* 31 (1969): 357–69.

Charlesworth, J. H. and Culpepper, R. A. "The Odes of Solomon and the Gospel of John." *CBQ* 35 (1973): 298–322.

Chesnut, G. F. *The First Christian Histories: Eusebius, Socrates, Sozomen, Theodoret and Evagrius.* Théologie Historique 46. Paris, 1977.

Chesnut, R. C. *Three Monophysite Christologies: Severus of Antioch, Philoxenus of Mabbug, and Jacob of Serug.* Oxford, 1976.

Chitty, D. *The Desert a City.* Oxford, 1966; London, 1977.

Clark, E. *Ascetic Piety and Women's Faith: Essays on Late Ancient Christianity.* Lewiston, 1986.

———. "Ascetic Renunciation and Feminine Advancement: A Paradox of Late Ancient Christianity." *Anglican Theological Review* 63 (1981): 240–57. (= *Ascetic Piety and Women's Faith*, 175–208.)

———. "Authority and Humility: A Conflict of Values in Fourth-Century Female Monasticism." *Byzantinische Forschungen* 9 (1985): 17–33. (= *Ascetic Piety and Women's Faith*, 209–28.)

———. "Piety, Propaganda, and Politics in the *Life of Melania the Younger*." In *Studia Patristica* 18.2, edited by E. A. Livingstone, Oxford, 1986. (= *Ascetic Piety and Women's Faith*, 61–94.)

Cochrane, C. N. *Christianity and Classical Culture.* 2d ed. London, 1944; London and New York, 1974.

Cohn, N. *The Pursuit of the Millenium.* Oxford, 1970.

Constantelos, D. J. *Byzantine Philanthropy and Social Welfare.* New Brunswick, 1968.

———. "Physician-priests in the medieval Greek Church." *Greek Orthodox Theological Review* 12 (1966–67): 141–53.

Cox, P. *Biography in Late Antiquity: A Quest for the Holy Man.* Berkeley and Los Angeles, 1983.

Daniélou, J. "Le ministère des femmes dans l'église ancienne." *La Maison-Dieu* 61 (1960): 70–96. (= "The Ministry of Women in the Early Church," trans. G. Simon. London, 1961.)

Darling, R. A. "The Patriarchate of Severus of Antioch 512–518." Ph.D. diss., University of Chicago, 1982.

de Gaiffier, B. "Intactam sponsam relinquens. A Propos de la Vie de S. Alexis." *Anal. Boll.* 65 (1947): 157–95.

Delcourt, M. *Hermaphrodite: Myths and Rites of the Bisexual Figure in Classical Antiquity.* Translated by J. Nicholson. London, 1961.

Delehaye, H. *Cinq leçons sur la méthode hagiographique.* Sub. Hag. 21. Bruxelles, 1934.

———. *The Legends of the Saints.* Translated by D. Attwater. New York, 1962.

———. "Les femmes stylites." *Anal. Boll.* 27 (1908): 391–92.

Dictionnaire d'histoire et de géographie ecclésiastiques. Edited by A. Baudrillart, A. Vogt, and U. Rouzies. Paris, 1912–.

Dictionnaire de spiritualité: Ascétique et mystique, doctrine et histoire. Edited by E. Mioni and D. Stiernon, et al. Paris, 1937–.

Dictionnaire de théologie catholique. 15 vols. Edited by A. Vacant, E. Mangenot, and E. Amann. Paris, 1901–50.

Diehl, C. *Théodora, impératrice de Byzance.* 3d ed. Paris, 1904; 1937.

Dillemann, L. *Haute mésopotamie orientale et pays adjacents.* Paris, 1962.

Dols, M. W. *The Black Death in the Middle East.* Princeton, 1977.

Douglas, M. *Purity and Danger: An Analysis of the Concepts of Pollution and Taboo.* London, 1978.

Downey, G. "The Christian Schools of Palestine: A Chapter in Literary History." *Harvard Library Bulletin* 12 (1958): 297–319.

———. "Ephraemius, Patriarch of Antioch." *CH* 7 (1938): 364–70.

———. *Gaza in the Early Sixth Century.* Norman, 1963.

———. "The Persian Campaign in Syria in A.D. 540." *Speculum* 28 (1953): 340–48.

———. "The Perspective of the Early Church Historians." *GRBS* 6 (1965): 57–70.

———. "*Philanthropia* in Religion and Statecraft in the Fourth Century After Christ." *Historia* 4 (1955): 199–208.

Draguet, R. "L'histoire lausiaque: une oeuvre écrite dans l'ésprit d'Evagre." *RHE* 41 (1946): 321–64.

Drijvers, H. J. W. *Bardaisan of Edessa.* Assen, 1966.

———. "The Byzantine Saint: Hellenistic and Oriental Origins." In *The Byzantine Saint,* edited by S. Hackel, 25–33. (=*East of Antioch,* chap. 4.)

———. *Cults and Beliefs at Edessa.* Leiden, 1980.

———. *East of Antioch: Studies in Early Syriac Christianity.* London, 1984.

———. "Facts and Problems in Early Syriac-speaking Christianity." *The Second Century* 2 (1982): 157–75. (=*East of Antioch,* chap. 6.)

———. "Die Legende des heiligen Alexius und der Typus des Gottesmannes im syrischen Christentum." In *Typus, Symbol, Allegorie bei den östlichen Vätern und ihren Parallelen im Mittelalter,* edited by M. Schmidt, 187–217. Regensburg, 1982. (=*East of Antioch,* chap. 5.)

———. "The 19th Ode of Solomon." *JTS* 31 (1980): 337–55. (=*East of Antioch,* chap. 9.)

———. "Spätantike Parallelen zur altchristlichen Heiligenverehrung unter besonderer Berücksichtigung des syrischen Stylitenkultus." *Göttingen Orientforschungen* 1, Reihe, Syriaca 17 (1978): 77–113.

Duchesne, L. *L'eglise au VIe siècle.* Paris, 1925.

———. "Les Protégés de Théodora." *Mélanges d'archéologie et d'histoire de l'école française de Rome* 35 (1915): 57–79.

Duval, R. *La littérature syriaque des origines jusqu'à la fin de cette littérature après la conquête par les Arabes au XIII siècle.* 3d ed. Paris, 1907; Amsterdam, 1970.

Ebied, R. Y. "The Syriac Influence on the Arabic Language and Literature." *Symposium Syriacum 1980, OCA* 221 (1983): 247–51.

Evelyn-White, H. G. *The Monasteries of the Wâdi 'N Natrûn 2: The History of the Monasteries of Nitria and of Scetis.* New York, 1932.

Every, G. "The Monophysite Question, Ancient and Modern." *ECR* 3 (1971): 405–14.

———. "The *Protevangelion of James* with Related Texts." Unpublished paper, 1982.

Festugière, A.-J. "Epidémies «hippocratiques» et épidémies démoniaques." *Wiener Studien* 79 (1966): 157–64.

———. *Les Moines d'Orient.* 4 vols. Paris, 1961–65.

———. "Lieux communs littéraires et thèmes de folk-lore dans l'hagiographie primitive." *Wiener Studien* 73 (1960): 123–52.

Fiey, J.-M. "Aonès, Awun, et Awgin (Eugène): Aux origines de monachisme mésopotamien." *Anal. Boll.* 80 (1962): 52–81.

———. "Cénobitisme féminin ancien dans les églises syriennes orientale et occidental." *L'orient syrien* 10 (1965): 281–306.

———. *Jalons pour une histoire de l'église en Iraq.* CSCO 310/Sub. 36. Louvain, 1970.

———. "Les laïcs dans l'histoire de l'église syrienne orientale." *POC* 14 (1964): 169–83.

———. "Les Marcionites dans les textes historiques de l'église de Perse." *Le Muséon* 83 (1970): 183–88.

Fiorenza, E. Schüssler. *In Memory of Her: A Feminist Theological Reconstruction of Christian Origins.* New York, 1983.

Fliche, A., and Martin, V., eds. *Histoire de l'église depuis les origines jusqu'à nos jours.* Vols. 1–4. Paris, 1935–50.

Flusin, B. *Miracle et histoire dans l'oeuvre de Cyrille de Scythopolis.* Études Augustiniennes. Paris, 1983.

Forster, R., and Ranum, O. *Biology of Man in History.* Baltimore and London, 1975.

Fouyas, M. *Theologikai kai Istorikai Meletai: Sylloge Demosieumaton* 1. Athens, 1979.

Frazee, C. A. "Late Roman and Byzantine Legislation on the Monastic Life from the Fourth to the Eighth Centuries." *CH* 51 (1982): 263–79.

Frend, W. H. C. "Eastern Attitudes to Rome during the Acacian Schism." In *The Orthodox Churches and the West,* SCH 13 (1976), 69–81.

———. "The Monks and the Survival of the East Roman Empire in the Fifth Century." *Past and Present* 54 (1972): 3–24.

———. "The Monophysites and the Transition Between the Ancient World and the Middle Ages." In *Passaggio del mondo antico al medio evo da Teodosio a san Gregorio Magno: Atti dei Convegni Lincei 45,* 339–65. Rome, 1980.

———. "Popular Religion and Christological Controversy in the Fifth Century." In *Popular Belief and Practice,* SCH 8 (1972), 19–29.

———. *The Rise of Christianity.* Philadelphia, 1984.

———. *The Rise of the Monophysite Movement: Chapters in the History of the Church in the Fifth and Sixth Centuries.* 2d ed. Cambridge, 1978.

———. "Severus of Antioch and the Origins of the Monophysite Hierarchy." *OCA* 195 (1973): 261–75.

Garitte, G. "Textes hagiographique orientaux relatifs à S. Leonce de Tripoli: 2. L'homélie copte de Sévère d'Antioche." *Le Muséon* 79 (1966): 335–86.

Garsoïan, N.; Mathews, T.; and Thomson, R. *East of Byzantium: Syria and Armenia in the Formative Period.* Washington, 1982.

Goldberg, A. M. *Untersuchungen über die Vorstellung von der Schekhinah in der frühen rabbinischen Literatur.* Berlin, 1969.

Gore, C. *The Church and the Ministry.* 2d ed. Edited by C. H. Turner. London, 1936.

Graef, H. *Mary: A History of Doctrine and Devotion.* 2 vols. London and New York, 1963.

———. "The Theme of the Second Eve in some Byzantine Sermons on the Assumption." In *Studia Patristica* 9.3, edited by F. L. Cross, 224–30. Berlin, 1966.

Graffin, F. "Jacques d'Edesse réviseur des homélies de Sévère d'Antioche." *Symposium Syriacum 1976, OCA* 205 (1978): 243–55.

Gray, P. T. R. *The Defense of Chalcedon in the East (451–553).* Leiden, 1979.

Gregorios, P; Lazareth, W. H.; and Nissiotis, N. A., eds. *Does Chalcedon Divide or Unite? Towards Convergence in Orthodox Christology.* Geneva, 1980.

Gregory, T. *Vox Populi: Popular Opinion and Violence in the Religious Controversies of the Fifth Century A.D.* Columbus, 1979.

Gribomont, J. "Le monachisme au sein de l'église en Syrie et en Cappadoce." *Studia Monastica* 7 (1965): 7–24.

Griffith, S. H. "Ephraem, the Deacon of Edessa, and the Church of the Empire." In *Diakonia: Studies in Honor of Robert T. Meyer,* edited by T. Halton and J. Williman, 22–52. Washington, 1986.

Grillmeier, A. *Christ in Christian Tradition from the Apostolic Age to Chalcedon (451).* Translated by J. S. Bowden. London, 1965.

Grillmeier, A., and Bacht, H., eds. *Das Konzil von Chalkedon: Geschichte und Gegenwart.* 3 vols. Würzburg, 1951–54.

Grosdidier de Matons, J. "La femme dans l'empire byzantine." In *Histoire mondiale de la femme,* edited by P. Grimal, 3:11–43. Paris, 1967.

Grumel, V. *La chronologie.* Traité d'études Byzantine 1. Paris, 1958.

Guilland, R. *Etudes de topographie de Constantinople byzantines.* 2 vols. Berlin, 1969.

Guillaumont, A. *Aux origines du monachisme chrétien. Spiritualité Orientale* 30 (1979).

———. "La conception de désert chez les moines d'Egypt." *Revue de l'Histoire des Religions* 188 (1975): 3–21.

———. "Le dépaysement comme forme d'ascèse dans le monachisme ancien." *Annuaire de l'Ecole Pratique des Hautes Etudes, Section des Sciences Religieuses* 76 (1968–69): 31–58.

———. "Monachisme et éthique judéo-chrétienne." *Judéo-Christianisme: Recherches historiques et théologiques offertes en hommage au Cardinal Jean Daniélou,* 199–218. Paris, 1972.

Gülcan, E. "The Renewal of Monastic Life for Women in a Monastery of the Tur Abdin." *Sobornost* 7.4 (1977): 288–98.

Hackel, S., ed. *The Byzantine Saint*. SSTS 5. London, 1981.

Halkin, F. *Bibliotheca hagiographica graeca*. 3 vols. 3d ed. Sub. Hag. 8a. Bruxelles, 1957.

———. *Novum auctarium bibliothecae hagiographicae graecae*. Sub. Hag. 65. Bruxelles, 1984.

Hardy, E. R. *Christian Egypt: Church and People*. New York, 1952.

Harvey, S. A. "Physicians and Ascetics in John of Ephesus: An Expedient Alliance." *DOP* 38 (1984): 87–93.

———. "The Sense of a Stylite: Perspectives on Simeon the Elder." *Vigiliae Christianae* 42 (1988): 376–94.

Hendriks, O. "L'activité apostolique du monachisme monophysite et nestorien." *POC* 10 (1960): 3–25, 97–113.

———. "La vie quotidienne du moine syrien oriental." *L'Orient Syrien* 5 (1960): 293–330, 401–31.

Hitti, P. K. *History of Syria*. London, 1951.

Hoffmann, R. J. *Marcion: On the Restitution of Christianity*. Chico, 1984.

Honigmann, E. *Évêques et évêchés monophysites d'Asie antérieure au VIe siècle*. CSCO 127/Sub 2. Louvain, 1951.

———. "L'histoire ecclésiastique de Jean d'Ephèse." *Byzantion* 14 (1939): 615–25.

Hopkins, K. "Contraception in the Roman Empire." *Comparative Studies in Society and History* 8 (1965–66): 124–51.

Hunt, E. D. *Holy Land Pilgrimage in the Later Roman Empire A.D. 312–460*. Oxford, 1982.

———. "Palladius of Helenopolis: A Party and its Supporters in the Church of the Late Fourth Century." *JTS* 24 (1973): 456–80.

———. "The Traffic in Relics: Some Late Roman Evidence." In *The Byzantine Saint*, edited by S. Hackel, 171–80.

Janin, R. *Constantinople byzantine: Dévelopment urbain et répertoire topographique*. 2d ed. Archives de l'Orient Chrétien 4a. Paris, 1964.

Jargy, S. "Les origines du monachisme en Syrie et en Mésopotamie." *POC* 2 (1952): 110–25.

———. "Les premiers instituts monastiques et les principaux représentants du monachisme syrien." *POC* 4 (1954): 109–17.

Johnson, A. C., and West, L. C. *Byzantine Egypt: Economic Studies*. Princeton, 1949.

Jonas, H. *The Gnostic Religion: The Message of the Alien God and the Beginnings of Christianity*. 2d ed. rev. Boston, 1963.

Jones, A. H. M. *The Later Roman Empire 284–602*. 3 vols. Oxford, 1964.

———. "Were Ancient Heresies National or Social Movements in Disguise?" *JTS* 10 (1959): 280–98.

Judge, E. A. "The Earliest Use of Monachos for 'Monk' (P.Coll.Youtie 77) and the Origins of Monasticism." *JAC* 20 (1977): 72–89.

Kallner-Amiran, D. H. "A Revised Earthquake-Catalogue of Palestine, 1." *Israel Exploration Journal* 1 (1950–51): 223–46.

———. "A Revised Earthquake-Catalogue of Palestine, 2." *Israel Exploration Journal* 2 (1952): 48–65.

Kirk, K. E., ed. *The Apostolic Ministry: Essays on the History and Doctrine of Episcopacy.* London, 1946.

Klijn, A. F. J. "The Influence of Jewish Theology on the Odes of Solomon and the Acts of Thomas. In *Aspects du Judéo-Christianisme,* edited by M. Simon, 167–79. Paris, 1965.

———. "The 'Single One' in the Gospel of Thomas." *JBL* 81 (1962): 271–78.

Kopecek, T. A. "The Social Class of the Cappadocian Fathers."*CH* 42 (1973): 453–66.

Kretschmar, G. "Ein Beitrag zur Frage nach dem Ursprung frühchristlicher Askese." *ZTK* 61 (1964): 27–67.

Kugener, M.-A. "La compilation historique de Pseudo-Zacharie le Rhéteur." *ROC* 5 (1900): 201–14, 461–80.

Labourt, J. *Le christianisme dans l'empire perse sous la dynastie sassanide.* Paris, 1904.

Lagrand, J. "How was the Virgin Mary 'Like a Man'?" *NT* 22 (1980): 97–107.

Lattke, M. *Die Oden Salomos in ihrer Bedeutung für Neues Testament und Gnosis.* 3 vols. Orbis Biblicus et Orientalis 25. Göttingen, 1986.

Lebon, J. "La christologie du monophysisme syrien." In *Das Konzil von Chalkedon,* edited by A. Grillmeier and H. Bacht, 1:425–580.

———. "Ephrem d'Amid, patriarche d'Antioche (526–544)." *Mélanges d'histoire offerts à Charles Moeller,* 197–214. Louvain and Paris, 1914.

———. *Le monophysisme Sévèrien.* Louvain, 1909.

Liebeschuetz, J. H. W. G. *Antioch: City and Imperial Administration in the Later Roman Empire.* Oxford, 1972.

Lietzmann, H. *A History of the Early Church.* 4 vols. Translated by B. L. Woolf. London, 1961.

McCullough, W. S. *A Short History of Syriac Christianity to the Rise of Islam.* Chico, 1982.

McLaughlin, E. "'Christ My Mother': Female Naming and Metaphor in Medieval Spirituality." *Nashotah Review* 15 (1975): 228–48.

McLaughlin, E., and Ruether, R. R., eds. *Women of Spirit: Female Leadership in the Jewish and Christian Traditions.* New York, 1979.

MacMullen, R. "Provincial Languages in the Roman Empire." *AJP* 87 (1966): 1–17.

McNeil, B. "The Odes of Solomon and the Scriptures." *Oriens Christianus* 67 (1983): 104–22.

———. "The Odes of Solomon and the Suffering of Christ." *Symposium Syriacum 1976,* OCA 205 (1978): 31–38.

Macuch, R. *Geschichte der spät- und neusyrischen Literatur.* Berlin, 1976.

Malone, E. E. *The Monk and the Martyr.* Washington, 1950.

Mango, C. "The Church of Saints Sergius and Bacchus at Constantinople and the Alleged Tradition of Octagonal Palatine Churches," *JÖB* 21 (1972): 189–93.

———. "The Church of Sts. Sergius and Bacchus Once Again." *BZ* 68 (1975): 385–92.

Mar Aprem. *Nestorian Missions.* Trichur, 1976; Maryknoll, 1980.

Mathews, T. *The Byzantine Churches of Istanbul.* University Park, 1976.

Meyendorff, J. *Byzantine Theology: Historical Trends and Doctrinal Themes.* 2d rev. ed. New York, 1987.

——. *Christ in Eastern Christian Thought.* New York, 1975.

Miller, D. A. "The Emperor and the Stylite: A Note on the Imperial Office." *Greek Orthodox Theological Review* 15 (1970): 207–12.

Mingana, A. *Catalogue of the Mingana Collection of Manuscripts* 1: *Syriac and Garshuni Manuscripts.* Cambridge, 1933.

Moeller, C. "La chalcédonisme et le néo-chalcédonisme en Orient de 451 à la fin du VIe siècle." In *Das Konzil von Chalkedon,* edited by A. Grillmeier and H. Bacht, 1:637–720.

Momigliano, A. ed. *The Conflict Between Paganism and Christianity in the Fourth Century.* Oxford, 1963.

——. "Popular Religious Beliefs and the late Roman Historians." In *Popular Belief and Practice,* SCH 8 (1972), 1–18.

Monks, G. R. "The Church of Alexandria and the City's Economic Life in the Sixth Century." *Speculum* 28 (1953): 349–62.

Mouterde, P. "Le concile de Chalcédoine d'après les historiens monophysites de langue syriaque." In *Das Konzil von Chalkedon,* edited by A. Grillmeier and H. Bacht, 1:581–602.

Murray, R. "The Characteristics of the Earliest Syriac Christianity." In *East of Byzantium,* ed. N. Garsoïan et al., 3–16.

——. "The Exhortation to Candidates for Ascetical Vows at Baptism in the Ancient Syriac Church." *NTS* 21 (1974–75): 59–80.

——. "Mary, the Second Eve in the Early Syriac Fathers." *ECR* 3 (1971): 372–84.

——. *Symbols of Church and Kingdom: A Study in Early Syriac Tradition.* Cambridge, 1975.

——. "The Theory of Symbolism in St. Ephrem's Theology." *Parole de l'Orient* 6–7 (1975–76): 1–20.

——. "What does a Catholic Hope from the Dialogue with Orthodoxy?" *ECR* 3 (1971): 178–81. [= *The Altar Almanach* (1970): 50–53.]

Nasrallah, J. "Survie de Saint Siméon Stylite l'alépin dans les gaules." *Syria* 51 (1974): 171–97.

Nau, F. "Deux épisodes de l'histoire juive sous Théodose II (432 et 438) d'après la vie de Barsauma le Syrien." *REJ* 83 (1927): 184–206.

——. "Etude sur les parties inédites de la chronique ecclésiastique attribuée à Denys de Tell Mahré (†845)." *ROC* 2 (1897): 41–68.

Nedungatt, G. "The Covenanters of the Early Syriac-speaking Church." *OCP* 39 (1973): 191–215, 419–44.

Nelson, J. L. "Symbols in Context." In *The Orthodox Churches and the West,* SCH 13 (1976), 97–119.

Neusner, J. *Aphrahat and Judaism: The Christian-Jewish Argument in Fourth Century Iraq.* Leiden, 1971.

————. *A History of the Mishnaic Law of Women Pt. 5: The Mishnaic System of Women.* Studies in Judaism in Late Antiquity 33. Leiden, 1980.

Nock, A. D. *Conversion.* London, 1933.

Nöldeke, T. *Sketches from Eastern History.* Translated by J. S. Black. London, 1892; Beirut, 1963.

Ortiz de Urbina, I. *Patrologia Syriaca.* Rome, 1965.

Patlagean, E. "À Byzance: Ancienne hagiographie et histoire sociale." *Annales: e.s.c.* 23 (1968): 106–26. (= "Ancient Byzantine Hagiography and Social History." In *Saints and their Cults: Studies in Religious Sociology, Folklore and History,* edited by S. Wilson, 101–21. Cambridge, 1983.)

————. "L'histoire de la femme déguisée en moine et l' évolution de la sainteté féminine à Byzance." *Studi Medievali* 17 (1976): 597–623.

————. *Pauvreté économique et pauvreté sociale à Byzance 4e–7e siècles.* Paris/La Haye, 1977.

————. *Structure sociale, famille, chrétienté à Byzance: IVe–XIe siècle.* London, 1981.

————. "Sur la limitation de la fécondité dans la haute époque byzantine." *Annales: e.s.c.* 24 (1969): 1353–69. (= "Birth Control in the Early Byzantine Empire." In *Biology of Man in History,* edited by R. Forster and O. Ranum, 1–22.)

Paulys Realenzyclopädie der classischen Altertumswissenschaft. Edited by G. Wissowa and W. Kroll. Stuttgart, 1894–.

Payne-Smith, R. *Thesaurus Syriacus.* 2 vols. Oxford, 1879–1901; New York, 1981.

Payne-Smith, J. (Mrs. Margoliouth) *Supplement to the Thesaurus Syriacus.* Oxford, 1927; New York, 1981.

Peeters, P. *Bibliotheca Hagiographica Orientalis.* Sub. Hag. 10. Bruxelles, 1910; 1954.

————. *Orient et Byzance: Le tréfonds oriental de l'hagiographie byzantine.* Sub. Hag. 26. Bruxelles, 1950.

Peña, I.; Castellana, P.; and Fernandez, R. *Les stylites syriens.* Studium Biblicum Franciscanum Collectio Minor 16. Milan, 1975.

Pigulevskaja, N. *Les villes de l'état iranien aux époques parthe et sassanide.* Paris, 1963.

Pomeroy, S. *Goddesses, Whores, Wives, and Slaves: Women in Classical Antiquity.* New York, 1975.

Quasten, J. *Patrology.* Vols. 1–3. Westminster, 1950–60.

Ramsey, W. M. "A Noble Anatolian Family of the Fourth Century." *CR* 33 (1919): 1–9.

————. *Pauline and Other Studies.* London, 1906.

Reallexikon zur Byzantinischen Kunst. Edited by K. Wessel. Stuttgart, 1966–.

Rosen, G. *Madness in Society: Chapters in the Historical Sociology of Mental Illness.* London, 1968.

Rosen, V., and Forshall, J. *Catalogus codd. mss. orientalium qui in Museo Britannico asservantur 1: Codices Syriacos et Carshuni amplectens.* London, 1838.

Rousseau, P. *Ascetics, Authority, and the Church in the Age of Jerome and Cassian.* Oxford, 1978.

————. "Blood-relationships Among Early Eastern Ascetics." *JTS* 23 (1972): 135–44.

———. "The Spiritual Authority of the Monk Bishop." *JTS* 22 (1971): 380–419.

Ruether, R. R. *Gregory of Nazianzus: Rhetor and Philosopher.* Oxford, 1969.

———, ed. *Religion and Sexism: Images of Women in the Jewish and Christian Traditions.* New York, 1974.

Rydén, L. "The Holy Fool." In *The Byzantine Saint,* edited by S. Hackel, 106–13.

Sanjian, A. K. *Colophons of Armenian Manuscripts 1301–1480.* Cambridge (Mass.), 1969.

Segal, J. B. *Edessa: The Blessed City.* Oxford, 1970.

———. "The Jews of North Mesopotamia Before the Rise of Islam." In *Sefer Segal,* edited by J. M. Grintz and J. Liver, Israeli Society for Biblical Research, 32–63. Jerusalem, 1964.

———. "Mesopotamian Communities from Julian to the Rise of Islam." *PBA* 41 (1955): 109–39.

Sellers, R. V. *The Council of Chalcedon: A Historical and Doctrinal Survey.* London, 1953.

———. *Two Ancient Christologies.* London, 1940.

Sigerist, H. E. *Civilization and Disease.* New York, 1943.

Smid, H. R. *Protevangelium Jacobi, A Commentary.* Translated by G. E. Van Baaren-Pape. Assen, 1965.

Stein, E. *Histoire du bas-empire.* 2 vols. Paris, 1949.

Strong, H. A., and Garstang, J. *The Syrian Goddess.* London, 1913.

Strycker, E. *La forme la plus ancienne du Protévangile de Jacques.* Sub. Hag. 33. Bruxelles, 1961.

Syrkin, A. Y. "On the Behavior of the 'Fool for Christ's Sake'." *History of Religions* 22 (1982): 150–71.

Tchalenko, G. *Villages antiques de la Syrie du nord.* 3 vols. Paris, 1953–58.

Teall, J. L. "The Barbarians in Justinian's Armies." *Speculum* 40 (1965): 294–322.

Torrey, C. C. "Notes on the Chronicle of Joshua the Stylite." *Hebrew Union College Annual* 23 (1950): 439–50.

Trethowan, W. H. "Exorcism: A Psychiatric Viewpoint." *JME* 2 (1976): 127–37.

Trible, P. *God and the Rhetoric of Sexuality.* Overtures in Biblical Theology 1. Philadelphia, 1978.

Trimingham, J. S. *Christianity Among the Arabs in Pre-Islamic Times.* London, 1979.

Turner, C. H. "The Lausiac History of Palladius." *JTS* 6 (1904–1905): 321–55.

Van Berchem, M., and Strzygowski, J. *Amida.* Heidelberg, 1910.

Van Millingen, A. *Byzantine Churches in Constantinople: Their History and Architecture.* London, 1912; 1974.

Van Roey, A. "Les débuts de l'église jacobite." In *Das Konzil von Chalkedon,* edited by A. Grillmeier and H. Bacht, 2:339–60.

Vasey, V. "John Moschus, Monk Marian Witness." *AER* 143 (1960): 26–34.

Vasiliev, A. A. *Justin the First: An Introduction to the Epoch of Justinian the Great.* Dumbarton Oaks Studies 1. Cambridge (Mass.), 1950.

Vikan, G. "Art, Medicine, and Magic in Early Byzantium." *DOP* 38 (1984): 65–86.

———. *Byzantine Pilgrimage Art.* Washington, 1982.

Von Rad, G. *Wisdom in Israel.* Translated by J. D. Martin. London, 1972.

Vööbus, A. *Celibacy: A Requirement for Admission to Baptism in the Early Syrian Church*. PETSE 1. Stockholm, 1951.

———. *History of Asceticism in the Syrian Orient*. CSCO 184/Sub. 14, 197/Sub. 17. Louvain, 1958.

———. *History of the School of Nisibis*. CSCO 266/Sub. 26. Louvain, 1965.

———. "The Institution of the *Benai Qeiama* and the *Benat Qeiama* in the Ancient Syrian Church." *CH* 30 (1961): 19–27.

———. "The Origin of the Monophysite Church in Syria and Mesopotamia." *CH* 42 (1973): 17–26.

Ward, B. *Harlots of the Desert: A Study of Repentance in Early Monastic Sources*. Cistercian Studies 106. Oxford and Kalamazoo, 1987.

Ware, K. T. "Chalcedonians and Non-Chalcedonians: The Latest Developments." *ECR* 3 (1971): 428–32.

Widengren, G. *Mani and Manichaeism*. Translated by C. Kessler. London, 1965.

———. *Mesopotamian Elements in Manichaeism (King and Savior* 2). Uppsala and Leipzig, 1946.

———. "Researches in Syrian Mysticism: Mystical Experiences and Spiritual Exercises." *Numen* 8 (1961): 161–98.

Wigram, W. A. *The Separation of the Monophysites*. London, 1923; New York, 1978.

Wilkinson, J. *Jerusalem Pilgrims Before the Crusades*. Jerusalem, 1977.

Wipszycka, E. *Les ressources et les activités économiques des églises en Egypt de IVe au VIIIe siècles*. Papyrologica Bruxellensia 10. Bruxelles, 1972.

Wright, W. *Catalogue of the Syriac Manuscripts in the British Museum*. 3 vols. London, 1872.

———. *A Short History of Syriac Literature*. London, 1894.

Young, F. M. "Christological Ideas in the Greek Commentaries on the Epistle to the Hebrews." *JTS* 20 (1969): 150–63.

———. *From Nicaea to Chalcedon: A Guide to the Literature and its Background*. Philadelphia, 1983.

———. "The God of the Greeks and the Nature of Religious Language." In *Early Christian Literature and the Classical Intellectual Tradition*, edited by W. R. Schoedel and R. L. Wilken, Théologie Historique 53, 45–74. Beauchesne, 1980.

———. "A Reconsideration of Alexandrian Christology." *JEH* 22 (1971): 103–14.

Zax, M., and Cowen, E. *Abnormal Psychology: Changing Conceptions*. 2d ed. New York, 1976.

Ziegler, P. *The Black Death*. London, 1969.

INDEX

Compositor:	G&S Typesetters, Inc.
Text:	10 x 13 Palatino
Display:	Palatino
Printer:	Braun-Brumfield, Inc.
Binder:	Braun-Brumfield, Inc.

DATE DUE